Open Source Database Driven
Web Development

CHANDOS
INFORMATION PROFESSIONAL SERIES

Series Editor: Ruth Rikowski
(email: Rikowskigr@aol.com)

Chandos' new series of books are aimed at the busy information professional. They have been specially commissioned to provide the reader with an authoritative view of current thinking. They are designed to provide easy-to-read and (most importantly) practical coverage of topics that are of interest to librarians and other information professionals. If you would like a full listing of current and forthcoming titles, please visit our web site **www.chandospublishing.com** or contact Hannah Grace-Williams on email info@chandospublishing.com or telephone number +44 (0) 1865 884447.

New authors: we are always pleased to receive ideas for new titles; if you would like to write a book for Chandos, please contact Dr Glyn Jones on email gjones@chandospublishing.com or telephone number +44 (0) 1865 884447.

Bulk orders: some organisations buy a number of copies of our books. If you are interested in doing this, we would be pleased to discuss a discount. Please contact Hannah Grace-Williams on email info@chandospublishing.com or telephone number +44 (0) 1865 884447.

Open Source Database Driven Web Development: A Guide for Information Professionals

Isaac Hunter Dunlap

Chandos Publishing
Oxford • England

Chandos Publishing (Oxford) Limited
Chandos House
5 & 6 Steadys Lane
Stanton Harcourt
Oxford OX29 5RL
UK
Tel: +44 (0) 1865 884447 Fax: +44 (0) 1865 884448
Email: info@chandospublishing.com
www.chandospublishing.com

First published in Great Britain in 2006

ISBN:
1 84334 161 1 (paperback)
1 84334 171 9 (hardback)
978 1 84334 161 1 (paperback)
978 1 84334 171 0 (hardback)

© I. H. Dunlap, 2006

Contents

Acknowledgements

I wish to thank the Western Illinois University community and my colleagues in the WIU libraries for creating an engaging environment in which to work, study, learn, teach and write. Thanks also to the Macomb Public Library staff for providing solitary research and writing opportunities on the 'wireless' second floor of the historic Carnegie structure.

A student can never adequately repay his teachers. From kindergartens to ivory towers, I have benefited from many outstanding individuals who committed themselves to sparking imaginations and offering light and sustenance along the way. All hail the teachers!

Thanks to Dr Randy Ralph for his generosity in providing initial HTML lessons long ago. I do not adequately know how to acknowledge Dr James Carmichael (University of North Carolina at Greensboro) for his style, good guidance and general encouragement.

I am appreciative for the pearls of wisdom shared by my former colleague, Bob Frasier, regarding PHP/MySQL development.

Weldon Payne, a good writer and friend, is once again owed a debt of thanks for agreeing to review another manuscript. However, the present author claims responsibility for the content, and any errors, oversights or omissions found within.

Eternal love and gratitude to Mom, Dad and 'E'.

Finally, and most significantly, I wish to thank Jill, Laura Katherine, Sarah Elizabeth (and yes, Windsor), for their patience, forbearance and encouraging support throughout the past year.

Isaac Hunter Dunlap
June 2006
Macomb, Illinois

List of figures and tables

Figures

Tables

About the author

Isaac Hunter Dunlap was born in Chapel Hill, North Carolina in 1966. A native of Chatham County, he is a graduate of Campbell University (BA, History), Southern Baptist Theological Seminary (Master of Divinity, Higher Education), and the University of North Carolina at Greensboro (Master of Library and Information Studies), where he was a Beta Phi Mu inductee. He is a tenured Associate Professor and Coordinator of Information Systems at Western Illinois University Libraries.

Dunlap is an experienced web developer, having created numerous websites, content management systems, online databases and information gateways over the last decade. He frequently writes and is invited to speak at state and national forums on database driven web development, web design and accessibility, open source software, library digitisation initiatives and other areas related to library and information systems.

Dunlap is actively involved in professional organisations including the American Library Association, the Association of College and Research Libraries and the Illinois Association of College and Research Libraries (IACRL). He currently serves on the IACRL Executive Committee and is Chair of the Publications Committee.

An avid golfer, music lover and traveller, Dunlap resides with his wife and two daughters in Macomb, Illinois.

The author may be contacted at the following:

E-mail: *ih-dunlap@wiu.edu*

Website: *www.isaachunter.net*

Preface

My introduction to the World Wide Web began in 1994 while pursuing a graduate degree in library and information studies at the University of North Carolina at Greensboro. A helpful colleague revealed the shrouded mystery of how to create a basic web page on a UNIX system with the rudimentary tools of Telnet, pico and a few HTML tags.

These were still the relatively early days of the Web when the Mosaic browser reigned and it was difficult to find an ISP who could deliver dial-up Internet service. Mostly unknown to the masses, the Internet was predominantly an e-mail tool used by universities and government-funded research institutes. The Web was just beginning to display some of the potential presaged by hypertext initiatives such as Ted Nelson's Xanadu project of the late 1960s. Like Martin Luther posting theses on a Wittenberg door, it is doubtful that CERN's Tim Berners-Lee could have ever imagined the information revolution he would unleash.

As my curiosity and determination to understand and use this exciting new technology grew, I began developing more complex websites and experimenting with supplemental tools such as HTML editors and digital imaging programs. Soon after my appointment as Reference Librarian and Web Coordinator at Western Illinois University Libraries, I quickly became aware of the shortcomings of the instruments in my web development toolbox. Creating an expansive website was not difficult. Providing over 13,500 students, faculty and regional citizens with substantial amounts of digital library information was more complex. Manual HTML coding of static pages could only be taken so far.

Figuring out how to enable keyword searching across the library website became my initial quest. Basic capabilities were realised via CGI scripts written in PERL, which also opened up possibilities for developing simple, searchable web databases and interactive forms. Sites such as Matt Wright's Script Archive and Solena Sol's Extropia offered free scripts that handled basic functions and introduced some measure of web interactivity. Some of these scripts were installed via brute determination and the painful manual filling of critical documentation gaps. More robust search systems were available in the late 1990s, but they usually required one or both of the following requirements (neither of which was part of my working environment): (1) additional funding for proprietary systems, and (2) root access to the campus web server.

Still, by the late 1990s developers began to provide more sophisticated applications which could be employed by anyone with a UNIX account. Extropia's WebDB package included 'Database Manager' and 'Database Search' features and was issued under an open source licensing model. These well-developed programs brought an attainable database dimension into the web development process.

With these simple database tools and a passing knowledge of PERL, one could create a search engine capable of querying a sizable library periodicals database and producing on-the-fly, non-static web pages with convincing success. Unfortunately WebDB relied on a 'flat-file' database structure as its backend. Each database's content lived in a single (huge) file delimited by pipes or tabs. As the library's electronic periodical holdings grew exponentially, the speed of title searches slowed at a commensurate pace. The system toiled under its own weight as simple search queries grinded away interminably. There had to be a better way.

Almost from nowhere, two powerful and eminently functional open source tools quietly emerged on the scene. MySQL (a relational database server) and PHP (a relatively new web scripting language) began to be mentioned on listservs, message boards and development websites. Simple online tutorials and guides began to appear describing basic concepts leading towards a more versatile approach to Web publishing and content management. These tools have been rapidly adopted by web developers from disparate (and desperate) organisations seeking to gain control of their information resources. Over the last five years these tools have provided me a stable platform on which to successfully develop numerous database driven web applications.

This book is an outgrowth of a professional journey bent on finding the most efficient, economical and effective means of managing and publishing information in a web environment. I have gleaned much over the years from anonymous PHP/MySQL online postings, often filled with rants, ravings, rebuttals and counter-rebuttals along with the occasional calm, competent contribution. Though I have benefited from specialised titles that focus on small strands of the subject, I have found few print resources that provide an adequate general overview along with the necessary details required to begin developing open source database driven web solutions. This book seeks to fill that gap.

The static Web I once knew is a fading memory. Today's dynamic, database driven Web is propelling us toward extraordinary new adventures and discoveries.

Visit this book's companion website at:

www.databasedrivenweb.net

Find valuable resources including:

- Source code and example scripts
- Accessibility resources
- Validation links
- Web development articles and tools
- Open Source software

Weighty worlds of wonder: whats, whys and wherefores of the Web

Seven hundred pounds and possibilities is good gifts.
(William Shakespeare, *The Merry Wives of Windsor* I.i)

The sage bard of Stratford knew well the value of the tangible in relation to the possible. Managing to stage (and survive) fantastically successful theatrical productions in a perilous age of political and religious conflict, William Shakespeare was well versed in effective information management. Recent scholarship has shown that while aspects of his life remain mystifyingly veiled, it is clear that he infused both his literary and literal worlds with imagination and a profound sense of the myriad pathways of possibility. Shakespeare understood that even good roads of promise and potentiality could be difficult to traverse without practical assistance and direction. In life and in tale the fulfilment of either a celestial vision or a worldly scheme each required a skilful handling of characters, events and information.[1]

Though Shakespeare's world was in many respects dissimilar to our own, the World (Wide Web) of Information in which we live also presents us with perplexing predicaments and spectacular possibilities. A hallmark of the globe's leading cultural, educational, commercial and governmental centres, the Web has revolutionised information generation and sharing, led to the establishment of countless virtual communities, and in many ways has brought the world closer together.

Comprising over 11.5 billion indexed pages and accessed by over one billion people worldwide, the Web is utilised by practically every major enterprise, organisation and institution of the modern age.[2] From the 'smallest town in the world' (Hum, Croatia) to some of the most remote outposts on the planet (Mount Everest or Broome, Western Australia) the Web has found a niche in daily life.[3] The Web's influence seems to have touched almost every sphere of human activity. In an article entitled 'The Net: Now Folks Can't Live Without It,' *Business Week Online* reported that:

> Every year, millions more people around the world are using the Internet to interact in more ways than ever before – to date, find old classmates, check on medical ailments and cures, to read and express alternative views of the news, and even to get live sales help online.[4]

The worldwide expansion of Internet access continues at a remarkable pace. Internet usage in North America currently exceeds the 68 per cent level of market penetration (227 million users) and has grown by approximately 110 per cent since 2000. With more than 205 million users, market penetration has reached almost 69 per cent in the USA and grown by 115 per cent over the same period. There are more than 230 million Internet users among the European Union's 25 member countries, with Germany, the UK, Italy and France representing more than 61 per cent of overall activity. Among these four, the UK leads in market penetration at almost 63 per cent (37.8 million users), followed by Germany at 59 per cent (48.7 million), Italy at 49 per cent (28.9 million) and France with 43 per cent (26.2 million). Almost 75 per cent of Sweden's population accesses the Internet (6.8 million). Total EU usage has grown by more than 147 per cent since 2000, while market penetration now approaches 50 per cent.

Asia already enjoys the world's largest number of users (364 million), but currently has only 10 per cent market penetration. These figures are certain to rise over the next couple of decades as massive numbers of potential users begin to obtain Internet access in China and India (already with 393 per cent and 912 per cent increases, respectively, since 2000). While Internet access in Africa remains extremely spotty, Latin American and Middle Eastern activity has grown significantly.[5] The Computer Industry Almanac estimates that by 2011 more than two billion people will be Internet users.[6]

Despite the so-called 'dot-com' bust of 2000, worldwide e-commerce continues to thrive. Gross online sales in the USA (including travel) totalled $176.4 billion in 2005 with estimates for 2006 topping the $211 billion mark. Through 2009, annual growth is projected to rise more than 18 per cent.[7] European e-commerce for 2001 totalled $95.6 billion with 2006 estimates in the $135 billion range. UK online sales represent approximately one-third of EU online totals and are projected in the $110 billion range by 2010. Germany represents almost another third of EU retail activity with $108 billion in projected e-sales for 2008. Continued growth is expected in Western Europe as the UK, Germany, France, Italy and Spain Could see combined e-commerce growth of 41 per cent between 2004 and 2008.[8] With reinvigorated venture capital investment and new revenue growth there is even active discussion of a 'Web 2.0' dot-com renaissance that will build on the lessons learned from the first boondoggle.[9]

While business fortunes rise and wane, the Web continues to be creatively employed in higher education and other fields of human endeavour. One group of educators discussing its influence wrote:

> To say that the Web has affected many societies and cultures is to understate its impact along several dimensions ... While it is possible to overstate or mis-state the Web's effect, whether on higher education or on other institutional clusters, the encompassing reach of the technology, used in every country on Earth by literally tens of millions of users, makes it clear that the Web truly has a revolutionary effect.[10]

The revolution is well under way in the USA as online distance education is booming. Undergraduate and master's level degrees in almost every imaginable discipline can be earned from accredited institutions with minimal, if any, physical visits to the host institution. Academic libraries have quickly embraced database driven web solutions to offer digital reserve desks and access to full-text articles, books and digital collections of primary source materials. During the 2000–2001 academic year more than three million US students participated in online courses and in excess of 2,800 college-level degrees (44 per cent graduate) were offered.[11] Although Web-based distance learning has not yet seen comparable activity in Europe, e-learning has been widely adopted by higher education institutions throughout Australia.[12]

While the Web's emergence as an information powerhouse is almost universally acknowledged, the last few years have witnessed a gradual cessation in the exuberant hyperbole that accompanied its earliest beginnings. Cybercrime, e-privacy concerns, cultural homogenisation and other social ills related to the Internet have also begun to be considered. The Web's actual influence continues to be a matter of debate. In a measured vein, one group of sociologists has noted that:

> utopian claims and dystopic warnings based on extrapolations from technical possibilities have given way to more nuanced and circumscribed understandings of how Internet use adapts to existing

patterns, permits certain innovations, and reinforces particular kinds of change … the ultimate social implications of this new technology depend on economic, legal, and policy decisions that are shaping the Internet as it becomes institutionalised.[13]

Though the Web's constructive possibilities remain vast, much of the early hype has dissipated and the 'ultimate social implications' of the Web appear somewhat murky. With each brilliant possibility that would seem to harken a new day of promise there loom nagging and intractable information problems threatening to undermine worthwhile initiatives, deplete resources and overwhelm participants.

The twin perils of our time

Every age has its share of predicaments. Shakespeare frequently captured the spectacle of Elizabethan characters grasping wealth, love or power only to be tragically undone by a trivial happenstance or unseen forces of collusion. An Einsteinian poet of our information age might similarly posit that every potential advance of technology is met with (at least) an equal and opposite series of forces bent on obstruction and/or incapacitation. While the Web has created enormous economic, educational and information-sharing possibilities, two seemingly antithetical conspirators have arisen who share a penchant for impeding and imperilling the constructive use of information. The modern antagonists might be described in this way:

Inaccessibility – inability to gain information access due to limited resources, skills, time, proximity, interest and/or permission. This condition is frequently experienced by end users (e.g. lacking Internet access), but can also be found in organisations with an insufficient capability to manage information, resulting in underutilisation of potential information assets.

Hyper-accessibility – easily obtainable information access often via broadband connections through multiple paths (wired/wireless/ satellite) and devices (desktop/laptop/cell/PDA/etc.), from numerous content providers via alternative media (HTML/RSS/blogs/streaming media/etc.), resulting in information overload and (ironically) underutilisation of potential information assets.

Inaccessibility

Even during the early stages of the information revolution of the 1990s, one of the most talked about and feared threats was the looming 'digital divide'. The Internet access statistics previously cited demonstrate that substantial and continuing gains are being made towards universal connectivity. While falling computer prices and Web access fees over the last decade have helped level the playing field, more than five billion global citizens remain disenfranchised. The top 15 countries in Internet usage represent 69 per cent of the worldwide total and the top seven (USA, China, Japan, India, Germany, UK, South Korea) hold a 53 per cent share.[14]

Census Bureau data indicate that computer ownership continues to be skewed along ethnic and socioeconomic lines in the USA.[15] A 2005 UK report found similar correlations between Internet access and socioeconomic status.[16] Despite public and private efforts to address Internet inequities (e.g. Clinton/Gore E-Rate legislation; 'Connecting the UK' initiative; Amsterdam's 'Fibre to the Home' project; Gates Foundation international library grants; Macedonia's 'mesh' network; Taiwan's 'M-Taiwan' project), there is continuing disparity. The digital divide was and remains a threat to social and information equality around the globe.

Although 'inaccessibility' is generally thought of in terms of non-existent Internet connectivity, it can hold other meanings. The term can also refer to unavailable informational content due to factors such as a lack of resources (both human and technical), minimal digitisation of physical content, deficient descriptors and access points, non-conformity with established web accessibility standards for persons with disabilities, ill-designed navigational processes, selection of improper technologies and ineffectual information management.

Hyper-accessibility

While many are unable to use the Internet or access existing digital information, at the opposing extreme of the Internet revolution are the world's citizens who are increasingly overwhelmed by the unprecedented torrent of information flowing through both narrow and broadband global networks. The International Data Corporation (IDC) recently predicted that:

> the volume of Internet traffic generated by end users worldwide will nearly double annually over the next five years ... By 2007,

IDC expects Internet users will access, download and share the information equivalent of the entire Library of Congress more than 64,000 times over, every day.[17]

A recent *New York Times* article discussing the developing field of interruption science noted that 'information is no longer a scarce resource – attention is'.[18] Behavioural psychologists and human–computer interaction scientists tell us that people are having difficulty coping with the influx of data and the accompanying distractions:

> The reason many interruptions seem impossible to ignore is that they are about relationships – someone, or something, is calling out to us. It is why we have such complex emotions about the chaos of the modern office, feeling alternately drained by its demands and exhilarated when we successfully surf the flood.[19]

Educators from many disciplines recognise that the tidal waves of information can be a mixed blessing. In 2001 *The Lancet*, the influential UK medical journal, published an article affirming the potential of information technology to transform medical education, but also warned that the 'rate of technological advancement is frighteningly fast'.[20] Commentator Gary Grate creates a vivid image of the confused state brought on by the disorienting onslaught of unorganised digital information by suggesting that an 'employee trying to work in this environment is a lot like a tourist in the middle of a strange city without a map':

> The street names mean little or nothing, and particular places have less meaning, though they may appear to hold great significance. The tourist is lost and befuddled amid the cacophony and apparent chaos of the unfamiliar city.[21]

Other writers have commented how the constant deluge of information has changed not only what we are seeking, but has also made us adapt our information seeking behaviour and modify our roles in the process. Indeed, one online observer noted that 'there is an information overload and within a small time, we can turn from learner to a researcher'.[22]

The World Wide Web's emergence as a 'fact of life' in the modern world has created new information demands for organisations of every kind. Due to the sheer availability of information and the related ease of digital acquisition, many organisations are generating vast amounts of information content at an enormous rate. Each day – perhaps as never before – decisions of consequence are determining how information is gathered, preserved, managed and distributed. The choices are determining whether information will remain untouched, unorganised, unused or underappreciated.

Effective stage management

If Shakespeare's observation that 'All the world's a stage' still holds true, the World (Wide Web) is in dire need of expert production management and directorial assistance. Library and information professionals who can creatively and effectively resolve difficult information issues are in high demand. Fortunately, these 'stage managers' can now use world-class information tools at minimal or no cost. Grass-roots software development communities comprised of both 'hackers' of previous generations and technophiles of the present are actively creating exciting open source database driven web technologies. Both content providers and end users are recalibrating to take advantage of this phenomenal surge in information management software.

Virtually any organisation, be it a corporation, social club, volunteer fire department or public library can (and does) employ open source technologies to create searchable web database applications. These systems can be used for a variety of purposes including inventory control, website administration, digital image management, event scheduling, blogging and more. One need not invest great sums or time to begin rapidly deploying powerful digital management solutions. Developing database driven web applications is exciting, rewarding and imminently doable. Anyone possessing relatively basic web development skills and a measure of determination and tenacity can learn quickly.

The chapters that follow explain what open source software is, where it came from, why it is being used, who is using it and how to take advantage of it. Open source software development is placed in historical context as it is critical to know why this type of software exists and how it continues to be maintained and developed. Later chapters provide guidance on tool selection, standards conformity, database design, basic coding practices and illustrative 'real-world' case studies. Throughout the reader is guided towards reliable open source tools and methods that have been proven to work. Specialised resources should be consulted for in-depth analysis and treatment of topics such as server installation, advanced relational database design and security. Many excellent technical resources are listed in the accompanying notes and bibliography.

There is a satisfying sense of accomplishment after successfully writing even a simple PHP script that, for instance, dynamically updates a web page on demand. Writing good scripts (or sonnets for that matter) becomes easier with the doing. Success breeds even greater success as well-written code can be used in subsequent projects again and again. What's more, effectively applying the technologies presented here for one project will likely suggest other application opportunities that can dramatically improve information management capabilities for any organisation. The possibilities are as expansive as one's imagination. Shakespeare, the quintessential information professional, might well exult:

> Prove true, imagination, O, prove true!
>
> (William Shakespeare, *Twelfth Night*, III.iv)

Notes

1   See the illuminating study by Greenblatt, S. (2004) *Will in the World: How Shakespeare Became Shakespeare*, New York: W.W. Norton.

2   Gulli, A. and Signorini, A. (2005) 'Indexable Web is more than 11.5 billion pages', available at: *http://www.cs.uiowa.edu/~asignori/web-size/* (accessed 1 June 2006); see also Internet World Stats (2006) 'World Internet Usage and Population Statistics', available at: *http://www.internetworldstats.com/stats.htm* (accessed 1 June 2006).

3   See 'Hum – the smallest town in the world', available at: *http://www.hum.hr* (accessed 1 June 2006) and BBC (2003) 'Search on for top net cafes', available at: *http://news.bbc.co.uk/2/hi/technology/3026348.stm* (accessed 1 June 2006).

4   Kharif, O. (2003) 'The Net: now folks can't live without it', *Business Week Online*, available at: *http://www.businessweek.com/technology/content/jun2003/tc20030610_1865_tc104.htm* (accessed 1 June 2006).

5   Internet World Stats (2006), op. cit.

6   Computer Industry Almanac Inc. (2006) 'Worldwide Internet users top one billion in 2005', available at: *http://www.c-i-a.com/pr0106.htm* (accessed 1 June 2006). Web usage and e-commerce activity are notoriously difficult to measure. Furthermore,

international data sources frequently utilise differing statistical methodologies. Most estimates of Web usage are based on general Internet access, which would typically include WWW/HTTP services. See Internet World Stats (2006), op. cit.; International Telecommunications Union (2006) 'Key global telecom indicators', available at: *http://www.itu.int/ITU-D/ict/statistics/atglance/ KeyTelecom99.html* (accessed 1 June 2006); US Census Bureau (2006) 'E-Stats', available at: *http://www.census.gov/estats/* (accessed 1 June 2006); European Commission: Information Society (2006) 'A dynamic e-business environment', available at: *http:// europa.eu.int/information_society/ecowor/ ebusiness/* (accessed 1 June 2006); and National Statistics Online (2006) 'Internet', available at: *http://www.statistics.gov.uk/cci/nscl.asp?id=8454* (accessed 1 June 2006).

7   Top Tech News (2006) 'Online sales grow by double digits', available at: *http://www.toptechnews.com/story.xhtml?story_id= 120000033TK0* (accessed 1 June 2006); Shop.org and Forrester Research (2005) 'Report: the state of retailing online 8.0', available at: *http://www.shop.org/press/05/052405.asp* (accessed 1 June 2006); Expanded Academic ASAP online database: June, W. (2005) 'Internet penetration analysis: the impact on global e-commerce', *Global Competitiveness* 13 (Annual): 9(16) (accessed 1 June 2006); eMarketer (2006) 'US retail e-commerce', available at: *http:// www.emarketer.com/Report.aspx?ecom_us_jun06* (accessed 1 June 2006); and Burns, E. (2006) 'Online retail revenues to reach $200 billion', available at: *http://www.clickz.com/stats/sectors/retailing/ article.php/3611181* (accessed 27 June 2006).

8   European Commission: EuroStat (2004) 'E-commerce and the Internet in European businesses (2002)', available at: *http:// ec.europa.eu/enterprise/ict/studies/entr-ict-2002.pdf* (accessed 1 June 2006); eMarketer (2005) 'Western Europe E-Commerce', available at: *http://www.mindbranch.com/products/R203-345.html* (accessed 1 June 2006); eMarketer (2006) 'UK Online', available at: *http:/ www.emarketer.com/Report.aspx?uk_jan06* (accessed 27 June 2006); and eMarketer (2006) 'Germany Online', available at: *http:// www.emarketer.com/Report.aspx?germany_mar06* (accessed 27 June 2006).

9   Said, C. (2005) 'Silicon Valley humming again; tech giants turn on their smarts and figure out where to take the Internet', *San Francisco Chronicle*, 30 October, BUSINESS, p. J1; LexisNexis Academic online database (2005) 'Leadpile.com says online commerce to

pass one trillion dollar mark by 2012: New "super younger Internet consumer" will lead the way'. *PR Newswire*, 21 September.

10 Clark, K., Parsia, B. and Hendler, J. (2004) 'Will the Semantic Web change education?', *Journal of Interactive Media in Education* No. 3, available at: http://*www-jime.open.ac.uk/2004/3* (accessed 1 June 2006).

11 Waits, T. and Lewis, L. (2003) *Distance Education at Degree-Granting Postsecondary Institutions: 2000–2001*, Washington, DC: National Center for Education Statistics.

12 Danish Technological Institute, Massy, J., Alphametrics Ltd and Heriot-Watt University (2005) 'Study of the e-learning suppliers' "market" in Europe', available at: *http://europa.eu.int/comm/ education/programmes/ elearning/doc/studies/market_study_en.pdf* (accessed 1 June 2006); and Jones, D. R. (2000) 'The distance education debate: an Australian view', *Change* 32(6): 32–3.

13 Dimaggio, P., Hargittai, E., Neuman, W. R. and Robinson, J. P. (2001) 'Social implications of the Internet'. *Annual Review of Sociology* (27): 307–6.

14 Computer Industry Almanac Inc. (2006), op. cit.

15 Keegan Eamon, M. (2004) 'Digital divide in computer access and use between poor and non-poor youth', *Journal of Sociology & Social Welfare* 31(2): 91–112.

16 Prime Minister's Strategy Unit and Department of Trade and Industry (2005) 'Connecting the UK: the digital strategy', available at: *http:// www.strategy.gov.uk/downloads/work_areas/digital_strategy/report/ pdf/digital_strategy.pdf* (accessed 1 June 2006).

17 CRM Today (2003) 'IDC finds that broadband adoption will drive Internet traffic growth', available at: *http://www.crm2day.com/ news/crm/EpuyuElZVAXSEEQgoH.php* (accessed 1 June 2006).

18 Thompson, C. (2005) 'Meet the life hackers', *The New York Times*, 16 October, Section 6, p. 40.

19 Ibid.

20 Ward, J., Gordon J., Field M. J. and H. P. Lehmann (2001) 'Communication and information technology in medical education'. *The Lancet* 357 (9258): 792–6.

21 Grate, G. F. (2005) 'Taking aim at information overload', *Communication World* 22(6): 22–4.

22 Khatri, R. (2005) 'The Internet and its origin', available at: *http:// www.gorkhapatra.org.np/pageloader.php?supp=2005/10/28/ fridaysuppliment/topics/topic4&file=2005/10/28/index* (accessed 11 November 2005).

2

The open source movement

The moon belongs to everyone, The best things in life are free,
The stars belong to everyone, They gleam there for you and me.
(Buddy De Sylva and Lew Brown, *Good News*, 1927)

The popularity of open source software has captured the imagination of developers, information professionals and computing enthusiasts around the globe. The Linux operating system, Apache web server, MySQL database management system, and PHP scripting language are leading examples of freely available software that have transformed the information technology used by non-profit organisations, universities and commercial industries. Frequently distributed together under the acronym LAMP, these four products have created the world's most popular web services platform.[1]

Each individual component of this platform, even standing alone, confirms the scope and significance of the open source movement. Implemented practically everywhere on the planet (and even on the space shuttle), approximately 29 million computer users have selected the Linux operating system. Amazingly, 65–70 per cent of all websites in operation are distributed by open source Apache web servers. The popularity of the MySQL/PHP combination has propelled each to amazing heights in the last five years. PHP has become the world's most deployed server-side scripting language while the 100 million distributed copies of MySQL are utilised by international entities as diverse as Google, Sony, UNICEF and France Telecom.[2]

Though it has risen quickly, the phenomenal growth, ubiquity and utility of open source software did not materialise magically. Its roots lie in the forerunning free software movement of the mid-1980s that continues to this day. The participants and developers in the open source and free software paradigms are an extremely energetic cadre of independent volunteers who have transformed how we access and utilise the World Wide Web. It is difficult to envision how the Web could have grown and become such a global force without open source resources leading the way.[3]

While untold thousands of Internet users regularly take advantage of 'free' software they download online, not everyone is familiar with why the open source and free software movements began, what they are, and how they continue to grow and evolve. Many computer users have become so accustomed and accepting of this 'open' and sharing cyber-environment that the distinct differences between the distribution terms of the myriad software projects available is frequently ignored, confused or forgotten. This isn't surprising as almost any discussion of open source code or free software is almost invariably fraught with difficulty due to the ambiguity created both by shifting definitions and wide-ranging methods of actual practice.[4]

Many individuals approach open source software with a pressing need to be resolved. They also come with varying expectations and philosophical viewpoints. The Internet's collective social structure and unique environment tend to blur the lines between ownership, cost and value. Likewise, the increased commercialisation of the Internet over the last decade has contributed to a kind of culture clash that reverberates throughout the open source and free software communities.

Much of the confusion concerning open source and free software probably lies in the casual language and terminology used to describe it. Depending upon one's perspective, simple statements concerning these resources are frequently evaluated quite differently. Table 2.1 captures some of the confusion. [5]

Suffice to say that subtle yet important nuances and distribution terms are sometimes the only factors that differentiate one 'free' piece of software from another. To understand the open source and free software movements (and how powerful, no-cost tools such as MySQL have come to be), it is necessary to review earlier developments that laid the foundation for many of the phenomenal computer innovations of recent years.

The rise of UNIX

Throughout the 1960s and early1970s, computer programming code developed in research labs was often shared among programmers.[6] As

Table 2.1	The confusing semantics of open source software		
Common assertions		**True**	**False**
1. Open source software is free		✓	✓
2. Open source software is available at zero-price		✓	✓
3. Open source software is equivalent to free software		✓	✓
4. MySQL is an open source product		✓	✓
5. 'Free software' is free		✓	✓
6. 'Free software' is similar to freeware or shareware		✓	✓

(1) Open source software may be distributed at no cost (though not necessarily), but its licensing terms do not always give the user the liberty to freely modify and redistribute the product. (2) Open source software may be distributed at zero cost or sold for profit. (3) In some cases they are equivalent, but free software often endows the user with certain liberties that open source software may not permit. (4) MySQL is an open source product that is licensed under the GNU General Public Licence. MySQL is also commercially licensed by the MySQL AB company in a proprietary version that is not publicly released. (5) Free software may be distributed at no cost or sold for profit. (6) Freeware and shareware products are neither free software nor open source as the underlying code is not publicly revealed, yet both free software and freeware may both be distributed at no cost.

hardware ruled the day, most software was written in machine language unique to each computer. The hardware was the primary mechanism that enabled the completion of information processing tasks. In some respects, the software was incidental. In this age before the personal computer, there were limited 'off-the-shelf' applications available. As it was the machines themselves that dominated the computing market, there was little profit motive or incentive to 'protect' programming code.[7]

In many respects, code was valued similarly to how the drivers that help computers and printers 'communicate' with one another are perceived today. For example, drivers (modules of code) can usually be downloaded free of charge from most printer manufacturer websites as a printer would otherwise be useless without them. Standing alone, the driver is of almost no value unless you have already purchased the company's printer.

Computer operating systems, tied as they were to each individual machine type, developed slowly and inefficiently during the mid-twentieth century for many reasons. One factor was the low processing speeds and lumbering size of the card-fed traditional mainframes that were available. Another was the relatively small number of engineers who were equipped to develop any given system as the available talent was spread across various machine platforms. By the late 1960s, a radically new approach was needed to harness the increasing power of quicker (and much smaller) computer processors. At this juncture of computing history such a bold undertaking could probably only be developed by an institution endowed with world-class technical expertise, technological resources and financial support. Such a place would also need to be blessed with a culture that prized and rewarded original research more dearly than product development. The famous Bell Labs, owned and supported by the American Telephone and Telegraph (AT&T) monopoly, was one of the few entities that could boast such assets.[8]

For decades a recognised world leader in 'pure' research, some of Bell Labs' 40,000-plus inventions and discoveries included the transistor (making the information age possible), the charge-coupled device (used in digital cameras and the Hubble space telescope), superconducting alloys, radio astronomy, high-powered lasers, solar battery cells and holograms.[9] Donald Rosenberg has noted that while some of the great centres of software development were located in the universities, Bell Labs was 'better than a university – there didn't seem to be a lack of money. In this rarefied atmosphere of abstract thought and pure research, work looked like play'.[10]

Furthermore, the Labs were 'generally regarded as the world's best single research institution in communications and electronics'.[11] Bell was heavily involved in computer research due to AT&T's need for sophisticated telephone switching systems. In the 1960s, Bell Labs worked to develop a multi-user, interactive operating system called MULTICS. While MULTICS advanced important theoretical ideas that would make later operating systems more dependable, the project ultimately failed due to its size and complexity. Nearly anywhere else that would have likely been the end of the story. At a place like Bell, however, the tale had only just begun, as 'this was the perfect place to invent the perfect computer system'.[12]

Ken Thompson, a Bell Labs programmer who had participated in the MULTICS development project, began to pine for the better aspects of the failed operating system. In 1969, he started work on a new generalised computing language (called 'B') that could run on top of machine assembly languages. With this rudimentary language he began developing a new operating system called UNIX. Colleague Dennis Ritchie joined Thompson in the effort and dramatically improved the underlying language (renamed 'C'). UNIX enjoyed a tremendous advantage by being written in a new, more abstract language. As UNIX was not tied to a specific machine language, it was destined to be a portable, platform-independent operating system that could be compiled to run on anything from a mainframe to a laptop.[13] In 1974, Thompson and Ritchie authored a paper that introduced UNIX and noted that 'the user will find that the most important characteristics of the system are its simplicity, elegance, and ease of use'.[14]

This revolutionary operating system began to take hold throughout Bell Labs. Following the norms of the day, the UNIX source code was shared freely with academic researchers, scientists and developers around the world. Attracted to the facility and elegance of the system, advanced users and programmers endowed UNIX with 'an almost cult-like status'.[15] Improvements and enhancements began to pour in from far-flung contributors with no ostensible relationship with Bell Labs except for an interest in improving this increasingly popular system. University computer science programmes readily adopted UNIX as it gave their students access to a powerful operating system that they could learn to use and actually tweak for themselves.[16]

The University of California at Berkeley became a major contributor to UNIX development and would later issue its own distribution of UNIX (Berkeley Software Distribution, or BSD UNIX) that included new networking protocols such as TC/IP that Berkeley had developed for the ARPANET project funded by the US Department of Defense. These protocols would provide the foundation for what is now known as the Internet. UNIX had set some important wheels in motion. However, its spectacular success also transformed the sociological and economic dynamics of the computing culture in which it emerged.[17]

Evolving environments

Throughout the 1970s, Richard M. Stallman was employed by the freewheeling artificial intelligence (AI) lab at the Massachusetts Institute of Technology (MIT). Graduate students and faculty at this computing centre were actively encouraged to share code and to build upon the efforts of their peers. The hoarding or password protecting of code was generally unknown. The AI lab represented an 'open' environment in which creativity and innovation were rewarded in the collective. No advantage was gained by hiding one's contributions to the community.[18]

It happened one day that Stallman's utopian bubble was pierced when he was unable to send a document to a printer via a new computer that had been recently acquired. Accustomed to tweaking printer control coding for improved performance and related purposes, Stallman sought to rectify the issue. He was horrified to discover that the proprietary code of the computer's printer control system could not be accessed. Even though MIT had purchased the computer, the company that developed the printer control module was unwilling to share or reveal the source code. By today's standards, the company's desire to protect its intellectual property assets might not seem terribly surprising, but for Stallman it was disturbingly incomprehensible. Stallman was also frustrated that a colleague at another university who possessed the driver's source code was unwilling to share it because he had signed a non-disclosure agreement with the company. An unsettling 'closed' software model was beginning to emerge.[19]

A dynasty unravels

As Stallman grappled with new realities within his own lab, seemingly unrelated matters at AT&T would soon impact computer software and systems development on a larger scale. In 1982, Judge Harold H. Greene of the Federal District Court for the District of Columbia approved a consent decree settlement between the US Justice Department and AT&T. The settlement required that AT&T (which held a monopoly on the US telephone services market), divest itself from its local operating companies. The underlying reasons for the settlement were complex, but an important aspect of the decision gave long-distance telephone customers the freedom to choose among competing service providers.[20]

While it would soon be possible to telephone 'grandma' for less, astute observers began to recognise that AT&T's devolution could heavily impact the computing industry and might come at a steep price. As part of the 1982 settlement, Judge Greene released AT&T from a 1956 court settlement that had prevented the telephone monopoly from entering the electronic and computer markets due to antitrust concerns. AT&T's management recognised this new ruling as a tremendous business opportunity. Though it was generally unknown to the outside world, AT&T had long been a national computing leader as it regularly developed and integrated innovative computing technologies into its complex switching systems. As the company had been under court order not to become involved in the computing industry, AT&T had always taken a very low profile in these areas or sought to emphasise their interdependence with 'communication services'.[21]

Meanwhile, other companies were trumpeting their success in launching a revolution in microcomputer development. By 1981, IBM had released its first personal computer and its new operating system was developed by a small startup company originally founded as 'Micro-soft' in Albuquerque, New Mexico. Numerous other companies were also interested in grabbing a piece of the emerging computing market. Although it faced new competitive realities, AT&T was no longer a telephone monopoly restricted to limited trade arenas. AT&T believed it had the resources and the expertise to make a dramatic impact in the high technology sector. Suddenly all of the old rules were turned upside down.[22]

For whom the bell tolls

Forced to divest itself from its local telephone service holdings, the 1982 settlement also called for AT&T to disassemble segments of its research centres. As a telephone services monopoly, AT&T had always taken a 'hands off' approach with its premier research and development labs. Taking tremendous pride in Bell Labs' achievements, for decades the parent company had directed astronomical resources towards continuing research and development efforts. Even as the settlement was being finalised AT&T was providing over $2 billion in annual support to Bell Labs.[23] During this period, AT&T began looking for creative ways to economically leverage its prior multi-billion dollar research investments. Judge Greene was more interested in equalising the playing field. He ordered AT&T to redistribute core research and development operations and to transfer significant portions of these assets to newly created local telephone service providers. The death knell began to sound for the famed Bell Labs.

The UNIX project had always been an informal and cooperative research development effort shared by many parties. Nurtured within Bell Labs' vibrantly creative 'ivory tower' environment, the remarkable operating system would soon become a target for commercial exploitation as the intellectual property rights associated with UNIX were claimed by the AT&T parent company. With UNIX defined as a commercial property, only the largest companies could afford the licences for its use.[24] AT&T began issuing non-disclosure agreements to everyone involved with the project. Not surprisingly, many UNIX users and developers around the world felt betrayed by AT&T's unilateral declaration of proprietary rights. One of those developers was MIT's Richard Stallman.[25]

A moral imperative

Stallman felt that it was fundamentally wrong for software source code to be withheld from the world. He wasn't opposed to money being charged for software distributions, but he felt that the underlying source should always be readily available to anyone. Stallman understood that it would be very difficult for the computing culture he had once experienced at MIT to be shared with an increasingly 'closed source' world without a competing non-proprietary operating system that could serve as a platform. As Stallman has written:

> The easy choice was to join the proprietary software world, signing nondisclosure agreements and promising not to help my fellow hacker ... Another choice, straightforward but unpleasant, was to leave the computer field. That way my skills would not be misused, but they would still be wasted ... I looked for a way that a programmer could do something for the good. I asked myself, was there a program or programs that I could write, so as to make a community possible again? The answer was clear: what was needed first was an operating system.[26]

Taking up the challenge in 1984, Stallman resigned from MIT and launched the GNU ('GNU is Not Unix') Project with the goal of creating a UNIX-like operating system. The arduous task began from scratch with the hope of developing small modules that could later be stitched together to form a complete operating system.[27]

One of the most compelling aspects of this story is Stallman's strong philosophical bent. Possessing the technical skills necessary to devise a new computer operating system is one matter. Having the vision to ensure its continuing survival is quite another. Stallman sought to preserve and protect his new undertaking by employing a novel legal strategy known as 'copyleft'. In a total reversal of traditional copyright law, Stallman used the legal tools intended to restrict the use of intellectual content as a means to ensure that content would be freely shared. The emerging GNU system was distributed under a revolutionary software licence he principally authored called the GNU General Public License (GPL). The GPL endowed software users with certain fundamental liberties instead of forcing them to comply with narrowly crafted licensing terms meant to constrain and limit software improvements and use.[28]

Stallman didn't stop there. In 1985 he founded the Free Software Foundation (FSF) to support the GNU project and propagate the ideals of the 'free software' movement. The FSF laid much of the intellectual groundwork for what would later be dubbed the open source movement. The GPL continues to serve as the primary distribution licence for thousands of open source software projects and provides a legal framework supporting the 'free software' that is continuously copied, revised and shared on the Internet.[29]

It is important to note that Stallman and the FSF insist on using the 'free software' designation as opposed to the currently more popular 'open source' terminology. Both 'open source' and 'free software' carry similar meanings and are interconnected on many levels, yet the values and objectives of the two movements sometimes diverge. When the FSF speaks of 'free' (i.e. 'libre') software, it is referring to the liberties that pertain to it rather than its monetary cost.[30] Under the GPL licence, 'free software' can be sold for profit. Stallman notes that 'Free software is a matter of the users' freedom to run, copy, distribute, study, change and improve the software'. These concepts are enshrined in four freedoms that FSF has identified:

- The freedom to run the program, for any purpose (freedom 0).

- The freedom to study how the program works and adapt it to your needs (freedom 1). Access to the source code is a precondition for this.

- The freedom to redistribute copies so you can help your neighbour (freedom 2).

- The freedom to improve the program, and release your improvements to the public, so that the whole community benefits (freedom 3). Access to the source code is a precondition for this.[31]

Over the next few years, Stallman and a committed group of fellow 'hacker' collaborators continued to develop critical components of the GNU system including a C language compiler, debugger, and text editor.[32] One of the last components of the system that had not yet been built was a complex component called the kernel. The GNU team intentionally planned to develop a kernel (named 'GNU Hurd') at the end of the process. The kernel essentially interconnects all of a system's components, providing a hardware interface and system resource management.

Frustrated that a free and complete operating system was unavailable, Linus Torvalds, a Finnish college student, took the GNU components and assembled them as a working unit by writing his own kernel in 1991. He called the resulting system 'Linux' and distributed it under the GPL.[33] Anyone with an Internet connection could now download an advanced, no cost, UNIX-like operating system that would run on virtually any machine. This event changed the course of computing and gave programmers from every nation a platform on which to develop countless open source software applications. Significant though it was, another humble project would make its own contribution to the information scene.

Free software re-imagined

The year 1991, perhaps the *annus mirabilis* ('year of wonders') of free computing and global information access, saw both the advent of Linux and the public release of Tim Berners-Lee's revolutionary invention – the World Wide Web.[34] The simultaneous and astonishing ascent of these endeavours created seemingly limitless new opportunities for connectivity, collaboration and liberation from the 'closed' computing paradigm. While Stallman and the Free Software Foundation continued their evangelistic activities in support of 'free speech' software, elements within (and outside) the diverse computer programming culture began to recognise the commercial implications of these new technologies.

While not wanting to totally abandon free software principles, some influential participants wanted to chart a more pragmatic course for the community. By recasting the movement it was hoped that collaboratively-built software would be viewed as more reliable, stable, efficient, (and yes) more cost-effective. The non-profit Open Source Initiative (OSI), founded by Bruce Perens and Eric Raymond in 1998, marked an attempt to 'mainstream' the free software movement by emphasising economic and technical factors over moral and ethical ideology.[35]

OSI was incorporated for the purpose of establishing and propagating the Open Source Definition (OSD), authored by Perens. OSI also hoped to codify the informal processes that characterised the collective sharing and mutual instincts of the free software movement. By crafting definitions, setting standards and approving licensing templates, OSI sought to preserve the future of open source and free software by protecting and extending its reach. OSI also sought to make open source software more palatable to business and commercial interests.[36]

Though the Free Software Foundation and the Open Source Initiative shared many of the same goals, each was rooted in distinct ideological perspectives and philosophical motivations that have shaped their missions and influence. One of the reasons OSI dropped references to 'free software' in favour of 'open source' software was to clarify some of the more ambiguous meanings associated with the word 'free'. There was a general feeling that software labelled as 'free' (despite the primary *libre* meaning) ironically diminished its appeal upon the presumption that anything given away must be of low quality or merit.

While Stallman conceded that it was a valid goal to avoid the confusion between 'free' and 'gratis', he saw in the larger split an attempt to:

> set aside the spirit of principle that had motivated the free software movement and the GNU project, and to appeal instead to executives and business users, many of whom hold an ideology that places profit above freedom, above community, above principle … 'Free Software' and 'Open Source' describe the same category of software more or less, but say different things about the software, and about values.[37]

Meanwhile, Perens, Raymond and others believed that information technology decision makers would never embrace non-proprietary software without higher confidence and better answers to the questions they were asking. For example, how could 'free' software that people were willing to simply give away be reliable? How could free software be trusted to run 'mission critical' aspects of businesses and organisations? What was this 'copyleft' GPL licensing scheme, and how would companies that had invested millions of dollars developing software be able to protect proprietary code? Weren't there security risks in enabling everyone to see exactly how a software product was put together?[38]

OSI set out to address such questions systematically by countering that many open source programs provide the foundation for the Internet and are proven reliable. Furthermore, open source software (and free software for that matter) is not necessarily given away at zero cost. Companies may take an open source product, modify or add to it, and then offer it for sale in retail stores. They need not reveal their own code if they use an approved OSI distribution license. Some companies (e.g.

MySQL AB) have opted to 'give away' a product's entire code under the GPL licence, but then license it separately to sell value-added services such as technical support or helpful documentation and instructions. Finally, OSI argued that software that faces full public scrutiny is actually far more secure than software that is protected merely by its supposedly 'hidden', non-disclosed status.[39]

The Open Source Definition is the plumb line by which OSI determines whether any given software distribution license is deemed 'open source' compliant. The OSD lists ten criteria that must be met by the software's distribution terms. These include: (1) free redistribution (no restrictions on selling or giving away the software); (2) the source code must be made accessible; (3) the licence must allow modifications and derived works; (4) the integrity of the author's source code must be respected; (5) the licence must not discriminate against persons or groups; (6) nor discriminate against fields of endeavours; (7) the rights attached to the program apply to all later distributions; (8) the licence must not be specific to a product; (9) the licence must not restrict other software; and (10) the licence must be technology-neutral.[40] Software that is distributed under these terms is termed 'OSI Certified Open Source Software'. OSI notes that the basic idea behind open source is very simple:

> When programmers can read, redistribute, and modify the source code for a piece of software, the software evolves. People improve it, people adapt it, people fix bugs ... We in the open source community have learned that this rapid evolutionary process produced better software than the traditional closed model, in which only a very few programmers can see the source and everybody else must blindly use an opaque block of bits. Open Source Initiative exists to make this case to the commercial world.[41]

OSI has certified that the GNU General Public License (GPL) conforms to the Open Source Definition. However, not many commercial interests have embraced the GNU GPL, as it has a 'viral' characteristic. If a product includes even a few lines of GPL licensed code within other software code, the entire product must be distributed according to the GPL conditions. This means that companies that combine GPL licensed code with their 'in-house' closed code are unable to protect their proprietary code set. Overcoming this kind of commercial obstacle is precisely why OSI was created. OSI seeks to approve alternative distribution licenses that allow companies to protect their 'closed source' code while encouraging them to use, share, improve and redistribute the modules of code deemed to be 'open source'.[42]

While much of the open source community wants to promote open source principles for the sake of improved products, some of its promoters have also embraced this model as a means of penalising competitors who attempt to monopolise the marketplace with proprietary software. It is no secret that the overwhelming majority of open source developers and participants view the Microsoft software dynasty with disdain (while in many cases still having to rely on Microsoft products to perform certain tasks). As so many applications and software products are developed solely for MS Windows operating systems, numerous open source adopters seek a way to avoid the Microsoft 'trap'.[43]

While the free software and open source communities share many of the same interests, at heart they have different philosophical motivations. OSI has sought to embrace commercial interests in the hope of expanding the reach of the open source community of developers. The Free Software Foundation, in contrast, views OSI as a business-friendly initiative that on occasion may undermine the culture of 'free' and 'open' sharing. While OSI understands its efforts as protecting and furthering the general open source/free software movement, FSF sometimes views its counterpart's activities as being detrimental to the ethos of keeping code 'free in every respect'. FSF argues that this fundamental 'freedom' is what created the 'open' environment in the first place. The two communities appear to have reached a sort of détente where they collaborate when they can, and agree to disagree when necessary.[44]

For all practical purposes most people probably care little whether the code they download from the Internet is 'open source' with the OSI imprimatur or 'free software' as defined by the Free Software Foundation. That is, as long as they can acquire and utilise the code at *no cost* and participate in a larger community of developers and users willing to share insights, tips, methods and procedures for enhancing the code and its reach. It is this critical value-added services ethos – offered at no charge – that makes the open source and free software communities interesting, engaging and useful.

Supported by volunteer programmers numbering in the thousands, open source and free software initiatives and products have thrived in the virtual Internet community. MySQL and PHP, two open source tools discussed throughout this book, are powerful information management tools available at no cost that anyone may download and use. These tools have grown and thrived in an open source and free software culture that is supported by substantial technical expertise and thoughtful distribution methods. We all benefit from the depth and breadth of the communities that build, sustain and enhance them.

Summary

Built upon the struggles of innovative 'hackers,' high-minded free software renegades and enterprising pragmatists, the open source software movement has transformed the information technology landscape. Multinational corporations, non-profit research institutes, university libraries, garden clubs and individual hobbyists are all using open source software to gather, organise and provide access to information. Powerful, no cost, and easy-to-use open source software such as MySQL and PHP has made it possible for individuals without significant resources and years of highly technical training to develop complex web applications. The creation of database driven websites, content management systems and searchable online databases are now all well within reach. Meanwhile the scope and variety of web application development continues to expand. Grounded in the culture and ideals of an innovative and long-standing global community, open source database driven web development promises to be a significant information management touchstone for years to come.

Notes

1   Due to its popularity and the many commonalities shared by the open source and free software movements, the phrase 'open source' is used as a convenience throughout this book to signify software generally identified with either or both movements. The PHP, Perl and Python programming languages are often used interchangeably for the 'P' in LAMP. On technical and ethical grounds, Richard Stallman has vigorously protested that the so-called 'Linux' operating system should be more accurately referred to as 'GNU/Linux' (see *http://www.gnu.org/gnu/linux-and-gnu.html* (accessed 1 June 2006)). For brevity (and as 'GAMP' seems phonetically injurious), this book (while acknowledging Stallman's objections) shall use the more popularly recognised 'Linux' moniker.

2 DiBona, C., Ockman S. and Stone, M. (eds) (1999) *Open Sources: Voices from the Open Source Revolution*, Cambridge, MA: O'Reilly, p. 101. The number of Linux users is an approximation by the Linux Counter website: *http://counter.li.org/* (accessed 1 June 2006). For Apache data see Netcraft's 'May 2006 Web server survey', available at: *http://news.netcraft.com/archives/web_server_survey.html* (accessed 1 June 2006). For PHP stats, see the 'Apache module report (June 2006)', available at: *http://www.securityspace.com/s_survey/data/man.200508/apachemods.html* (accessed 1 June 2006). See MySQL usage information at 'MySQL customers by industry', available at: *http://www.mysql.com/ customers/* (accessed 1 June 2006).
3 Rosenberg, D. K. (2000) *Open Source: The Unauthorized White Papers*, Foster City, CA: IDG Books, pp. 31–2; Overly, M. (2003) *The Open Source Handbook*, Silver Spring, MD: Pike & Fischer; i.
4 Rosenberg (2000), op. cit. pp. 18–25.
5 The differences and similarities between the free software vs. open source movements and associated definitions are perhaps best articulated in the writings of Richard M. Stallman: *http://www.fsf.org/licensing/essays* (accessed 1 June 2006); *http://www.gnu.org/philosophy/* (accessed 1 June 2006); and 'Categories of free and non-free software', available at: *http://www.gnu.org/philosophy/categories.html* (accessed 1 June 2006). See also Rosenberg (2000), op. cit.; 'Open Source Initiatives FAQ' available at: *http://www.opensource.org/advocacy/faq.php* (accessed 1 June 2006); and Wendel De Joode, R. van, Bruijn, J. A. de, and van Eeten, M. (2003) *Protecting the Virtual Commons*, The Hague: TMC ASSER Press.
6 Wayner, P. (2000) *Free For All: How Linux and the Free Software Movement Undercut the High-Tech Titans*, New York: HarperBusiness, p. 27; Rosenberg (2000), op. cit. p. 8.
7 Kavanaugh, P. (2004) *Open Source Software: Implementation and Management*, Amsterdam: Elsevier, pp. 1–17; Peterson, R. L. (1999) *UNIX Clearly Explained*, San Diego: Academic Press, pp. 3–12; Stallman, R. M. (1999) 'The GNU operating system and the free software movement', in DiBona et al. (1999), op. cit. pp. 53–70.
8 Much has been written about the illustrious Bell Labs, the 'greatest research lab of the twentieth century' and the 'crown jewel of AT&T'. Scientists who valued the pursuit of primary research

found Bell Labs superior to a university appointment as they enjoyed unrivaled resources, freedom and could even place unlimited long-distance business telephone calls – see Gehani, N. (2003) *Bell Labs: Life in the Crown Jewel*, Summit, New Jersey: Silicon Press; and Crandall, R. W. (1991) *After the Breakup: US Telecommunications in a More Competitive Era*, Washington, DC: Brookings Institution, p. 18.

9   Eleven Bell Labs researchers have received Nobel Prizes in Physics while 28 have garnered the IEEE Medal of Honor. See 'Bell Labs Awards' available at: *http://www.bell-labs.com/about/awards.html* (accessed 1 June 2006); 'History' available at: *http://www.bell-labs.com/about/history/* (accessed 1 June 2006); and Noll, M. (1987) 'Bell system R&D activities', *Telecommunications Policy* 11(2): 164.

10   Rosenberg (2000), op. cit. p. 9.

11   Jackson, C. L. (1984) 'The anchor of the Bell system', in Shooshan, H. M. (ed.) *Disconnecting Bell: The Impact of the AT&T Investiture*, New York: Pergamon, p. 71.

12   Rosenberg (2000), op. cit. p. 9.

13   Ritchie, D. and Thompson, K. (1974) 'The UNIX time-sharing system', *Communications of the ACM* 17: 365–75; Dunphy, E. (1991) 'The UNIX industry: evolution, concepts, architecture, applications, and standards', Boston: QED, pp. 23–4; Raymond, E. S. (1999) 'A brief history of hackerdom', in DiBona et al. (1999), op. cit. pp. 22–3; Sobell, M. G. (1989) *A Practical Guide to the UNIX System* (2nd edn), Redwood City: Benjamin/Cummings; and Bach, M. J. (1986)'*The Design of the UNIX Operating System*', Englewood Cliffs, NJ: Prentice Hall.

14   Ritchie (1974), op. cit.; Salus, P. H. (1994) *A Quarter Century of UNIX*, Reading, MA: Addison-Wesley.

15   Dunphy (1991), op. cit. p. 21; and Salus (1994): 119–36.

16   Dunphy (1991), op. cit. pp. 25–7.

17   McKusick, M. K. (1999) 'Twenty years of Berkeley Unix', in DiBona et al. (1999), op. cit. pp. 31–46.

18   Rosenberg (2000), op. cit. pp. 6–9.

19   Rosenberg (2000), op. cit.; Stallman (1999), op. cit.

20   Greene delivered his opinion on 11 August 1982: United States *v.* AT&T (Civil Action No.82-0192). For a detailed look at the issues and decision makers involved in the famous settlement see Cole, B. G. (1991) *After the Breakup: Assessing the New Post AT&T*

Divestiture Era', New York: Columbia University Press; Crandall, R. W. (1991) *After the Breakup: US Telecommunications in a More Competitive Era*, Washington, DC: Brookings Institution; and Noll (1987), op. cit. Coincidentally, during the writing of this book AT&T was purchased by SBC (formerly Southwestern Bell, one of the seven 'Baby Bell' regional telephone operating companies created by the original AT&T breakup). In March 2006, this 'new' AT&T (SBC kept the AT&T moniker), continued its reconsolidation efforts by announcing a $67 billion plan to purchase Bell South, the fourth 'Baby Bell' to be acquired/reunited by SBC. Meanwhile, France's Alcatel announced plans in April 2006 to purchase Lucent Technologies (an AT&T 'spinoff' company founded in 1996 that operates what remains of the original Bell Labs). See Young, S. (2005) 'SBC completes AT&T purchase', *Wall Street Journal* 246:109:A8 (19 November); Searcey, D. (2006) 'A reborn AT&T to buy Bell South', *Wall Street Journal Abstracts* A:1:4 (6 March); and Mohammad, A. (2006) 'Alcatel agrees to buy Lucent', *The Washington Post* A:A09 (3 April).

21 Crandall (1991), op. cit. pp. 37–40; Cole (1991), op. cit. pp. 2, 36; Irwin, M. R. (1984) *Telecommunications America*, Westport, CT: Quorum, pp. 81–110; and Stone, A. (1989) *Wrong Number: The Breakup of AT&T*, New York: Basic Books, pp. 200–35.

22 Dunphy (1991), op. cit. pp. 28–9.

23 See Noll (1987), op. cit.; and Cole (1991), op. cit.

24 For an introduction to the history of the UNIX controversy and beginnings of the free software and open source Movements, see Rosenberg (2000), op. cit.; Wendel De Joode (2003), op. cit.; DiBona et al. (1999), op. cit.; Overly (2003), op. cit.; Wayner (2000), op. cit.; the essays by Richard Stallman at *http://www.gnu.org* (accessed 1 June 2006); and the Open Source Initiative website at *http://www.opensource.org* (accessed 1 June 2006).

25 Wayner (2000), op. cit. pp. 33–9.

26 Stallman, R. M. (2002) *Free Software, Free Society: Selected Essays of Richard M. Stallman*, Boston: GNU Press, p. 17.

27 'GNU' is a recursive acronym, pronounced 'guh-NEW'.

28 Dixon, R. (2004) *Open Source Software Law*, Boston: Artech House, pp. 17–39.

29 Stallman (1999), op. cit.; Rosenberg (2000), op. cit.

30 Stallman notes that 'Free software is a matter of liberty, not price. To understand the concept, you should think of "free" as in "free

speech", not as in "free beer"'. See Stallman (2002), op. cit. p. 41.

31   The first numeral in computer indexing is generally '0', which helps explain FSF's unusually numbered list of freedoms. See Stallman (2002), op. cit. p. 41.

32   For an overview of the storied 'hackers' (not to be confused with present-day computer outlaws) and their prodigious work, see Levy, S. (2001) *Hackers: Heroes of the Computer Revolution*, New York: Penguin; Raymond, E. S. (1996) *The New Hacker's Dictionary* (3rd edn), Cambridge, MA: MIT Press; and Raymond (1999), op. cit. pp. 19–29.

33   While acknowledging Torvald's contribution in authoring an important system component, Stallman argues that the resulting operating system should be referred to as 'GNU/Linux'. See Stallman's 'Linux and the GNU Project', available at: *http://www.gnu.org*. While events (i.e. Linux) seem to have overtaken it, work continues on the GNU Hurd, though it was still not ready for production use by 2006 (see *http://www.gnu.org/software/hurd/hurd.html* (accessed 1 June 2006)).

34   See W3C (1995) 'About W3C: History' available at: *http://www.w3.org/History.html* (accessed 1 June 2006).

35   Kavanagh (2004), op. cit. p. 2; Perens, B. (1999) 'The Open Source Definition', in DiBona et al. (1999), op. cit. pp. 171–88.

36   Perens (1999), op. cit.; See also OSI (2006) 'The open source case for hackers', available at: *http://opensource.org/advocacy/case_for_hackers.php* (accessed 1 June 2006).

37   Stallman (1999), op. cit. pp. 69–70.

38   Rosenberg (2000), op. cit.; Wendel De Joode (2003), op. cit.; Perens (1999), op. cit.

39   Perens (1999), op. cit.; and OSI (2006) 'The Open Source Definition' (version 1.9), available at: *http://www.opensource.org/docs/definition.php* (accessed 1 June 2006).

40   OSI (2006), op. cit.

41   See the OSI website: *http://www.opensource.org* (accessed 1 June 2006).

42   Wendel De Joode (2003), op. cit. pp. 74–82; Wayner (2000), op. cit. pp. 88–93.

43   Rosenberg (2000), op. cit. pp. 37–38.

44   See 'Why free software is better than open source', in Stallman (2002), op. cit. pp. 55–60.

3

Six reasons to consider open source

Man is a tool-using animal ... Without tools he is nothing,
with tools he is all.

(Thomas Carlyle, *Sartor Resartus*, 1834)

Open source software is a highly attractive option for organisations seeking to improve how they manage and deliver digital information. Many of the leading open source software applications now available are on a par with (or even superior to) their finest proprietary counterparts. Low-cost open source options boasting huge support communities have led many companies and government institutions that were initially leery of adopting these 'untested' resources to fully embrace and integrate them into their operations. While open source software has made major inroads, proprietary software still has an important role to play and will likely remain a constant for the foreseeable future. Open source software can often complement or enhance proprietary software applications giving the user significant flexibility and expanded capabilities.[1]

This chapter makes the case for open source software and encourages anyone selecting between various software options to consider the nature of their information needs carefully. There are at least six key factors that make open source software a 'live' option that most organisations should explore. The following discussion addresses many of the general characteristics of open source software and what makes it unique. As the focus of this book is database driven web development, PHP and MySQL will be frequently highlighted examples of useful open source options.

Stability and improvements

The high levels of stability, security and continuing enhancement found in major open source software initiatives are well known. Committed, talented and experienced developers have come in droves to participate in open source communities. With their number has come stability, attention to detail, continuously incoming 'fresh blood' to pursue exciting possibilities, and speedy responses to bugs and security holes. These characteristics are among the primary reasons open source products have been so successful.

Eric S. Raymond's influential treatise 'The Cathedral and the Bazaar' has made the seminal case for why open source software development is superior to the closed source proprietary model used by most corporations. His general philosophy holds that the more programmers who interact and work with any given piece of code will invariably improve it ('many eyeballs tame complexity'). Raymond argues that with open source software 'given a large enough beta-tester and co-developer base, almost every problem will be characterised quickly and the fix obvious to someone'.[2] He goes on to compare the cathedral (proprietary) approach to programming with the bazaar (open source) method:

> In the cathedral-builder view of programming, bugs and development problems are tricky, insidious, deep phenomena. It takes months of scrutiny by a dedicated few to develop confidence that you've winkled them all out. Thus the long release intervals, and the inevitable disappointment when long-awaited releases are not perfect. In the bazaar view, on the other hand, you assume that bugs are generally shallow phenomena – or, at least, that they turn shallow pretty quickly when exposed to a thousand eager co-developers pounding on every single new release. Accordingly you release often in order to get more corrections, and as a beneficial side effect you have less to lose if an occasional botch gets out the door.[3]

The pool of potential developers is quite large as the source code for any given project is available for anyone to access and review. Highly motivated people around the world can rapidly gain knowledge and skill by installing the 'free' code on inexpensive machines and begin experimenting.[4] Electronic bulletin boards, listservs, blogs and other modes of e-communication are frequented by thousands of online volunteers interested in addressing both basic and advanced development and implementation issues. New articles and tutorials are constantly being created and shared on the Web. These resources address multiple skill levels and provide ways for organisations to train staff and develop applications at low cost.

Much has been written about the unique nature of open source communities and the factors that predispose developers to so willingly share their time and contribute their expertise to global strangers whom they will likely never meet. Open source communities tend to approach software development differently than proprietary organisations.[5] Open source researcher Walt Scacchi has noted that:

> open software development practices are giving rise to a new view of how complex software systems can be constructed, deployed, and evolved. Open software development does not adhere to the traditional engineering rationality of virtues found in the legacy of software engineering life cycle models or prescriptive standards ... [rather it] is inherently and undeniably a complex web of socio-technical processes, development situations, and dynamically emerging development contexts ... [which] continually emerge through a web of community narratives.[6]

Franke and Shah state that a 'community-based innovation system works on the basis of generalised exchange'.[7] The authors identify reasons why it might make sense to reveal software enhancements and innovations including the desire to 'induce improvements by others' and that 'reputation effects and expectations of reciprocity' may further promote the free disclosure and contribution of their work.[8] Instead of two-party 'quid pro quo' conditions found in commercial markets, open source communities frequently assist innovators they may not know. Some of the strongest motivations for assisting may include:

> the enjoyment gained from working with others, the presence of community norms supporting providing assistance for free, and the idea that helping others in the community is what should be done – are reflective of social processes not personal benefit ... In brief, a community-based innovation system compared with a market system seems to offer significant advantages.[9]

Raymond argues that open source communities cannot be understood within the rubric of voluntary 'generalised exchange' or the broader environment of 'free markets'. He focuses on the economic and anthropological characteristics of 'gift cultures' as a way of understanding the motivations of open source developers. Raymond argues that gift cultures are 'adaptations not to scarcity but to abundance':

> They arise in populations that do not have significant material-scarcity problems with survival goods. We can observe gift cultures in action among aboriginal cultures living in ecozones with mild climates and abundant food ... [and] in certain strata of our own society, especially in showbusiness and among the very wealthy ... In gift cultures, social status is determined not by what you control but by *what you give away*.[10]

Raymond believes that the principle of self-selection weighs heavily in the culture of the open source community. He notes that the open source 'social milieu selects ruthlessly for competence'. Only those with sufficient skill and talent are likely to recommend themselves for active participation. Indeed:

> open source developers are volunteers, self-selected for both interest and ability to contribute to the projects they work on (and this remains generally true even when they are being paid a salary to hack open source) ... The success of the open-source community [provides] hard evidence that it is often cheaper and more effective to recruit self-selected volunteers from the Internet than it is to manage buildings full of people who would rather be doing something else.[11]

Wendel de Joode notes that many researchers have identified the uncommon characteristic of 'joy' as a significant motivation for many open source developers. The sheer joy one experiences in developing software may not always offset some of the more prosaic undertakings that are involved. Still, it seems plausible that joy could help compensate for the nettlesome issues and aggravations that sometimes accompany complex hacking. The 'user's direct need' for functioning and improved software is perhaps the primary benefit of revealing code and encouraging other developers to participate in a project. Finally, the pursuit of 'reputation' may help explain why people may choose to freely contribute their time and talent to open source projects. Individuals can gain status within their development communities by writing outstanding (sometimes called 'elegant') code, repeatedly solving thorny issues, authoritatively and accurately answering questions, and by documenting and managing projects.[12]

Raymond summarises how open source communities can produce superior software to closed source commercial developers by pointing out that:

> While coding remains an essentially solitary activity, the really great hacks come from harnessing the attention and brainpower of entire communities. The developer who uses only his or her own brain in a closed project is going to fall behind the developer who knows how to create an open, evolutionary context in which feedback exploring the design space, code contributions, bug-spotting, and other improvements come from hundreds (perhaps thousands) of people ... Perhaps in the end the open-source culture will triumph ... because the closed-source world cannot win an evolutionary arms race with open-source communities that can put orders of magnitude more skilled time into a problem.[13]

It is unlikely that so many major corporations, governments, and other large organisations would migrate to open source technologies if they were not found to be dependable, innovative and secure. The unique and remarkable character of open source development communities continues to provide stability and foster enhancements of major open source software projects and initiatives.

Standards

Open source products tend to be based on internationally recognised standards. Proprietary software companies frequently create their own 'standards' to differentiate their products from competitor offerings. Without good cause, open source developers do not typically deviate from recognised standards because an important goal is to make the software less complicated and more universal. For example, with each new version, the developers of the MySQL database are moving towards 'supporting the full ANSI/ISO SQL (Structured Query Language) standard' as it evolves.[14] SQL is the language that database management systems use to create, modify and retrieve data. To increase speed and performance, MySQL does add some extensions to the basic SQL standard. These extensions are documented and revealed in the open source code so implementers do not face 'closed source' surprises.

MySQL is compliant with the ODBC (Open DataBase Connectivity) 3.5x standard created by SAG (SQL Access Group). This means that any data residing in MySQL can be easily exported to any another ODBC compliant database (such as Microsoft Access). It is very simple, for example, to 'back-up' an entire MySQL database that lives on a remote server to a MS Access database on a PC. A simple ODBC connection can download a sizable amount of MySQL data and its tabular structure in a matter of seconds. This flexibility is not available in some proprietary database products. Indeed, some 'closed' database systems do not even provide an 'export' feature.[15] It is important to never 'lock' data into a closed system (nor into a closed or static format) that restricts access and publishing opportunities.

The developers of open source systems tend to design interoperable software that conforms to recognised standards for the good of the larger 'community'. Strict adherence to rigid standards may sound exclusionary on the surface, but it actually permits greater product integration, promotes flexibility and choice. Commercial software firms do not always share this general sensibility. They tend to enforce allegiance to their own 'dogma' unless there is a competitive advantage in seeking compliance with rules established by broader collections of users, developers and institutions.

Scalability

The term 'scalability' is understood in a variety of ways within the information world. In the context of database driven web development, scalability primarily relates to the level of performance that is retained while expanding database content and increasing the number of database end users. It is also associated with the relative ease and cost of adding application features, cumulative levels of ongoing maintenance and security, and the development time required to make enhancements.[16]

The PHP scripting language and MySQL database system have been shown to deliver secure, exceptional performance and support the growth of demanding projects. PHP makes rapid database connections, processes content quickly and rapidly serves web pages. This is a critical aspect of database driven web development as practically every web user, be they a kindergartener or experienced developer, wants immediate feedback.

Users understandably want web pages to load quickly and PHP holds up its end of each transaction. Likewise, MySQL completes the 'handshake' as it can process queries at enormous speeds. MySQL has been shown to manage terabyte-sized databases containing millions of rows effectively.[17] Both resources are flexible and easy to manipulate, making them solid long-term development tools.

The Nickelodeon cable television channel is an example of a large enterprise that has adopted the LAMP (Linux, Apache, MySQL, PHP) open source platform with great success. Its MySQL implementation holds several million database entries and has reported 'brilliant' performance.[18] Other major enterprises such as Sabre, Google and DaimlerChrysler have all migrated to MySQL to handle 'mission-critical, heavy-load production systems' that are continually evolving.[19] PHP and MySQL work together to provide powerful, flexible components that can keep up with the expanding database driven development needs of virtually any organisation, large or small.

Portability

Portability is often tied to the standards that have been adopted by any given software product. Not surprisingly, many open source developers specifically design their software for open source operating systems such as Linux. While this trend continues, a growing number of sophisticated open source applications are being ported to run on proprietary and a variety of open source platforms.[20] Much of this activity has been made possible by the growing creation and institutional acceptance of international standards.

Both PHP and MySQL run on most major operating systems including Microsoft Windows 9x, NT, 2000, XP; Mac OSX; Linux 2.0+; and numerous UNIX-like varieties. MySQL can be ported to any system that has a C++ compiler and conforms to POSIX threading standards (international, though not open source standards developed primarily for UNIX systems).[21] When software has been ported to run effectively on a variety of software systems, it is a good sign that the application is being actively used and has been widely adopted. This in turn makes it more likely that the software is stable and functions well.

In a database driven content management context, 'portability' also relates to the relative ease of migrating data from one system to another. Data can be easily imported into MySQL from proprietary databases and exported back out again. As discussed earlier, avoiding proprietary formats is an area where open source software excels. Whereas many proprietary products are attempting to 'lock in' their users (and their user's data) in one way or another, open source software tends to pursue conformity with universal standards. Most information professionals are keenly aware of the need to avoid proprietary 'lock in' of content. Systems come and systems go. It is important to always store valuable data in ways that enhance portability and keep all options open for future content migration.

Cost effectiveness

Open source technology provides the means for organisations of any size, but particularly those with limited financial resources, to use powerful tools that traditionally were only available to major corporations. Commercial enterprise, non-profit groups, state governments and educational institutions are increasingly adopting open source tools.

With many institutions of higher education receiving inadequate funding, it is no wonder that open source tools are frequently being used to address increasing student and faculty demands for improved technology resources and services.

Corporate IT managers must have a high degree of confidence in any software product before they will consider deploying it for 'mission critical' applications. Business information technology departments have become more comfortable with open source resources as they have begun to mature and deliver high levels of stability and satisfaction. This can be seen in the well-known popularity and growth of Linux. It can also be found in the database arena with MySQL being selected over far more established proprietary rivals such as Oracle to perform many important tasks.

Total cost of ownership (TCO) is a metric frequently used in determining not only short-term expenditures for software, but long-term outlays regarding administration, maintenance, upgrades, technical support and end-user assistance. IT managers on a worldwide basis are flocking to open source software (especially the LAMP platform) as a means of lowering TCO measures.

Lycos Europe, a popular Web destination for 25 million users on a monthly basis, recently announced that its migration to MySQL reduced its TCO costs by 90 per cent.[22] The initial software acquisition and future upgrades generally cost nothing or are available in low-cost distributions. Neither are there ongoing licensing fees nor legal audits. Open source software also tends to run more effectively on older hardware equipment than the latest proprietary versions that often demand the newest hardware processors and highest memory levels. A recent study found that the TCO for Linux was 36 per cent less than Microsoft's Windows platform when run on existing hardware.[23]

The actual TCO for any piece of software always depends upon how it is used and deployed. As the initial cost and licensing of open source software is almost always less expensive than 'closed source' commercial software, it is not unusual to see proprietary software vendors releasing estimates indicating the TCO of open source software is higher. These estimates can be misleading if the open source product is unnecessarily installed on expensive hardware, if special services (typically 'proprietary-based') are added to the open source column, or if open source development, training or support costs are elevated based on proprietary norms.[24]

'Incumbent' systems always have a short-term cost advantage as training and staffing are already in place. It is also easy to inflate the initial training and staffing costs of a new open source product due to speculative user satisfaction and error rates. When taking a longer view, open source costs are likely to track more favourably. As established open source software (e.g. Linux, MySQL, PHP) is well known and widely used, there are many skilled, and geographically dispersed individuals available to provide support and training at reasonable costs. While open source (and proprietary) training and administration rates could be higher in given regions, proprietary costs are likely to rise over time as its 'closed' system becomes more specialised and less likely to easily interface with other evolving systems. Having carefully investigated these variables, organisations of every size have come to the conclusion that embracing open source solutions is a cost-effective way to run information management operations.[25]

Access

One of the more obvious benefits of open source software is its availability. As a child of the Internet, open source software can be found at large online repositories and is easily downloaded. Well-known repositories such as SourceForge.net list thousands of software projects being developed by volunteer contributors around the world. Unlike 'closed' software development efforts, open source participants have the ability to participate, contribute code, make suggestions and influence the future direction of any given project.

Both PHP and MySQL are available at 'no-cost' and all source code is available for review. Both of these resources are supported by enormous open source communities that work to develop and enhance reliability and performance. Access means that security holes can be fixed more quickly than with proprietary products as so many programmers have access to the code and can collectively craft a reliable solution.[26] Access also means that thousands of contributors are routinely using and learning more about any given software project. This helps guarantee ongoing project support and development as implementers seek to enhance and strengthen software they have adopted.

Other considerations

For many organisations seeking to improve information management, adopting well-regarded open source software such as the LAMP platform makes a lot of sense. The benefits of adoption often outweigh proprietary alternatives. It is not accidental that IT managers around the world are aggressively implementing the LAMP platform.[27]

However, there are almost always exceptions to most rules. Commercial enterprises, for example, may be reluctant to adopt certain types of open source licensing agreements (e.g. General Public License) that could have the effect of legally obliging the company to release proprietary code if integrated with open source code. Corporations invest significant resources of time and money to protect their intellectual property interests. Not many are inclined to release all of the profitable software source code they constructed at considerable cost. Due to legal liability concerns, companies may also tend to prefer software that has been 'certified' by some responsible party. Open source software does not always come with such an imprimatur, though some open source vendors are building their business plans around just such a model (e.g. MySQL AB, Red Hat). Outside of the commercial realm, most organisations would not find legal objections such as these persuasive.

While there are thousands of open source programs available (and well supported systems such as Linux to run them on), there are some classes of software that the open source community is unlikely to ever develop or seek to address. Adopters must realise that an 'open source solution' may not be available for every computing need. It is important to investigate options, as many proprietary products are indeed superior to their open source counterparts. This may be due to numerous factors including software development time, project stability, commitment and wherewithal of the associated development community, and the perceived importance (and general interest in) any given open source project.[28]

Developing an open source version of an obscure application with limited appeal may not seem compelling or worthwhile to volunteer programmers seeking to provide useful tools to the masses. For example, there will probably always be specialised proprietary drivers and arcane directive software needed to run commercial networks. Most open source programmers are likely to find greater fulfilment in contributing code towards the improvement of a groundbreaking web browser, universal operating system, or a graphics-imaging program than to write code that will primarily be used in the commercial world to supplement legacy systems and processes.

One of the major concerns that critics often discuss is the level of support and service that may (or may not) accompany open source products. Is there a toll-free number that can be dialled when something does not work? Can someone be e-mailed? Is there a responsible person or entity that stands behind the product and guarantees support when the software fails or operates erratically? A question or message can always be posted to an online bulletin board, but will anyone with the sufficient expertise required to resolve your organisation's specific situation actually respond? These are important questions that organisations adopting open source products should consider.

One of the ways to mitigate the 'service and support' concern is to adopt only established open source software with a proven track record and that has been widely adopted by diverse varieties of not-for-profit institutions and commercial enterprises. Software such as Linux, Apache, MySQL and PHP have been thoroughly tested under 'real world' conditions and offer demonstrated reliability and stability. 'Newer' open source projects are more likely to be supported by fewer developers, have more bugs and may generate greater unforeseen issues and difficulties. Projects with limited scope are less likely to have developed a network of skilled programmers and implementers to improve the software and who are willing to share their expertise. Substantial numbers of tutorials, guides, manuals, tips and other resources are readily accessible for popular, oft-implemented open source resources such as Linux, MySQL and PHP.[29]

Some organisations may feel they have neither the technical expertise nor the wherewithal to acquire personnel needed to develop and maintain open source systems. In some cases, it may seem more sensible to purchase a proprietary product that comes with 24-hour technical support and an extended warranty. On the other hand, even commercial technical support does not always address every issue quickly and accurately. The sheer size of the open source community makes it probable that many people have already experienced most issues likely to occur with established applications.

A growing number of small companies are rapidly entering the open source distribution, services and support arena. These service providers can be contacted around the clock and are skilled at troubleshooting and resolving technical issues that may occur. As open source components are so widely implemented, it is often convenient and quite cost-effective for individuals and not-for-profit groups to outsource certain functions such as server and website hosting. Off-site ISPs can be easily contracted to maintain technical server infrastructure, register domain names, physically host websites and provide access to dynamic services such as MySQL and PHP. This frees the organisation and its technical personnel to focus on creating and managing information content instead of worrying about ongoing network and security issues.

Open source software has brought powerful information management tools within reach of organisations that could have never afforded to purchase comparable commercial products. Entities lacking database driven web capabilities of any kind will want to seriously consider adopting open source resources such as MySQL and PHP. The cost is right and the fundamental technical specifications are in place for serious web development activities. But if open source software sounds agreeable in principle, how can it be practically applied in a web environment? Developing database driven websites and applications may sound like dynamic activities, but what are the distinct advantages of actually pursuing them? What is the 'database driven model' and how can it enhance information management activities? The answers to these questions are now pursued.

Notes

1   See Babcock, C. (2006) 'Does open source matter? To IT, it does', *Information Week* (14 February), available at:

http://www.informationweek.com/software showArticle.jhtml? articleID=180201693 (accessed 1 June 2006); Taft, D. K. (2006) 'CIOs: open-source software offers cost, quality benefits', *eWeek* (13 February), available at: *http://www.eweek.com/article2/ 0,1895,1926444,00.asp* (accessed 1 June 2006); and Anthes, G. (2005) 'Reaching out: as their options multiply, companies will increasingly look beyond the boundaries of their own organizations to procure IT', *Computerworld* 39 (7 March), available at: *http:// www.computerworld.com/printthis/2005/0,4814,100170,00.html* (accessed 1 June 2006).

2   Raymond, E. S. (2001) *The Cathedral and the Bazaar*, Cambridge, MA: O'Reilly, pp. 30, 33; also available at: *http://www.catb.org/ ~esr/writings/cathedral-bazaar/* (3.0: 1997–2000), (accessed 1 June 2006).

3   Ibid. p. 31.

4   Kavanagh, P. (2004) *Open Source Software*, Amsterdam: Elsevier, pp. 50–2.

5   For a review of the literature regarding the motivation of open source developers, see Kakhani, K. R. and von Hippel, E. (2003) 'How open source software works: 'free' user-to-user assistance', *Research Policy* 32: 926–8. For an analysis of the costs and benefits of developing open source software, see Lerner, J. and Tirole, J. (2002) 'Some simple economics of open source', *The Journal of Industrial Economics* 50(2): 197–234.

6   Scacchi, W. (2002) 'Understanding the requirements for developing open source software systems', *IEEE Proceedings – Software* 149(1): 24–39.

7   Franke, N. and Shah, S. (2003) 'How communities support innovative activities: an exploration of assistance and sharing among end-users', *Research Policy* 32: 172.

8   Ibid.

9   Ibid. pp. 172–3.

10 Raymond (2001), op. cit. 'Homesteading the Noosphere', p. 81.

11 Raymond (2001), op. cit. p. 57–8.

12 Wendel De Joode, R. van, Bruijn, J. A. de, and van Eeten, M. (2003) *Protecting the Virtual Commons*, The Hague: TMC ASSER Press, pp. 38–41.

13 Raymond (2001), op. cit. pp. 50–1, 54.

14 See MySQL 5.1 Reference Manual (1.9.1), available at: *http:// dev.mysql.com/doc/refman/5.1/en/standards.html* (accessed 1 June

2006). A stated exception is that concessions will not be made to 'speed and quality of the code'.

15 Dunlap, I. H. (2005) 'Open source digital image management' *Computers in Libraries* 25(4): 6–8, 46–8.

16 Herrington, J. (2003) 'The PHP scalability myth', available at: *http://www.onjava.com/pub/a/onjava/2003/10/15/php_scalability.html* (accessed 1 June 2006).

17 See MySQL 5.1 Reference Manual (1.9), available at: *http://dev.mysql.com/doc/refman/5.1/en/compatibility.html* (accessed 1 June 2006).

18 See Gedda, R. (2005) 'Open source MySQL database all child's play', available at: *http://www.computerworld.com.au/index.php?id=1708870374* (accessed 1 June 2006).

19 See MySQL 5.1 Reference Manual, available at: *http://dev.mysql.com/doc/refman/5.1/en/introduction.html* (accessed 1 June 2006).

20 For thousands of open source application examples, visit SourceForge: *http://www.sourceforge.net* (accessed 1 June 2006); FSF and UNESCO's Free Software Directory: *http://directory.fsf.org/*(accessed 1 June 2006); the Open Source Software Directory: *http://www.osdir.com/Downloads.phtml* (accessed 1 June 2006); and Yahoo's listings: *http://dir.yahoo.com/Computers_and_Internet/Software/Open_Source/*(accessed 1 June 2006). The European Union's IDABC initiative maintains the 'Open Source Observatory', a clearinghouse of best practices and useful resources, available at: *http://europa.eu.int/idabc/en/chapter/452* (accessed 1 June 2006).

21 For a list of MySQL-compatible operating systems, see MySQL 5.1 Reference Manual (2.1.1), available at: *http://dev.mysql.com/doc/refman/5.1/en/which-os.html* (accessed 1 June 2006).

22 See MySQL case study 'Lycos Europe migrates to MySQL', available at: *http://www.mysql.com/why-mysql/case-studies/mysql-lycos-casestudy.pdf* (accessed 1 June 2006).

23 Cybersource (2004) 'Linux vs. Windows: total cost of ownership comparison', available at: *http://members.iinet.net.au/~cybersrc/about/linux_vs_windows_tco_comparison.pdf* (accessed 1 June 2006).

24 Kavanagh (2004), op. cit. pp. 48–9.

25 Ibid. pp. 41–65; Wheeler, D. (2005) 'Why open source software', available at: *http://www.dwheeler.com/oss_fs_why.html* (accessed 1 June 2006); Hochmuth, P. (2005) 'Big business technologists

talk up Linux', *Network World* (30 May), available at: *http://www.networkworld.com/news/2005/053005-linux-world.html* (accessed 1 June 2006); Ferguson, C. (2005) 'How Linux could overthrow Microsoft', *Technology Review*, available at: *http://www.technologyreview.com/read_article.aspx?id=14504&ch=infotech* (accessed 1 June 2006); Vaughan-Nichols, S. J. (2005) 'Open Source Goes Main Street', *eWeek* (3 August), available at: *http://www.eweek.com/article2/0,1895,1843633,00.asp* (accessed 1 June 2006); Shankland, S., Kane, M. and Lemos, R. (2001) 'How Linux saved Amazon millions', *CNET* (30 October), available at: *http://news.com.com/2100-1001-275155.html* (accessed 1 June 2006); Roy, R. (2006) 'Open source's mainstream future', *Insurance & Technology* (1 February): p. 37, from *LexisNexis Academic* online database.

26 For example, see Vaughan-Nichols, S. (2005) 'Firefox still tops IE for browser security', *eWeek* (29 September), available at: *http://www.eweek.com/article2/0,1895,1865087,00.asp* (accessed 1 June 2006). Others argue that despite its reputation open source software has not yet been proven inherently more secure, see Viega, J. (2004) 'Open source security: still a myth', available at: *http://www.onlamp.com/pub/a/security/2004/09/16/open_source_security_myths.html* (accessed 1 June 2006).

27 Babcock, C. (2006) 'What's left of Unix?', *InformationWeek* (23 January), available at: *http://www.informationweek.com/story/showArticle.jhtml?articleID=177102427* (accessed 1 June 2006).

28 Anthes (2005), op. cit.

29 For example, a search of the OCLC *WorldCat* Catalog for the 2003–2005 publication years finds 683 titled books on Linux, 173 on Apache, 174 on MySQL and 400 on PHP. A February 2006 Google search for "+MySQL +tutorial" amassed 15 million hits while "+PHP +tutorial" produced over 53 million.

4

The database driven web

It is always safe to assume, not that the old way is wrong,
but that there may be a better way.

(Henry R. Harrower, 1883–1934)

It is not accidental that numerous non-profit organisations, governmental entities and some of the world's largest and most successful online enterprises have selected open source relational databases to drive their information management processes. Information technology managers have found database systems such as MySQL to be cost-efficient, reliable and easy to implement. With database driven web operations obviously functioning well in high-profile institutions, it is not surprising that numerous organisations with mounting information needs are rushing to deploy new systems.[1]

Still, anyone contemplating the migration of a general website or other content to a database driven platform should move deliberately and in an organised fashion. While there is certainly no need for fear or excessive caution, there should be recognition that the creation of database driven web applications requires planning and time for development and implementation. There are varying levels of complexity that may be pursued depending on the nature of the project. In any case, well-spent time and effort expended at the beginning of the process will be rewarded at the conclusion.

But what does 'database driven web development' actually mean? How does the database driven approach differ from traditional web development? Why is it necessary? What are the pros and cons of migrating to a database driven model?

Static vs. database driven

In the early days of the World Wide Web, one of the most common ways of introducing newcomers to this startling new information environment was teaching the basic principles of Hypertext Markup Language (HTML).[2] Learners were often led to simple online tutorials such as the 'Beginner's Guide to HTML' which provided straightforward examples of placing HTML tags around content (e.g. text, digital images, URLs) for optimum display in the leading browsers of the time.[3] Early browsers such as Mosaic and Spyglass ruled the Web, as did rudimentary 'homepages' offering black text, blue hypertext links and a stark grey-coloured default background. In this era before cascading style sheets (CSS) and other browser extensions, designers had only a handful of ways to format and present content.

'White space' was created between lines of text and other content by creatively interspersing the '<p>' (paragraph), '<br>' (line break) and ' ' (space) tags in assorted groupings. Header tags (e.g. <h1>) caused layout problems because indiscriminate regions of white space that could not be controlled automatically surrounded them. The most 'advanced' web designers began to creatively employ HTML tables, not as holders for statistical data, but to control presentational layout. All of this detailed design work occurred within the bounds of a single computer file. Each file was subsequently uploaded via FTP (File Transfer Protocol) to a public web server directory where it could be downloaded and 'read' online via a browser. A multi-page 'website' was strung together by connecting individual files to one another via hard-coded hypertext links. Maintaining a website's presentational consistency across multiple pages meant identically hand-coding the stylistic features of each file. Even today, probably most websites in existence continue to rely on this primary method of online publishing.

Files (and websites) of this type are considered 'static'. Each page is an individual construct completely separate from all others. Making a minor content change means manually opening, modifying and then uploading a specific file to a web server. Instituting a stylistic change across multiple pages necessitates manually opening and modifying each file individually. Besides being time-consuming and tedious, this process almost invariably leads to coding errors and inconsistencies as a website grows larger and more dispersed.

The database driven model takes web development to another level (see Figure 4.1). Instead of linking a multitude of static files together,

Figure 4.1 The database driven model

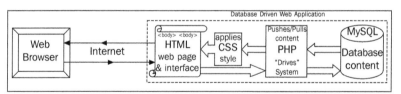

Source: based on 'Abstract view of a dynamic request'; Andreolini, M., Colajanni, M. and Lancellotti, R. (2006) 'Websystem reliability and performance', in Mendes, E. and Mosley, N. (eds) *Web Engineering*, Berlin: Springer-Verlag, p. 189.

the database driven model can use a single file to generate dynamic, 'on-the-fly' web pages. For example, a designer can create a 'canvas' for a website by embedding a single stylistic layout (headers, footers, colours, general formatting) into a single file. The file defines the site's basic style and provides a place for the 'body' of each page on the site to appear. Each individual page of the site is created dynamically by pulling text, images, and other content from a database field into the 'body' of the page. Site navigation in the database driven model is achieved via a dynamic querying process.

Instead of targeting other static files on the web server (which must all be independently maintained), navigational links are designed to pull specific content residing in database rows into the body of the appropriate page. Freed from the bonds of the static page, the content can be called to appear on demand and only when necessary. Even in this basic example, the webmaster's work has become a lot less arduous.

New possibilities

Maintaining the 'body' of each page in a database instead of in a series of hard-coded files creates a number of exciting opportunities. Perhaps the most obvious is that a single file (or a small group of files) can now provide access to the entire website's content. The constant struggle of opening, closing, and juggling multiple independent files in numerous directories can draw to a close.

Separating the website's content from its stylistic layout also makes it easier to update. Website redesigns are no longer so tortuous as aesthetic modifications can be applied on a global basis without affecting the intellectual content of the site. Design changes that once had to be performed on every page of the site can now be configured in a single place. This ensures that no page on the website will be 'forgotten' and left with the 'old' design. It also means that the content can be stripped of old proprietary browser code that was once needed to establish font sizes, colours and other formatting. Cleaning up the intellectual content that will 'live' in a database also means that the content can be more easily published in other media. Uncluttered, the content can be more easily streamed via audio, RSS feeds, PDAs and other devices.

Maintaining the intellectual content within a database increases the webmaster's flexibility on several fronts. With the static file approach, the webmaster is frequently left with the ordeal of shuffling files and e-mail attachments from one format to another. By default, a webmaster may unnecessarily be forced to become an organisation's primary web editor for no other reason than they are the last person to 'touch' all the files before upload.

As the individual authorised to upload files to the server, the webmaster may also feel trapped by time constraints and security issues. Many webmasters have felt the pressure of multiple content contributors wanting today's late arriving copy to be already uploaded 'yesterday'. With many other duties to perform it can be difficult for a webmaster to 'stay on top' of this file transfer routine. Letting all contributors have 'write' access to the server (or even to a specific directory) is not a solution that very many web administrators would deem wise. This approach opens up far too many opportunities for overwrites, unintended mistakes and high-value security concerns.

Employing a database driven model removes many of the structural issues that cause web-publishing difficulties in the first place. The webmaster now has the capability to establish normalised security and publishing protocols. Contributors need not be permitted direct access to the web server or its files. They can now be granted access to a database at whatever level is appropriate, be it a cluster of tables, a specific table or perhaps to only a designated column or row. This type of security arrangement assists (and protects) all parties as the chances for inadvertent error (or even intentional sabotage) are minimised and dispersed.

Contributors can submit and modify data on their own schedule instead of waiting for the webmaster to respond. More people can be included in the web authoring process as no one is required to understand HTML, CSS, PHP or any other coding language. Once a web contributor has submitted new content, anyone within the organisation (or multiple individuals) can be assigned the responsibilities of editorial review. Where once the publication process was slowed by file swapping, cutting and pasting, and last minute HTML modifications, now any reviewed content is a mere 'button click' away from being published to the Web.

Big believers

Configuring a single file to interface with a database for the purposes of publishing web pages is only a limited example of what a database driven web platform can achieve.

Global non-profit organisations, corporations and government entities of all sizes use open source databases to help gather, organise, manage and distribute information. While there are several open source database varieties available, this book focuses on the MySQL Relational Database Management System (RDBMS) for several reasons. Its speed, reliability and performance are comparable with world-class 'closed source' RDBMS systems developed by companies such as Oracle. Powerful enough to efficiently process millions (even billions) of database rows, MySQL is also simple enough to be effectively used by database beginners.

The international list of entities that have adopted MySQL as their RDBMS of choice reads like a who's who of every field. Leading search engine and web portals such as Google, Yahoo! and Lycos Europe; news outlets such as Reuters, Associated Press and BBC; broadband and telecommunications providers such as Cox Communications, Siemens, Nokia, Sweden's Bredbandsbolaget (B2) and Germany's T-Systems; electronics companies like Motorola and Sony International; manufacturers such as Caterpillar, DaimlerChrysler and Yamaha; health, research and not-for-profits like UNICEF, CERN, Canada's Genome Sciences Centre, Médecins Sans Frontières (Doctors Without Borders) and Institut Curie; and college and university research libraries around the world all use MySQL to power critical applications. Indeed, MySQL has over six million active installations.[4]

Seven reasons for pursuit

With so many well-known organisations using MySQL and adopting database driven web strategies it's not surprising that even casual website maintainers have begun to see the advantages of migrating away from the static model. While every situation is unique, here are some of the leading reasons to pursue open source database driven technology.

Cost-effectiveness

It is difficult to beat almost anything that's 'free' (especially when it means zero price). As discussed previously, 'open source' and 'free software' are frequently available at no cost. The MySQL open source database option can be downloaded free of charge online and is generally included with most popular Linux distributions such as Red Hat, SUSE, Debian GNU/Linux and others. Besides the monetary savings from obtaining non-proprietary software, other costs can be avoided as well. The organisational costs of relying on a static web publishing model can be viewed in economic terms, but also in measures of overall productivity and human potential.

Countless potential content providers have been discouraged from submitting worthwhile articles or news items due to arcane HTML coding requirements, technological challenges or a daunting bureaucratic process established for the sole purpose of keeping a static website functioning.

Actual human beings also live on the receiving end of any given web page transmission. It is poor 'public relations' for an organisation to let its Web presence falter. Sometimes relatively minor considerations can undermine the public's trust and confidence in an organisation. Websites that are out-of-date and poorly maintained can have a highly negative impact. While businesses may lose profits, worthy causes and public service organisations performing good work can also forfeit sorely needed voluntary contributions due to a struggling website. There are other real costs associated with a website that is continually 'down' or sporadically updated. Besides the toll of inconvenience, the effects of denying public access to information can be significant.

Available at zero cost and benefiting from testing throughout the world, database solutions such as MySQL have a proven track record of stability and reliability.

Adopting a database driven model can also improve cost-effectiveness in some of the critical areas that rarely appear in a line item of an annual report. Protecting and enhancing an organisation's human 'capital' (both internally and externally) can ultimately deliver big dividends.

On the clock

The well-known cliché 'time is money', conveys a certain economic truth, yet time is also a human resource that organisations can 'spend' in different ways. Unless an organisation is running a very modest website that is rarely updated, much time may unnecessarily be directed to continual page re-coding, file manipulation and transfer, and other unwieldy tasks related to the 'static' web model. It would be misleading to suggest that the development of database driven web applications does not require a front-end time commitment. However, the time expended in initial development can be quickly recouped by the time saved performing functions on behalf of the static approach.

Though a webmaster's skill and expertise will continue to be required, pursuing a database driven model can free up time for the individual to address other information management and technology issues. Information management projects that once seemed almost impossible for smaller organisations to imagine can be earnestly pursued once an individual develops the basic skills needed to create database driven web solutions.

Ease of skill acquisition

Related to the savings of money and time is the moderate slope of the database driven model's learning curve. Though perhaps helpful, it is not necessary to complete extensive coursework or training to construct a database driven web application. Anyone possessing HTML coding skills and a basic familiarity with the UNIX environment (which most webmasters already enjoy) can quickly acquire the necessary PHP and MySQL skills.[5] The construction of information management projects that once seemed almost impossible for smaller organisations to imagine can be earnestly pursued once an individual develops the basic skills needed to create database driven web solutions. Likewise, database driven technology empowers people with little or no interest in HTML or coding to make important ongoing contributions to an organisational website.

Templates

The separation of intellectual content from web page layout and design makes the development of reusable templates a distinct possibility. Many large organisational websites make use of a template-based format so that new content can be plugged into existing frameworks. Perhaps the best examples can be found at large online news operations where writers and reporters routinely submit articles directly into a web-based database driven content management system (CMS).

Many CMS modules provide text-entry services via a WYSIWYG editing field that mimics a full-featured word processor.[6] The click of a button submits the story either directly to the news bureau's website or may signal an editor to review the article before posting it online. Neither the writer nor the editor needs to know anything about HTML or web page creation as the CMS can insert the news content directly into the body of an existing web page template 'on the fly'. The awaiting template will have already been crafted, sporting navigation schemes, images, advertising banners and links to additional information. Many of these other 'content elements' may themselves have been directed to the same web page template by contributors with different responsibilities (e.g. ad designers and photographers). Templates and CMS applications can be developed to streamline virtually all aspects of data entry and web page creation.

Fresh data

The quickest way to lose a website visitor is to display stale, outdated information.

Static pages tend to grow old quickly because someone must manually add or rotate new data in and out of an HTML file. The database driven approach allows new content to be rotated automatically from a collection of sources. Fresh stories can rotate on the front page of the website or can be strategically sprinkled throughout the site in appropriate contexts. Even if your site doesn't always have that much fresh content to offer, setting up a rotating delivery system displaying interesting information can at least leave the impression that there is movement, change and ongoing activity in the life of the organisation.

Diverse publishing options

Separating content from design empowers organisations to use materials in new and innovative ways. An article coded on a static HTML page for web delivery has frequently seen its last premiere. An article that resides in a database, however, can live on to see subsequent appearances in a variety of media. RSS (really simple syndication) feeds are an excellent means of re-publishing content in an accessible format. Major news organisation websites (e.g. Reuters, BBC and CNN) and extremely small personal websites have embraced this easy-to-use publishing technology. Digital content residing in a database can be routinely transmitted to PDAs and cellular phones, and can even be converted into MP3 audio files for podcasts.[7] Managing information via database driven technology opens a wide array of content distribution options.

In addition to new publishing opportunities, the database driven approach may help the content itself to become more accessible to a variety of users. Content that is laden within outdated and proprietary HTML browser code can make access difficult for people with disabilities. The process of stripping the data (removing the old, invalid HTML code from the content) before inserting it into a database can greatly enhance accessibility for individuals using screen readers and other interpretive software. While completing the stripping task, this is also the perfect time to adopt cascading style sheets and to confirm that all code conforms to international standards for accessibility (e.g. Web Accessibility Initiative).[8] Migrating from the static model to the database driven model improves the quality of the content and expands audience reach.

Data management

When content is locked into static web pages it becomes difficult to organise and redistribute. Content residing in a database can be effectively managed with a web CMS built for local requirements with MySQL/ PHP or with a variety of open source CMS systems available for free download.[9] The CMS can be basic in design or remarkably complex depending upon organisational needs. Anyone who learns the basic principles of using MySQL and PHP can begin developing an array of information management tools that will help an entire organisation become more productive. Upon embracing the database driven approach it will soon become obvious that this technology can do far more than generate sophisticated websites – it can transform how organisations perform day-to-day operations and share information.

Seven excuses for delay

Before undertaking any project it is generally wise to consider such factors as monetary cost, the planning, development and implementation time that will be required, what resources (e.g. materials, personnel, and expertise) will be needed, ongoing support and maintenance issues, the likelihood of success versus failure and the consequences of inaction. While these factors are worth reflection, sometimes the mere suggestion of introducing a new technology can grind the wheels of innovation to a screeching halt. On occasion, an overwhelming desire for caution or a predilection for maintaining the status quo may outweigh a basic understanding of the technology or exaggerate the complexity of the task. In such cases, the following excuses for delay may also need to be addressed.

Apprehension

Fear has been known to drive the decision-making process within many organisations. This isn't terribly surprising as sustaining even a well-established organisation typically requires considerable assemblages of quality personnel, time, planning, astute investment, education, effective communication, external support and ongoing energy. Both the love and comfort of 'order and tradition' and the opposing forces of disorganisation, disorder and loss of purpose may propel both leaders and followers to embrace the status quo and avoid any action that could potentially fracture established processes.

The fear of new technology can lead an otherwise progressive soul to stick his head in the sand and wish for the days of the library card catalogue or punch card programmed mainframe computers. To embrace something called 'database driven web development' can sound intimidating or even somewhat terrifying to anyone who is not technically oriented. For the uninitiated user, the World Wide Web even now remains a mysterious or almost magical realm that is barely comprehended. Likewise the static HTML page provides a sense of security for the apprehensive. After all, it is the very model of stability. It is positioned on a web server as an unmovable object. It is concrete, neither desiring change nor capable of change on its own. Any modification made to the file must explicitly be performed on a manual basis, usually by a single party. It is a constant and a known commodity.

Database driven web pages represent motion, activity and change. Pages can be generated 'on the fly' based on content that is updated by contributors located anywhere in the world. Content can be added, modified or removed on a 24-hour basis without having to continually request that a lone 'webmaster' upload an unending series of files.

It may be the notion of placing web page content 'in motion' that makes some people uncomfortable with migrating from the static model. While they may psychologically lean upon the perceived stability of the static web page file, they conveniently ignore the staggeringly complex process that has always made web page viewing possible. Running over electrical currents switched with mind-boggling precision, strings of bits and bytes and digits are propelled effortlessly and flawlessly through interconnected nodes and hubs. Flowing through a worldwide matrix of fibre-optic lines and strands of twisted copper, the data are transmitted onward via a series of interrelated packets. Streaming inexorably toward some final destination, the data navigate through untold network protocols and standards designed by 'hackers' of past generations before gathering and reassembling into a 'static' web page viewable to anyone in the world.

Viewed in this light, the trifle of pulling a little content from a highly reliable database into the body of a simple file is a 'stroll through the park'. Fear is a poor excuse for not embracing such a powerful and relatively simple technology. Building a database driven web page is satisfying, imminently doable and provides a firm foundation for developing even more interesting and useful web applications.

Size

The objection 'Our website just isn't big enough to warrant a database driven approach' could only apply to the absolute smallest of sites. A 'website' consisting of fewer than ten pages could be a definite candidate for a database backend depending upon the nature of the site, its content and intended audience. The same database technology that supports world-class websites is also what drives simple 'five page' blogging sites devoted to every ephemeral hobby, trend and philosophy under the sun. While a website's total number of pages could be minimal, its content might lend itself to being maintained within a database structure.

Content rarely modified

It is probably a truism that a rarely updated website (and thus likely a seldom viewed website), probably does not merit the application of a database driven approach. However, why would any organisation that believes itself significant enough to maintain a web presence not want to entice more people to visit the site, learn more about the organisation, and potentially contribute to its success? A webmaster intent on increasing traffic, keeping interest up and demonstrating the vitality of the parent organisation can be assisted by adopting even a minimal database driven model. Automated and rotating news items, pictures and other content can be an effective way to keep a site fresh, entertaining and interesting.

Skill sets

The creation and maintenance of a static website generally requires a webmaster to be adept at certain tasks. Most people possessing web maintenance responsibilities can code a document in HTML, know how to FTP a file to a remote server, and can sufficiently find their way around a UNIX system to change permissions, rename files and do occasional 'live' editing via Telnet. Anyone who has obtained even this much ability can learn how to deploy a database driven website.

Of course, basic skills must be acquired in using web development resources such as PHP and MySQL. One of the primary reasons for the great popularity of the MySQL/PHP tandem is their ease of use. Some basic computer programming training can be useful, but it is by no means required. PHP is a simple scripting language that is intuitive and can be assimilated quickly. Similarly, MySQL is a very straightforward database management system. Understanding and applying advanced database normalisation principles will speed query times and improve performance, but MySQL is so fast that even databases not fully normalised can deliver surprisingly rapid results.

There are some information systems and management tasks that only highly experienced personnel should ever attempt. Using database driven technology to deploy a website, create a searchable online database or organise digital content is not one of them.

Personnel

Organisations of every shape and size depend on a diverse array of knowledgeable, talented people to attain goals and pursue their respective missions. The same can certainly be said for successful libraries and information management operations. It would be a mistake, however, to assume that one needs an entire staff of full-time system administrators, programmers and database developers to take advantage of open source database driven technology. An organisation that runs its own web server may already have the tools in place to begin pursuing web database development. Groups with a local webmaster that rely on an external Internet service provider (ISP) to host their web presence can find a multitude of providers offering inexpensive access to database development tools such as MySQL and PHP.

Though an entire support team is rarely needed, it is important to have at least one person on staff that is generally interested and motivated to learn web database development principles and techniques. Almost anyone holding the skill sets previously noted can learn how to proceed. Individuals possessing a certain degree of determination, a willingness to experiment, a sense of fulfilment with the process of coding and finding solutions, and who find joy in a job well done will likely excel. If working with new technology frustrates more than energises or is more drudgery than fun, then acquiring web database development aptitude is probably not the best pursuit. Persons who seek exciting new ways to gather, organise, distribute and provide access to virtually any type of digital information are likely to enjoy learning the database driven model.

Technical barriers

As a local server or even a remote web hosting service can provide all of the resources required for database driven web development, the threshold for adoption is quite low. As most fee-based web hosting services provide access to 'no cost' open source database resources, they do not have to pass on expensive commercial fees and licensing charges. Anyone with an Internet-accessible computer can fully administer a database driven operation without the overheads of buying, installing and maintaining a server. All data and PHP scripting can be backed up locally and easily uploaded to an alternative server if rates increase or services decline.

Time

Admittedly, a substantial amount of time is required to turn a moderately-sized static series of web pages into a full-fledged database driven website. Planning, development and implementation activities all require time to complete. However, keeping a static website up and running calls upon the webmaster (and various contributors) to expend considerable time, energy and effort completing wasteful, redundant activities.

With the database driven model, the time invested at the beginning of the development cycle is paid back many-fold. A great many processes that were once mandatory under the static approach may no longer be necessary. In addition, applications written in PHP can be built on a modular basis so that functions contributing to one implementation can be easily reused for other projects. Important sections of code that perform specific tasks (e.g. editing a database entry) can be divided into smaller 'chunks' or modules and 'called' to perform certain tasks only when needed. This modular tactic makes applications run faster. Perhaps more importantly, once any given module is proven to run effectively, it can be used again and again. The ability to build upon past success makes it much easier and quicker to develop subsequent database driven applications. Developers can soon address a wide variety of information management problems using code that has been tested and proven to work.

Summary

Creating static web pages from scratch is a wonderful way to begin learning about web development. The skills learned can be successfully applied elsewhere. Coding static HTML also continues to be a perfectly reasonable exercise if a single page or a small number of pages need to be placed online for a simple objective. However, the Web's dynamic nature and the pressing need for most organisations to manage an ever-growing avalanche of information soon render this method impractical if not obsolete. The database driven model is far superior for general publishing purposes and is absolutely indispensable for information managers needing to organise and provide access to both large quantities of data and small pieces of granular content. The tools are fully developed and available for use. The task at hand is to creatively and effectively use them to overcome the information challenges of the day.

Notes

1　*Business Wire* (2005) 'MySQL 5.0 now available for production use; enterprise platform vendors express enthusiastic support for world's most popular open source database', *Business Wire* (24 October), available from *LexisNexis Academic* online database (accessed 2 June 2006).

2　Learning HTML remains an invaluable exercise for anyone serious about web development. Despite progress being made in designing web authoring programs for the masses, there is no substitute for the ability to quickly manipulate HTML code on a page or in a PHP program.

3　For over a decade, the National Center for Supercomputing Applications (NCSA) at the University of Illinois sponsored Marc Andreessen's classic 'A Beginner's Guide to HTML'. Becoming dated, it was archived and later removed from the NCSA site by 2006 (formerly at: *http://archive.ncsa.uiuc.edu/General/Internet/ WWW/*). The resource lives on at many online sites including: *http://www.ee.surrey.ac.uk/localcopy/ HTMLPrimer.html* (accessed 2 June 2006).

4　See *http://www.mysql.com/customers/* (accessed 2 June 2006).

5　MySQL and PHP can also be utilised in the Windows environment.

6　WYSIWYG stands for 'what you see is what you get'. A number of open source WYSIWYG editors are available for integration into MySQL/PHP CMS applications. See *http://www.htmlarea.com* (accessed 2 June 2006) for selected examples of open source WYSIWYG editors.

7　For an overview, see *http://www.engadget.com/entry/ 5843952395227141/* (accessed 2 June 2006).

8　For more information about the W3C's Web Accessibility Initiative see *http://www.w3.org/WAI/* (accessed 2 June 2006).

9　Numerous CMS examples can be tested online, see *http:// www.opensourcecms.com* (accessed 2 June 2006).

5

Building block I: cascading style sheets

The web, then, or the pattern; a web at once sensuous and logical, an elegant and pregnant texture: that is style, that is the foundation of the art...
(Robert Louis Stevenson, 'Elements of Style', 1885)

One of the most exciting aspects of developing open source database driven web applications is the relatively low threshold of expertise required to begin. It never hurts to be a professional programmer with extensive UNIX experience, but neither is this a prerequisite for learning how to begin designing database driven applications. On the contrary, most webmasters with the HTML and UNIX skills needed to build a static website and keep it running probably have the necessary foundational skills.

The next five 'building block' chapters explore some of the major components needed for developing database driven web applications. Naturally, some computer experience on behalf of the reader is presupposed. As a matter of course, there are a few software and connectivity requirements that most information professionals will also understand as a given including Internet connectivity, web server access, and pre-installed development software such as PHP and MySQL.

While the learning curve is relatively modest, a few important skill sets need to be developed. One 'building block' area of expertise that some might consider tangential is the ability to use cascading style sheets (CSS) for presentation purposes. CSS is actually a significant area of concern for a variety of reasons, not the least of which is improved accessibility to web resources by disabled computer users. Another obvious skill area to acquire is the use of the PHP language for coding applications. PHP is a language that can be picked up 'as you go'. While formal training is not necessary, it always helps to have a good grounding in any language before more advanced techniques are attempted. Some concepts will be understood more quickly if languages such as Java or Perl have previously been studied, but using PHP to perform desired tasks is generally straightforward and can be quickly rewarding. With some inquisitiveness and the desire to make it happen, it is almost always possible to use PHP to make an application behave as it should.

A third building block worthy of discussion is the use of relational databases. Relational databases provide a powerful means of organising information in a defined structure. These databases can be easily accessed and queried to efficiently send content to web pages. Database normalisation, a building block closely connected to the third, offers developers a reliable procedure for properly organising pieces of information within a relational database framework.

Finally, the MySQL relational database management system will be introduced. General database experience is always helpful when learning about a new database system, but MySQL lends itself to use by beginners and intermediate developers in ways that some relational databases cannot begin to approach.

A brief introduction to each of these areas follows along with some basic examples of how to begin exploring these tools and concepts. While it is beyond the scope of this book to address these building blocks in a comprehensive way, it is possible to focus on the most important and valuable concepts that will actually help you begin developing web database applications. The examples that have been included were carefully designed to demonstrate the key ideas and methods that are required to begin.

One of the challenges in picking up and reading any book on PHP, MySQL or general web development, is determining what is really important to know up front, and what can wait until a problem presents itself to be overcome. For instance, it is important to know how to manipulate strings, perform complex regular expression matching and use advanced arrays with PHP. However, if the goal is to begin developing working code that can actually be used, it is not particularly important to know everything that can be known about these tasks. This book 'cuts to the chase' and focuses on practical techniques that are foundational. There is always more to learn, and the supplemental resources referenced throughout this book are highly recommended for additional background, techniques and solutions.[1]

Web services platforms

Obviously, it is difficult to build a database driven web application without a platform on which to get started. This book makes the gentle assumption that the reader has access, or can gain access, to a web server running PHP and MySQL. Most Linux distributions include the Apache web server, MySQL database and PHP language (LAMP) installed by default.[2] Consult your local system administrator for more information. Luckily, even if these web services are not provided on site, it is relatively inexpensive to purchase access from a commercial Internet service provider (ISP) or web hosting service. The level of competition between high profile web hosting services has become increasingly fierce. Many web hosts now offer 'bundled package' deals that include free domain name registration, multiple e-mail accounts, permission to set up several MySQL databases, PHP privileges, FTP access and much more for a nominal monthly fee.[3]

Compare the web hosting services carefully, including any extra charges that may be levied for such things as exceeding specified levels of bandwidth (either by user downloads or by administrative uploads to the site). Most intermediate ('developer' or 'business') packages, and even many entry level ('beginner') packages offer PHP and MySQL support. There has probably never been a better time to easily and inexpensively experiment with PHP and MySQL. Developers who are new to these technologies can always upgrade to higher levels of web hosting service as their coding skills develop and database needs expand.

Once a web services platform has been established, attention can turn to the primary building blocks that are required to begin building a database driven web application. Most webmasters and developers have made the shift from pure HTML to a hybrid HTML/CSS approach within the last five years, but some holdouts have still not chosen to 'take the leap'. The value of converting pages from HTML to CSS cannot be emphasised enough. The wisdom and benefit of CSS formatting is perhaps brought into greatest clarity in the context of migrating from static web pages to database driven web pages and other web-based applications.

Cascading style sheets

The use of CSS to perform general web page layout is an intelligent way to go about web development in general, and database driven web development in particular. CSS empowers a web page designer to establish uniform rules for how every page on the website will be displayed. Font styles, sizes and colours can be specified, link characteristics can adjust in response to cursor movements, margins can be set, background and sidebar colours selected, table characteristics globally fixed, and much more. The CSS rules are specified in a single plain text file with a .css filename extension. Generally, each page of the website engages these rules by 'calling' the external CSS file near the beginning of the HTML document. CSS tags corresponding to the external file's specifications are then embedded into the HTML of every web page, establishing uniformity of presentation throughout the site. Perhaps the most obvious benefit of employing CSS is that changing the 'look and feel' of the site can be achieved extremely easily. Changing the formatting specifications in the single external style sheet instantly transforms the entire website.

Some webmasters still 'get by' without using style sheets, but they pay a heavy price by not migrating to the CSS model. The first 'browser wars' of the late 1990s saw Netscape and Internet Explorer (IE) fighting for market share and designing their own format standards. While it was theoretically desirable to use CSS at that time, in practice it was a nightmare. As the browsers did not uniformly implement the CSS specifications of the World Wide Web Consortium (W3C), pages that looked spectacular in one browser could look like a train wreck in another.[4] Understandably, many web developers at that time were slow to embrace a mechanism that was so fraught with inconsistencies and challenges.

One difficulty was that the browsers were still relatively new pieces of software, and the Web itself was just a few years in the making. Engineers at Microsoft and Netscape duelled by adding new proprietary extensions and sought to continually 'push the envelope' by releasing a new browser version every three to four months.[5] Another challenge was that the CSS standards themselves were in the process of creation and revision. The CSS1 specification was created in 1996 and revised in 1999 with the CSS2 specs recommended in 1998 (at times in response to the ongoing browser enhancements). Confusion begat confusion. A number of websites were created in the late 1990s and early 2000s to document the lack of CSS browser conformity, suggest workarounds, and offer 'clever' hacks designed to make presentation more uniform across multiple browsers. Unfortunately, as the 'non-standardised' hacks were targeted at continually evolving browser specifications, they quickly became outdated and even began to cause problems themselves in the subsequent browser versions that were continually re-engineered.[6]

Despite IE's imperfect conformity with CSS standards and its reliance on numerous proprietary protocols, website presentation became (by default) more stable and predictable as Internet Explorer gained near total dominance of the browser market by 2000. The resulting status quo (and the 2003 release of IE6) began to provide a standardised platform of sorts, and enough CSS stability that most professional designers have actively embraced this formatting mechanism.

More recently, the rapid growth and enormous popularity of the Mozilla Foundation's open source Firefox browser, (along with its objective of ever-increasing CSS conformity), has led some industry observers to declare the beginnings of a second browser war.[7] Microsoft representatives have conceded that its current browser (i.e. 6) is 'behind the game' in terms of full CSS support; however, the forthcoming Internet Explorer 7.0 browser is expected to adhere to CSS standards more closely.[8] The good news for web developers is that some of the current browser battles appear to finally be about which can more fully embrace CSS standardisation. After all, a designer should be able to take for granted that valid code will display predictably and uniformly in any browser. Ideally, any remaining competitive battles ought to be waged over improved browser functionality for the user.

Luckily, the CSS platform has taken hold over the last several years and is now a professional web design standard. It is also an important component of database driven applications as it allows the developer to focus on effectively processing content instead of getting bogged down in design and formatting issues while writing scripts. In important respects, database driven web development is all about working to separate content from design. Generally speaking, intellectual content should be kept in 'pure and pristine' form, residing in a database that is unencumbered by cluttering design and format tags. However, database web development is also about pulling together content and design into a seamless, holistic presentation that communicates effectively.

Migrating from a static HTML only model to a database model can be a perfect opportunity to adopt CSS.[9] An important aspect of the migration process involves cleaning or 'stripping' the often proprietary HTML tags that browsers traditionally used to format and visually present data. For example, though it has been deprecated in the official HTML 4.0 standards, the ubiquitous font size tag (<font size=1>this is a small font</font>) is still recognised by most browsers and continues to be in widespread use.[10] CSS users can now employ tags such as <span class=smfont>this is a small font</span> within the HTML of a web page, and then associate 'smfont' with a specific font size in the style sheet (e.g. smfont = 10pt). Without CSS, every single page that held a <font size> tag would have to be modified. When using CSS, the point size of the 'smfont' can be easily adjusted in a single style sheet so that all fonts are uniformly altered. Figure 5.1 provides a sample of a CSS style sheet.

While this flexibility sounds extremely appealing, it is also true that a great deal of initial work may lie in store for the webmaster who has amassed several years' worth of pages written in static HTML. Each and every page has to be 'touched' and re-coded so that the outdated HTML tags are removed and the more 'universal' CSS tags are put in place. One of the techniques that will be discussed later in this book is the development of a PHP script that will automatically delete outmoded HTML tags or convert them into a standardised CSS tag set (see

Figure 5.1   Example CSS style sheet

	Discussion
```1 /* CSS Style Sheet Example */ 2 3 body { 4 font-size: 12px/15px; 5 font-family: Geneva, Verdana, 6 Arial, Helvetica, sans-serif; 7 } 8 9 .smfont { 10 font: 10px Geneva sans-serif; 11 }```	• Style sheets can be used to control every aspect of web page presentation including fonts, colours and spacing. • This example shows how to set a global font size and font style (12 pixel font with up to 15 pixels between lines; Geneva style preferred, but if unavailable the remaining styles follow in sequence). • Although the popular 'pixel' (px) size is displayed here, many CSS experts recommend using relative font sizes (% or em) as pixel sizes can vary depending on monitor resolution. • Lines 10–11: for spans of text requiring a smaller font, the .smfont class is declared (using the abbreviated CSS format that groups two or more properties in a string).

Chapter 16). This kind of script can be run immediately before the content of each page is inserted into a database. Such an approach can dramatically ease the process of 'stripping' old code and readying content for use.

Some really good news is that once the conversion is made, maintaining and updating the design of the site need never be a chore again. The long-term benefit of stripping the code of outdated, non-standard tags creates numerous new possibilities for the content. The elegance of the CSS approach is extended even further with the database driven model. As all intellectual content resides in a database, the 'clean' content (devoid of outdated tags and uni-dimensional formatting) can be pulled into a predefined CSS layout presentation, into multiple web layouts simultaneously, and can even be distributed by multiple media (e.g. Web, RSS, podcasting, cellular, PDA, etc.).

Converting a traditional 'static' website into a database driven site provides a perfect opportunity for webmasters to learn CSS, globally implement it, and ensure that all style sheets conform to W3C standards with a CSS validator.[11] Starting this content conversion process does require some front-end work, but the long-term benefits of having clean data in a database are well worth the trouble. All content is now ready for any kind of publication or distribution, creating stunning opportunities for accessing and making full use of important information.

The battles for web browser market share are not likely to end soon. Fortunately, the competitive playing field is encouraging (forcing) the major players towards increased conformity with international CSS standards. This trend (and the obvious benefits of separating content from design), argues persuasively for designing all web pages with CSS to ensure consistent display and presentation. With CSS now charged to oversee all expressions and flourishes of style and fashion, we turn to the exploration of another building block – a spirited and sprightly scripting language that drives the data and brings the Web to life.

Notes

1   The most important resources for understanding and using the major components discussed in this book are the official documentation available online: CSS (*http://www.w3.org/Style/CSS/* (accessed 2 June 2006)); MySQL (*http://dev.mysql.com/doc/* (accessed 2 June 2006)); and PHP (*http://www.php.net/docs.php* (accessed 2

June 2006)). Larry Ullman's series of books on PHP web development are highly recommended, and include: Ullman, L. (2004) *PHP for the World Wide Web* (2nd edn), Berkeley: Peachpit Press; and Ullman, L. (2001) *PHP Advanced for the World Wide Web*, Berkeley: Peachpit Press.

2 MySQL and PHP source code can be downloaded for installation at no charge: *http://dev.mysql.com/downloads/* (accessed 2 June 2006) and *http://www.php.net/downloads.php* (accessed 2 June 2006).

3 For example, to identify some of the larger web hosting services available in Europe and the USA see commercial directories (e.g. *http://webhost.thelist.com*; *http://uk.webhostdir.com/* (accessed 2 June 2006)); or consult Google with the terms '+web +host'.

4 View the W3C's CSS specifications and other helpful resources at: *http://www.w3.org/Style/CSS/* (accessed 2 June 2006).

5 Levy, S. (2003) 'The killer browser', *Newsweek* (21 April): 37.

6 See Lehman, D. (2000) 'Netscape 6 beta released; Users: too little, too late; some say browser wars over, and IE wins.' *Computerworld* (10 April), available at: *http://www.computerworld.com/news/2000/story/0,11280,44392,00.html* (accessed 2 June 2006). For an overview of CSS development history see: Lie, H. W. and Bos, B. (1999) 'The CSS Saga' *Cascading Style Sheets, Designing for the Web* (Chapter 20), Reading, MA: Addison Wesley, available at: *http://www.w3.org/Style/LieBos2e/history/* (accessed 2 June 2006). The downside to workarounds is described in Koch, P.-P. (2003) 'Keep CSS Simple', *Digital Web Magazine* (November), available at: *http://digital-web.com/articles/keep_css_simple/* (accessed 2 June 2006). See also Koch, P.-P. (2005) 'Quirks mode and strict mode', available at: *http://www.quirksmode.org/css/quirksmode.html* (accessed 2 June 2006). Browser comparison charts emerged quickly as designers realised that CSS standards conformity was implemented on an ad hoc basis. For example, see: RichinStyle.com (2000): *http://www.richinstyle.com/bugs/table.html* (accessed 2 June 2006); UseYourBrain (c. 2002) 'Browser comparison': *http://www.useyourbrain.co.uk/internet-browser-comparison-chart.htm* (accessed 2 June 2006); CSS Pointers Group (2006) 'CSS bugs and workarounds': *http://css.nu/pointers/bugs-ie.html* (accessed 2 June 2006); and Position is Everything (2005) 'The weird and wonderful world of Internet Explorer': *http://www.positioniseverything.net/explorer.html* (accessed 2 June 2006).

7 O'Reilly, D. and Spanbauer, S. (2005) 'Browser Wars II: Firefox's

grassroots cure for internet insecurity.' *PC World* 23(2): 67; Larkin, E. (2006) 'Browser face-off', *PC World* 24(1): 18.

8   See Wilson, C. (2005) 'Standards and CSS in IE', available at: *http://www.google.com/search?q=cache:W6tjDXTFpeQJ: blogs.msdn.com/ie/archive/2005/07/29/445242.aspx+ %22Standards+and+CSS+in+IE* (accessed 2 June 2006).

9   See Schmitt, C. (2002) 'Web page reconstruction with CSS', *Digital Web Magazine* (July), available at: *http://www.digital-web.com/ articles/web_page_reconstruction_with_css/* (accessed 2 June 2006). Other noted CSS resources include: Briggs, O., Champeon, S., Costello, E. and Patterson, M. (2004) *Cascading Style Sheets: Separating Content from Presentation* (2nd edn), Berkeley: Friends of ED; and primarily as a tool for advanced users, Meyer E. (2001) *Cascading Style Sheets 2.0 Programmer's Reference*, Emeryville, CA: McGraw-Hill Osborne Media.

10   Though now somewhat dated, see Warren Steel's cogent explanation for why the well-intentioned '<font>' tag became to cause much confusion: *http://www.mcsr.olemiss.edu/~mudws/font.html* (accessed 2 June 2006).

11   CSS validation is free and simple via online tools such as W3C's 'CSS Validation Service', available at: *http://jigsaw.w3.org/css-validator/* (accessed 2 June 2006).

Building block II: PHP

There's a cool web of language...

(Robert Graves, 'The Cool Web', 1927)

Driving the data

Originally released by Rasmus Lerdorf in 1995 under the moniker 'Personal Home Page Tools' (thus confirming its modest beginnings), PHP has developed into a wildly popular and stable scripting language that is accessible for weekend hobbyists and sufficiently powerful for professional web developers.[1] The language has become very attractive because it is specifically designed for web development activities. Later renamed PHP (for PHP: Hypertext Preprocessor – yet another recursive acronym), the language was totally reworked by Zeev Suraski and Andi Gutmans to produce PHP version 3, and later PHP 4.[2]

Although initially implemented as a simple scripting language, the open source community has quickly developed it into practically a full-scale programming language as of the PHP 5 release. PHP may not yet have the sophistication and pedigree of some of the more established computer programming languages, but its functionality in creating database driven web applications is widely known. The beauty of the language for newcomers is its simplicity and functionality. Probably because of this, PHP's growing popularity as an open source web development language is unparalleled. PHP is included in most Linux distributions and is installed at over 1,278,000 IP addresses and more than 20,475,000 domains.[3]

Static web pages coded in HTML have traditionally been assigned filenames with either the .htm or .html suffix. Pages written in PHP must typically be given a filename ending in .php (servers may be configured to recognise other extensions). File extensions tell the web server how to handle the file. Files ending in .php are sent through a PHP module which processes the code and submits any plain HTML to the user's client browser.

Webmasters who have a good grasp of how to code documents in HTML will quickly appreciate the ease of embedding PHP commands directly within the HTML code of a page. Likewise, HTML can also be interspersed within PHP code, making it easy to drop in or out of either language as needed. Whitespace in both languages is essentially ignored. Figures 6.1 and 6.2 present an example of a simple PHP script (let's call it happy.php) that will send some basic HTML tags and the phrase 'Happy days are here again' to a web browser.

This inherent flexibility to easily intersperse PHP with HTML code (not found in more complex, traditional languages such as Java and Perl), makes PHP an extremely versatile option that is perfect for web development activities. Web browsers do not display PHP code embedded within HTML documents (even if the source code is viewed), as all PHP commands are processed on the server before any resulting HTML is transmitted to the browser. PHP can be used to insert the current date anywhere on a web page or present alternative data based on a user's selections, but it can also establish direct connections with online relational database management systems such as MySQL. The results of database queries can then be returned to the browser for presentation in HTML (with CSS formatting).

Figure 6.1   The source code of a web page showing PHP embedded within HTML

Code	Discussion
| ```
1  <HTML>
2  <HEAD>
3  <TITLE>Example 1</TITLE>
4  </HEAD>
5  <BODY>
6
7   Happy days
8   <?php
9     //PHP finishes the phrase:
10    print (" are here again.");
11  ?>
12
13 </BODY>
14 </HTML>
``` | • Quality open source text editors (e.g. HTML Kit), offer automatically numbered lines and can display PHP code and HTML in different colours. These capabilities are helpful when debugging code. <br><br>• The syntax <?php (or simply <? ) is used to start a PHP sequence, while ?> ends it. <br><br>• Comments within PHP code are left unprocessed if prefaced by double slashes // or the pound (hash) sign #. <br><br>• A semicolon must appear at the end of every PHP statement (line 10). |
```

Figure 6.2 The resulting browser display

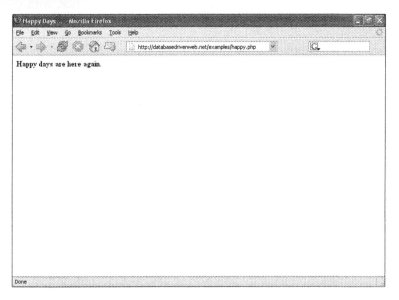

Most readers of this book likely have at least a basic understanding of how to code web pages manually using HTML. Anyone who has done much coding in this markup language is familiar with the routine of coding a document in a text editor, switching to a web browser and refreshing the page to see how it looks, and then switching back again to view the code and make necessary changes. Although this can sometimes be a tedious exercise, it is also a discipline that comes in handy when developing web applications. The fun part about building web applications is that instead of only refreshing pages to check line breaks and general layout, you are now refreshing the page to see if a script is dynamically making something happen.

PHP is a facile 'natural' language that uses commands with names that tend to describe the functions they perform. This tendency makes learning PHP easier than more advanced programming languages. Beginners can test and review a piece of working code and more quickly learn how to achieve similar results. The pursuit of functionality is an important key for PHP newcomers. At least initially, it is more important to pursue 'working code' that actually does something than to attempt a complete appreciation of why the code works at every stage. Novices should first focus on becoming conversant with basic PHP interactivity (e.g. using PHP to print text to a web page or creating a MySQL connection) before getting bogged down in more advanced concerns. Deeper appreciation and understanding comes with practice, with trial and error, and with the necessity of learning more in order to achieve more.

Basic coding principles

As an advanced scripting language, PHP can perform functions that markup languages such as HTML were never intended to do. Whether sorting or comparing user input, processing conditional statements, or querying a database and returning results, PHP provides a straightforward solution. The mastering of just a few general skill sets can quickly transform a novice PHP coder into a builder of increasingly sophisticated, web-based applications. Understanding the principle of how a segment of code functions can be extraordinarily useful. Code that works well can be modified to solve the kinds of problems that frequently appear when developing a program. Numerous online tutorials offer free access to PHP code segments that can be easily modified for specific purposes. Many of these resources are cited in this book including print resources that provide detailed theory and examples. This chapter focuses on some of the more basic aspects of beginning to code in PHP. The principles can be easily extended to write more complicated scripts.

Variables

Most programming languages designate certain 'containers' into which the coder can safely place defined pieces of information. Once distinct data are placed inside the container (called a *variable*, as it can store many kinds of information), the enclosed information can be easily named, referred to, stored in a database and displayed on a web page. Variables can be moved around, strung together with other variables, used to query a database, assigned values (e.g. true or false), and can be manipulated in a variety of ways.

For example, one piece of information might be the title of the book, while another could be the author. Other pieces of information could include the publisher, date of publication and perhaps several subject headings. As PHP is a loosely formed language, variables can be declared (and assigned to a piece of data) at any point within a stanza of code.

This capability is extremely handy, but it also means the coder must be careful not to overwrite variables used earlier in the script. In the PHP stanza in Figure 6.3, pieces of information related to a book are assigned to specific variables.

Besides being used to send information to a page, variables can also be used as a way to control what happens next in a sequence. Practically all Web users are now familiar with the myriad online submission forms that are the hallmark of e-commerce sites and technical support gateways. Several years ago, Perl was frequently used to process incoming web data from these types of forms. Many web developers now use PHP to manage submitted form data because of its accommodating simplicity in handling variables. As each text box, check box and drop-down menu on a form is created for a certain purpose, each 'piece of information' submitted through these mechanisms can be controlled. If a 'piece of data' can be controlled, it can be easily assigned to a unique variable. Once a collection of variables is established, PHP offers a multitude of tools to massage, manipulate and creatively manage the incoming data.

> **TIP** Variables are transient. They only exist during the running of a PHP script (which often produces a web page). If the variables will be needed for the creation of a subsequent page, they must have been 'kept alive' by being embedded in the original web page. This passing forward of variables enables PHP to 'remember' the data previously entered so that it can be re-used later in the chain.

Figure 6.3   Assigning variables

```
1  <?
2   // Let's put these pieces of information into separate
3   // containers (or "assign each piece to a variable"):
4
5   $title = 'The Name of the Rose';
6   $author = 'Umberto Eco';
7   $pub_date = '1980';
8
9   // Let's reorder the containers and print the
10  // information held within to a webpage:
11
12    print ("$author published <i>$title</i> in $pub_date.");
13
14 ?>
```

Conditional statements

A commonly used PHP variable management tool is the conditional statement. Using basic logic, a script can be directed to perform specific tasks based on the variables that are submitted. Though extremely basic, the 'if' conditional statement ranks high among the techniques used to control variables and the flow of the script. Here is the basic idea:

if x occurs, then do y

When processing incoming form data in the context of an interactive web application, it quickly becomes clear that this kind of technique has real potential. Indeed, conditional statements of this kind frequently recur in PHP variable processing due to their convenience and performance value. For example, imagine a simple web form that asks users to submit the first idea that occurs to them. If data are submitted, the resulting web page will thank the user and display the submission (Figure 6.4).[4]

The simple 'if' conditional statement can be extended to create flexible scripting options. When a greater number of variables are involved, the slightly more complex 'if/elseif/else' conditional statement is often used to direct the processing of a script (Figure 6.5).[5]

The 'if/elseif/else' loop sequences can be further extended to allow for the possible simultaneous submission of multiple variables. For instance, see Figure 6.6.

Comparison operators

Variables may also be assigned specific values that can be used to trigger an event or display information based on user input. A comparison

---

Figure 6.4 The resulting web page display: Thanks! You submitted Seven Fuzzy Rabbits

```
1 <?
2
3   if ($data)
4   {
5   print ("Thanks! You submitted $data.");
6   }
7
8 ?>
```

Discussion

- This statement declares that if the $data variable is submitted ('Seven Fuzzy Rabbits' first occurred to our intrepid user), then activate the function within the brackets { }.

- The print function sends the words within the double quotes "" (and the information represented by $data) to the browser for display on the web page.

Figure 6.5   An 'if-elseif-else' statement

```
1  <?
2
3   if ($author)
4    {
5     print ("The book\'s author is $author.");
6    }
7
8   elseif ($title)
9    {
10    print ("The title of the book is $title.");
11   }
12
13  else { }
14
15  ?>
```

Discussion

An implicit 'then' appears after each conditional statement. Read naturally, the logic goes like this: If there is a variable named $author, then display a sentence along with the variable's contents. But if only the $title variable exists, then print a sentence with its contents. Finally, if neither variable exists (else), then display nothing on the page.

Line 5: PHP reserves certain characters (quotation marks, apostrophes, backslashes and the dollar sign) that it needs for special purposes. These characters may need to be 'escaped' before being printed to the screen. To escape a character, simply place a backslash before it: book\'s.

Figure 6.6   An 'if-elseif-else' statement with multiple variables.

```
1  <?
2
3   if (($author) AND ($title))
4    {
5     print ("$title was written by $author.");
6    }
7
8   elseif (($title) AND (!$author))
9    {
10    print ("The book's title is $title.");
11   }
12
13  elseif (($author) AND (!$title))
14   {
15    print ("The book\'s author is $author.");
16   }
17
18  else
19   {
20    print ("Neither a title nor an author");
21    print (" was selected. <br>");
22    print ("<a href=\"author_title.php\">");
23    print ("Please try again</a>.");
24   }
25
26  ?>
27
28
```

Discussion

- Lines 3–6: If both variables are submitted (PHP recognises the Boolean operators AND, OR, NOT), then print both $title and $author variables.

- Lines 8–11: Else, if $title is submitted without the $author variable (the exclamation point (!) is a symbol equivalent to NOT), then print the $title variable.

- Lines 13–16: Else, if the $author is submitted, but there is no $title variable, then print the $author.

- Lines 18–23: Else (neither variable was submitted), print an instructional message to the user. Note that long sentences may be divided across multiple print statements. Line breaks (<br>), hyperlinks and other HTML/CSS formatting tags may be included within the print statement.

- Note that the double quotes within the anchor tag are escaped on line 22.

operator (such as the double equal sign: ==) provides an easy way to compare the value of a variable with some other numeral or string of text. Agreement (or disagreement) of the values can then be used to make certain defined events happen. For example, consider a scenario where you are maintaining a database of pianos that you are currently offering for sale. As soon as each piano is sold, you no longer want the listing to appear on your piano website. One way of toggling the pianos that are available or unavailable is to assign each piano a 'status' value in a database. For simplicity, the value could be set to '1' if available or set to '0' if it had already been sold. Later we will explore how to configure settings such as these in a database and to query for such values. But for now, consider that you had already established the present value of the variable $status and had relayed this information to your program. Figure 6.7 presents one way code could be written to display appropriate information on a web page based on the value of $status:

It could be desirable to modify the potential status of your pianos in other ways. For instance, you might sell out of a certain piano model but sometimes be able to back-order that model for a potential customer. An additional status could be assigned (e.g. backorder equals '2') in the database, so that the customer could request such an order if the model can be acquired. Expanding the PHP code to compare the value of $status to achieve alternative displays would require a simple loop, such as that in Figure 6.8.

Debugging error messages

When learning a new programming or scripting language such as PHP, there is nothing more helpful than actually writing code and experimenting with the results. Though writing code that runs successfully can build confidence and spur further achievement, the educational process is substantially about learning from mistakes and finding ways to avoid

Figure 6.7   Example of a comparison operator

Code	Discussion
```1 <?``` ```2 if ($status == '1')``` ```3 {``` ```4 print ("$piano_info");``` ```5 }``` ```6``` ```7 else {``` ```8 }``` ```9 ?>```	**Discussion** • The double equal sign '==' is a comparison operator. It compares the value of the $status variable with the number '1' to see if they agree. If they do, then the information about the piano is printed. • In PHP, a single equal sign '=' would declare equality and assert that the $status variable actually equals '1' – not wanted in this situation.

Figure 6.8 An 'if-elseif-else' loop with multiple comparison operators

	Discussion

1 <?
2 if ($status == '1')
3 {
4 print ("$piano_info");
5 }
6 elseif ($status == '2')
7 {
8 print ("This model is not in stock:");
9 print ("$piano_info");
10 print ("<a href=\"order.php\">");
11 print ("Let us order it for you</a>!");
12 }
13 else { }
14 ?>
	• $piano_info represents all the data about this particular piano. In practice, there would likely be multiple variables created to 'hold' each characteristic about the piano.
	
	• Line 6: The value of $status is compared with the number '2'. If they match, then the user has an opportunity to request a backorder by clicking the link.
	
	• Line 13: If the value of $status is neither '1' nor '2' (the piano is unavailable for sale or by order), it is not listed on the site.

Figure 6.9 Example of a PHP error message

Parse error: parse error in **/home/account/webpage.php** on line **6**
Status: 400 Bad Request Content-Type: text/html

them. Like most computer languages, PHP can be demanding in its exactness. Even a relatively minor inconsistency in coding can generate an error message in the browser window. One of the more frequently seen errors often looks something like that shown in Figure 6.9.

At times it can be frustrating to see error messages of this ilk appear on the screen. On the other hand, the good news is that the PHP command interpreter excels at alerting the writer to coding problems and can often provide hints that lead to successfully debugging. The PHP error message in Figure 6.9 may appear redundant and oblique, but it provides extremely helpful clues for determining how to correct the difficulty.

For instance, parsing errors are almost always caused by a misuse of PHP 'syntax', much like making a grammatical error in an English language sentence. In the case of PHP, the most important grammatical rules tend to deal with the proper spacing and use of semicolons, quote marks (single and double), parentheses and brackets: ; '' "" () {}. Virtually all PHP statements must end with a semicolon, and any clause opened with a quotation mark, parentheses, or bracket must be dutifully closed in like manner. The Figure 6.9 error message tells us to begin searching for these types of syntax irregularities, and it even goes so far as to tell us precisely where to begin looking (line 6). A quick review of the code that generated this message reveals a missing quotation mark within a print statement.

TIP When debugging an error message, go about it in a methodical way. Instead of trying to make multiple changes and then retesting, make one modification at a time. A single change may correct the problem while the second or third in a single sequence may actually create other difficulties. After making an alteration and saving the file to the server, be sure to refresh the browser's cache so the original error message does not reappear. With Internet Explorer and Firefox, holding down the <CTRL> keyboard button and tapping the F5 key forces the browser to reload and obtain a 'fresh' copy of the script's output.

Minor parsing errors probably account for the majority of mistakes made when writing PHP code. Admittedly, not all parsing errors are so easily addressed as in the preceding example.[6] Mistakes involving brackets can be particularly difficult as the PHP interpreter may not recognise an error until much later in the script when it fails to properly resolve. Cases such as this can make the interpreter identify 'ghost' errors on lines that are perfectly formed. Again, through writing and gaining experience with PHP, coders can gain an intuitive sense for how to spot and debug issues more rapidly.

Summary

After struggling with snippets of code, it can be quite satisfying to finally have 'breakthrough' moments that help make the process illuminating, rewarding and worthwhile. Take some time to review the above examples and experiment with embedding a few lines of PHP into your HTML pages. Assign some text to a variable and make it print to a browser screen, or give some variables alternative values and make a page display text based on an evaluation of a changing variable.

A number of foundational PHP concepts and techniques have been addressed in this chapter, including:

■   embedding PHP code into the HTML of a web page (Figure 6.1);

Panel 6.1: Integrating PHP and HTML – four steps

- Use a regular HTML text editor, just as you would when manually coding a simple web page in HTML. No-cost editors such as HTML-Kit (*http://www.chami.com/html-kit/*) provide a number of useful features including integrated FTP, code validators and other PHP/HTML aids.

- Save your code to a file with the extension .php (e.g. my_webpage.php).

- FTP the file to your web server (PHP capabilities must be previously installed by the system administrator).

- Call the file with your browser like any other web page on your site (*http://www.mywebsite.net/my_webpage.php*). If you receive a parsing error (your code likely used incorrect PHP syntax), debug the code and try again.

- using PHP to print (send) plain text to a browser for display (Figures 6.1 and 6.2);

- declaring and assigning values to variables (Figure 6.3);

- 'printing' (sending) both text and the contents of variables to a web page for display (Figure 6.3);

- using 'if' conditional statements to test the existence of a variable (Figure 6.4);

- using 'if/elseif/else' loops to trigger different events based on the existence (or non-existence) of multiple incoming variables (Figures 6.5 and 6.6);

- embedding HTML code (e.g.
 line breaks; <a href></a> anchor tags) into PHP print statements (Figure 6.6);

- using comparison operators to evaluate the value of single and multiple variables (Figures 6.7 and 6.8);

- triggering alternate displays based on comparison operator evaluations (Figure 6.8);

- identifying PHP syntax errors (Figure 6.9).

The more you are able to achieve, the more you will want to attempt. The possibilities for developing web applications with PHP are practically limitless. While PHP is a fine web development tool unto itself, combining it with a web-connected database can lead to innovative applications that can gather, manage, preserve and distribute information in truly remarkable ways. With CSS catering the style and PHP energetically driving the data, our journey turns toward a crucial building block in the search for effective web content management – a high-powered relational database management system.

Notes

1   Lerdorf's original PHP release and description can be viewed at: *http://groups.google.ch/group/comp.infosystems.www.authoring.cgi/ msg/cc7d43454d64d133* (accessed 2 June 2006).
2   For a good introduction as to why and how PHP was developed see Bakken, S. S. (2000) 'Introduction to PHP', available at: *http:// www.zend.com/zend/art/intro.php* (accessed 2 June 2006). One observer has noted that PHP is perhaps more like a recursive abbreviation than a recursive acronym, as acronyms are pronounced as words (as in NASA or RADAR), but abbreviations as letters (as in IBM or PHP): *http://www.php.net/manual/en/faq.general.php* (accessed 1 November 2005).
3   Based on April 2006 data provided by Netcraft, as cited by php.net, available at: *http://www.php.net/usage.php*.
4   The echo() construct, slightly different from print(), may also be used to output data for display (see *http://www.php.net/manual/en/ function.echo.php* and *http://www.php.net/manual/en/ function.print.php* (accessed 2 June 2006)).
5   A system-level PHP feature called 'Magic Quotes' is implemented in some server environments. If the Magic Quotes feature is turned 'on' by the system administrator, all quotations marks are automatically 'escaped' with a backslash (\" \", \' \'), so it is not necessary to manually escape them before display or upload to a database. If Magic Quotes is disabled, the PHP addslashes() function can be useful for escaping quotes within segments of text; if enabled, stripslashes() can be employed to remove all escapes. Some developers (if they have a choice), prefer to have the feature disabled, allowing them to retain full control over how their content is manipulated (e.g. see Fuecks, H. 'Magic quotes and add slashes in PHP', available at: *http://www.webmasterstop.com/63.html* (accessed 2 June 2006).

6 See, for example, Bechor, E. (2002) 'Making sense of PHP errors', available at: *http://www.devarticles.com/c/a/PHP/Making-Sense-Of-PHP-Errors/* (accessed 2 June 2006); and Ullman, L. (2004) 'Debugging', in *PHP for the World Wide Web* (2nd edn), Berkeley: Peachpit Press, pp. 233–48.

Building block III: relational databases

A relationship, I think, is like a shark, you know? It has to constantly move forward or it dies. And I think what we got on our hands is a dead shark.

(Woody Allen, *Annie Hall*, 1977)

A basic grasp of introductory relational database principles is a prerequisite for beginning development work with MySQL or any other database management system (DBMS). Relational databases are all about establishing and maintaining connections between various pieces of information. If these relationships are solid and stable, the varied pieces can be reliably extracted, efficiently manipulated and even leveraged to form new interdependent linkages with subsequent emerging data. If the relationships become tenuous or somewhat estranged, it becomes more difficult to keep the entire system of interconnections in harmony.

The best way to keep disparate pieces of data in mutual accord is to pay close attention, handle with care, and not create opportunities for them to clash, become dissonant or in variance.

Database definitions

The following definitions and discussion may assist newcomers (and perhaps refresh the memories of veterans) in understanding basic database concepts. The simple SQL query examples that follow introduce how to go about extracting relational database content. Virtually all major database management systems employ relational structures to organise data. By taking advantage of these interconnected frameworks, efficient and powerful database systems such as MySQL are capable of processing millions of records in the blink of an eye. A familiarity with general database terminology provides a foundation for exploring more advanced relational database principles:

- *Database*: a structured repository where information (e.g. text, numbers, web content) can be stored and organised for later querying, manipulation or retrieval.

- *Simple database*: often called a 'flat-file' database, where each set of information is placed on a single row of a text file. Distinct pieces of text on each line are generally separated by pipes or commas (e.g. | someone's name | someone's address | someone's city |). Flat-file databases tend to be very slow and contain numerous redundancies.

- *Relational database*: a database organised by the grouping of distinct pieces of related information (e.g. authors, titles, publishers) into structured, sub-divided 'containers' called tables (e.g. an author container, a title container, and a publisher container). The established relationship between a piece of information in one table (an author's name) to a piece in another table (a title by that author) is generally maintained by an indexed numbering system (see primary key) that databases can use to process information extremely rapidly.[1]

- *Table*: a database's largest 'container' for storing information. Tables are divided into columns and rows (similar to the format of a spreadsheet).

- *Column*: also called an 'attribute,' columns are structures for organising and formatting the pieces of data within a table. Whenever a table is created, each column is given a specific name (e.g. 'author_name') and is assigned a data type (which describes the format and size of the information to be contained in the column).

- *Row*: a sub-divided container for storing related pieces of information within the columns of a table. Rows are formally called 'tuples' (rhymes with couples). Each row in a table has the same structure as every other row.

- *Data type*: a declaration of the format (e.g. text or numerals) and the maximum size of the information permitted for each column (e.g. 50 characters of text or 10 digits). Assigning appropriate data types for the kinds of content expected to be held in each column helps improve speed and conserve space. Some of the major data types in MySQL are:

- INT (a numeric data type often used to define auto-incrementing integers for a primary key);

- CHAR (a fixed-length text field of less than 256 characters);

- VARCHAR (a variable-length text field useful for storing general data of inconsistent size);

- TEXT (a field for storing large amounts of data);

- TIMESTAMP (YYYYMMDDHHMMSS – year, month, day, etc.; the value is updated each time the row is changed).

■ *Primary key*: a special column containing values used for identifying each unique row in a table. A unique number is typically assigned to each row within the column. This number can be used to identify specific rows for deletion or modification, or can connect related pieces of information that may be stored across numerous tables. A primary key stored in the column of another table is called a foreign key. Keys are generally indexed (separately organised and sorted) to improve database performance.

■ *SQL*: a computer language specifically designed to create, query, retrieve and manipulate data in relational database systems such as MySQL. The language is recognised by the American National Standards Institute (ANSI) and International Organization for Standardization (ISO).

Flat-file versus relational databases

Flat-file databases are straightforward representations of information and are easy to understand as each row of data contains an entire set of information. The flat-file database in Figure 7.1 consists of four authors, the titles they have written, and the year each book was published.

Figure 7.1 A 'flat-file' database

Isaac | Brooks | Sun of the Clouds | 1996 |
Samuel | Chatham | Beaches of Sand | 1974 |
Samuel | Chatham | Mountain Dreams | 2006 |
James | Taylor | Winds of Hope | 2003 |
Susan | Overton | High Dwellers | 1999 |

While effective for managing small amounts of simple data, flat-file databases are known for their lack of responsiveness and efficiency. Flat-file database management systems have to 'read' the entire file when running a query even though the query may be looking for only a single piece of information (e.g. Overton) from a single field (e.g. field 2). Numerous redundancies are also likely to occur. In this example, the author's name must be explicitly provided for every entry even if it has already been stated (Samuel and Chatham). Significantly, the only way to connect one piece of information with another is to include both pieces on the same row. The flat-file format makes it difficult to create relationships between data that may occur on multiple rows.

For a variety of reasons, relational databases are much better information management tools. They provide increased flexibility as pieces of data can be separated into smaller components and then quickly reassembled based on the format and information needs of the user. Relational databases are far speedier than the flat-file approach as only the pieces of information that are needed must be accessed and processed. Redundancies are also reduced as a single piece of information can be easily referenced instead of needing to be continually re-stated. Tables 7.1 and 7.2 display how the same data in the flat-file database could be structured in a relational database.

The author table (Table 7.1) contains four rows of information, as

Table 7.1 An author table

author_id	author_first	author_last
1	Isaac	Brooks
2	James	Taylor
3	Samuel	Chatham
4	Susan	Overton

Table 7.2 A title table

title_id	author_id	title_name	title_date
1	2	Winds of Hope	2003
2	1	Sun of the Clouds	1996
3	3	Beaches of Sand	1974
4	3	Mountain Dreams	2006
5	4	High Dwellers	1999

enumerated by the primary key (author_id). The primary key assigns a unique number to each row in the table. The title table (Table 7.2) has its own primary key (title_id) and contains five rows of data. The relationship (or link) between the two tables is created by the insertion of the author_id field into the title table. A primary key inserted into another table is called a foreign key, so author_id is the primary key of the author table and is the foreign key of the title table. The title table is sorted by its primary key as each new title is added which explains why the numbers in the title table's foreign key (author_id) do not appear in order. Of course, this is expected as the sole purpose of a foreign key is to make connections between related pieces of information in separate tables (in this case between authors and their respective titles).

Notice that the author_id keys link author Isaac Brooks with a single title, *Sun of the Clouds*. Likewise, Samuel Chatham is the author of two books, while Taylor and Overton have each published a single title. If Overton publishes a book next year, the database can be easily updated by adding a new row to the title table that includes her unique author_id (number 4).

TIP There is perhaps no perfect convention for naming tables and column fields. The most important matter is to pick a style and stick with it. A method that is used throughout this book is to re-use the table name within the name of the column. This can be helpful when designing complex SQL queries because common column names can lead to confusion. Embedding the table name in each column makes it immediately obvious which column belongs to each table.

Once all of the authors and titles are entered into their respective tables and assigned unique keys, an important question arises: how will we pull all of this information back out of the database again and reconstitute it in a way that makes sense? Fortunately, this is not very difficult. Most relational database management systems use the SQL computer language to interact with information stored in a database. Though powerful, SQL uses a simple 'plain English' syntax that is understandable, descriptive and easy to pick up. SQL can be thought of as a way to ask a database specific questions about its content and retrieve the answers. The language can also be used to add, modify or delete database content. [2] In later chapters, it will be shown how SQL statements can be embedded within PHP code to perform database operations and return the results to a web page.

The most basic and probably the most frequently used SQL query is the SELECT statement. Let's say we would like to see a list of all the authors in the database. The SELECT statement `SELECT * FROM author;` would retrieve the information shown in Table 7.3.

This query asks the DBMS to SELECT (retrieve) all of the rows (everything = *) FROM the table named 'author'. This includes the information contained in both the author_first and author_last fields. If we only wanted to see a list of the last names of each author, we could use the query `SELECT author_last FROM author;` (Table 7.4).

More likely, we would want to ask the database to provide more extensive information. Instead of a list of all authors, we would like to see a listing of all the books written by a specific author along with their publication dates. Thus, to retrieve all available information concerning the books written by Samuel Chatham from the author and title tables, the following statement could be used (Table 7.5):

```
SELECT author_first, author_last, title_name,
title_date
FROM author, title
WHERE (author.author_id = 3) AND (title.author_id
= 3);
```

Table 7.3 Information retrieved from the SELECT statement 'SELECT * FROM author;'

author_id	author_first	author_last
1	Isaac	Brooks
2	James	Taylor
3	Samuel	Chatham
4	Susan	Overton

Table 7.4 Information retrieved from the SELECT statement 'SELECT author_last FROM author;'

author_last
Brooks
Taylor
Chatham
Overton

Table 7.5	Information retrieved from the SELECT statement 'SELECT author_first, author_last, title_name, title_date FROM author, title WHERE (author.author_id = 3) AND (title.author_id = 3);'

author_first	author_last	title_name	title_date
Samuel	Chatham	Beaches of Sand	1974
Samuel	Chatham	Mountain Dreams	2006

Breaking down this statement into smaller pieces, we are instructing the DBMS to SELECT the main rows and fields (the ones holding actual author/title data) FROM the tables named 'author' and 'title'. However, we also want to place a condition (WHERE) on this query. We only seek the rows that match a certain key (Samuel Chatham was assigned number 3). Specifically, we want all the rows where the number '3' appears in both the author_id column of the author table AND the author_id column of the title table. The AND operator is used to attach more than one condition to the WHERE clause. Note that multiple tables are called by separating each with a comma (,). A field from each table is explicitly called by placing a period (.) between the table name and the field name. It is permissible to 'wrap' statements at convenient junctures instead of entering them on a single line. MySQL statements always end with a semicolon (;). This is easy to remember as PHP statements always end with a semicolon as well.

NOTE When a query is run, MySQL conveniently outputs a field name header and creates a grid to display the results (see below). This output is particularly helpful when running test queries. Fortunately, none of this supplemental output is ever transmitted via PHP for display to a web page. The actual content from each retrieved row can be rearranged with PHP and HTML in almost unlimited ways and then formatted with CSS for attractive presentation to the Web.

author_first	author_last	title_name	title_date

It is easy to sort the database results for display by using the SQL 'ORDER BY' clause. Perhaps we would like to see all available information about the authors and their titles, displayed in chronological order (Table 7.6):

Table 7.6	Information retrieved from the SELECT statement 'SELECT author_first, author_last, title_name, title_date FROM author, title WHERE author.author_id = title.author_id ORDER BY title_date;'

author_first	author_last	title_name	title_date
Samuel	Chatham	Beaches of Sand	1974
Isaac	Brooks	Sun of the Clouds	1996
Susan	Overton	High Dwellers	1999
Samuel	Chatham	Winds of Hope	2003
James	Taylor	Mountain Dreams	2006

```
SELECT  author_first,  author_last,  title_name,
title_date
FROM author, title
WHERE author.author_id = title.author_id
ORDER BY title_date;
```

Note that by default, the ORDER BY clause sorts the rows in ascending order. To generate a list of the books in descending order (newest titles first), the DESC keyword can be appended to the ORDER BY clause:

```
SELECT  author_first,  author_last,  title_name,
title_date
FROM author, title
WHERE author.author_id = title.author_id
ORDER BY title_date DESC;
```

The output from the above query would display the 2006 entry first, followed by the other author and title rows in chronological sequence. The ORDER BY clause can also be used to sort multiple columns and is an effective means of alphabetising lists of results. For example, a list of titles could be generated based on an alphabetical sort of the author's last name, followed by a secondary sort on the title_name column (Table 7.7):

```
SELECT  author_first,  author_last,  title_name,
title_date
FROM author, title
WHERE author.author_id = title.author_id
ORDER BY author_last, title_name;
```

Table 7.7	Information retrieved from the **SELECT** statement 'SELECT author_first, author_last, title_name, title_date FROM author, title WHERE author.author_id = title.author_id ORDER BY author_last, title_name;'

author_first	author_last	title_name	title_date
Isaac	Brooks	Sun of the Clouds	1996
Samuel	Chatham	Beaches of Sand	1974
Samuel	Chatham	Winds of Hope	2003
Susan	Overton	High Dwellers	1999
James	Taylor	Mountain Dreams	2006

Table 7.8	Information retrieved from the **SELECT** statement 'SELECT title_name, title_date FROM title ORDER BY title_date DESC LIMIT 3;'

title_name	title_date
Mountain Dreams	2006
Winds of Hope	2003
High Dwellers	1999

There are times when it may be useful to retrieve only a limited number of rows from a large database, based on certain criteria. Combining the ORDER BY and LIMIT clauses can be an effective technique in these situations. Perhaps someone would like to see a list of only the three newest titles in the database (Table 7.8). A query could be written that retrieves the desired results:

```
SELECT title_name, title_date
FROM title
ORDER BY title_date DESC LIMIT 3;
```

Summary

This chapter explored basic concepts and introduced foundational principles concerning relational databases. 'Flat-file' databases are no match for powerful relational databases represented by DBMS systems such as MySQL. Breaking data into small pieces makes it easy to update specific tables of information and speeds delivery times as data that are not requested do not need to be processed. Using primary and foreign keys for organisation, these smaller pieces of information can be quickly extracted and reconstituted precisely when they are needed.

The SQL computer language provides a powerful means for effectively targeting and retrieving data. The basic building blocks presented here introduced common SELECT statements along with conditions, operators, sorting functions and limits. This is by no means a comprehensive examination of all SQL SELECT functions, but these examples provide a foundation for creating more advanced statements as needed. There are many additional SQL operators and elements that can provide enormous flexibility and control over how data are managed and retrieved.[3] Some of the more important of these SQL constructs will be explored later. However, the following discussion turns to a review of significant concepts related to effective database design. Much depends on how soundly data are organised and arranged within each database table. Taking care to create a well-conceived information framework speeds data processing and makes it that much easier to develop SQL statements that get the work done.

Notes

1   MySQL, a database management system (DBMS), is sometimes referred to as a relational database management system (RDBMS) as are other relational databases such as Oracle, DB2, and PostgreSQL.
2   SQL is a standardised language generally recognised across all of the major DBMS systems. A SQL query of one DBMS should typically function the same way with any other. In practice, each system may implement the language somewhat differently. The SQL statements used in this book conform to MySQL's implementation (versions 3.23 to 5.1, inclusive).
3   Consult the official MySQL online reference manual (*http://dev.mysql.com/doc/* (accessed 2 June 2006)) and supplemental resources such as DuBois, P. (2005) *MySQL* (3rd edn), Indianapolis: Sams; Williams, H. and Lane, D. (2002) *Web Database Applications*, Cambridge, MA: O'Reilly; and Kofler M. (2005) *The Definitive Guide to MySQL 5*, Berkeley: Apress.

Building block IV: database design and normalisation

Success is a science; if you have the conditions, you get the result.

(Oscar Wilde, 1883)

Effective database design and normalisation, very important aspects of database driven web development, require analysis and at least a moderate degree of foresight. Well-designed databases tend to make the entire web application development process run more smoothly. Design flaws made early in the development process can lead to unending workarounds, wasted effort and unnecessarily complex code. Even the smallest prospective database with a handful of tables deserves attention to detail. While not terribly glamorous, making the effort to sketch out a general framework (even on a paper napkin over morning coffee), will save time in the short term and reduce later headaches due to unexpected database expansion requirements. Naturally, the size and complexity of the proposed project will determine the level of planning and care that is required. Detailed schemata should be created for more ambitious projects requiring numerous interconnected tables of data.

During a project's early development stages, the value of effectively communicating with the end-users of the proposed web application cannot be overstated. This consideration is also addressed in Chapter 12, but it deserves attention at the database design phase as well. It is important to envision all potentialities and communicate effectively with those who will be providing, preparing, entering and accessing database content. The database designer needs to know precisely what data elements will be going into the database and how they will need to be retrieved out of the database. Ask lots of questions, ask the same questions in varying ways, and don't forget to rephrase and ask them politely again (and then again, on a different day of the week).

Almost invariably, an element that was assumed, not mentioned or not initially deemed significant will emerge later in the process. Sometimes these 'surprises' are not severe and can be easily remedied. On other occasions they can create multiple challenges. Optimally, it is best if you can identify *all* of the pieces of information that will be 'in play' and how these pieces need to be used. This is definitely worth striving for and perseverance usually pays off. However, experience also suggests that unintended miscommunications, late-arriving realisations, practical workflow issues, someone's last-minute 'must have' concept, the effects of introducing a new technology to solve an old problem, and other unforeseen variables sometimes make the ideal difficult to attain. A deep breath before speaking, a kind word, and a good sense of humour are always helpful additions to your database development toolbox if you can find them.

Database normalisation

In the early 1970s, Edgar F. Codd proposed a formal methodology for organising pieces of information in a relational database.[1] Called database normalisation, the process focused on eliminating redundancy of data and increasing data integrity. Codd's general theory was that redundancy should be eliminated if at all possible. Redundancy slows down processing and makes it more likely that some 'good' data will be inadvertently lost and that over time erroneous data will begin to creep into the data stream. For instance, if a database is created so that a person's name must be manually entered multiple times, it is more likely that someone will eventually misspell the name. A name could even be misspelled multiple times and in multiple ways which could lead to considerable confusion. However, if the database is designed so that a single field in a single table is designated for the person's name, this considerably reduces the opportunity for error. Any error that does occur only has to be updated at a single access point. By reducing redundancy, data integrity is maintained and the database is more likely to be kept free of errors.

Redundancy also makes it more difficult to make the database scalable. Numerous duplicate entries take up valuable storage space and are an indication that the database has been poorly designed. Databases that lack a consistent overall framework are hard to expand upon and enhance.

It is far preferable to prepare for future growth at the front end (even if it is not really expected), than to regret not having done it later. Many books have been written on database design and the principles of normalisation. Obviously, the following overview cannot do justice to such a complex area, but it does cover some of the more important concepts necessary for building a dependable database driven application.

First normal form

Codd ultimately envisioned five levels of normalisation, which he called 'normal forms'. Each form (level) is progressive and builds upon the earlier form. The first normal form (1NF) involves removing redundant information from horizontal rows. Each column should hold the most basic amount of information possible. This is sometimes called 'atomising' the data (reducing the data to its most essential or singular part). Each row at the 1NF level should also have a primary key that assigns a unique identifier. Table 8.1 provides a starting point to begin considering how a poorly designed database design can be improved.

Table 8.1 contains significant and pertinent information, but fails to comply with the 1NF. Notice that a unique identifier (a primary key) is missing. In addition, there are multiple pieces of information appearing on rows in the subject column. Table 8.2 attempts to remedy this.

Table 8.2 is an improvement and meets the minimum 1NF conditions. The table now contains a primary key to identify each row uniquely. Most databases (including MySQL) can enable this field to be 'auto-incrementing'. As each new entry is added, the key automatically increments to a higher number, ensuring that every row will always have its own unique identifier. Finally, the subjects in the original table

Table 8.1 A starting point to begin considering how a poorly designed database design can be improved

author	title	pages	publisher	subjects
Chatham	Beaches of Sand	204	XYZ	shells, fish
Brooks	Sun of the Clouds	456	XYZ	rain, rays
Taylor	Winds of Hope	270	QRS	air, joy
Overton	High Dwellers	352	XYZ	glimmers
Chatham	Mountain Dreams	339	QRS	visions

Table 8.2 An improved table, meeting the minimum 1NF conditions

author_id	author	title	pages	publisher	subjects
1	Chatham	Beaches of Sand	204	XYZ	shells
2	Chatham	Beaches of Sand	204	XYZ	fish
3	Brooks	Sun of the Clouds	456	XYZ	rain
4	Brooks	Sun of the Clouds	456	XYZ	rays
5	Taylor	Winds of Hope	270	QRS	air
6	Taylor	Winds of Hope	270	QRS	joy
7	Overton	High Dwellers	352	XYZ	glimmers
8	Chatham	Mountain Dreams	339	QRS	visions

have now been favourably reduced to basic elements (atomised) and placed in their own independent columns. This is the final requirement for 1NF conformity.

Second normal form

Still, all is not right. We now have increased redundancies and are now bumping up against the strictures of the second normal form (2NF). By definition, the 2NF meets all the conditions of 1NF and then expands upon them. Whereas 1NF addressed horizontal row redundancy, 2NF is concerned with improving vertical column redundancy. The 2NF can be achieved if each of the columns is dependent on the primary key. As a practical matter, moving from 1NF to 2NF means grouping duplicate sets of information appearing within single columns into separate tables and assigning them a foreign key. For example, Table 8.2 shows multiple redundant entries in the author, title and publisher columns. This situation can be improved by creating a new table for each group. A single entry for each respective group reduces the likelihood that future conflicts will develop in the database.

In a sense, moving toward conformity with the next levels is about recognising and defining relationships with the data. Several kinds of relationships can exist between pieces of information: (a) one-to-one, (b) one-to-many, and (c) many-to-many. An example of a one-to-one relationship is the connection between an ISBN number and a book. There is generally only one ISBN assigned to each book and only one book per ISBN. A one-to-many relationship exists between a single publishing house and the numerous titles it produces. The multiple titles can also be mapped back to the single publisher. Instances of many-to-many relationships frequently occur between authors and titles as multiple authors can contribute to a book, and an author can write multiple titles. Identifying these kinds of relationships between various pieces of information becomes significant when working to design an effective database.

First, it is important to clean up the 'author' column as there is too much redundancy. A quick way to achieve this is to simply pull the unique author data out of the table and create a separate author table (Table 8.3).

Table 8.3 conforms to 1NF and puts us in position to establish many future relationships. Likewise, the redundancy displayed in the title column of Table 8.2 calls for the establishment of a separate table for titles (Table 8.4).

Though the table in Table 8.4 will still require some attention, its creation (along with Table 8.3) holds promise for the budding of numerous many-to-many relationships over the course of time. A supplemental 'linking table' (Table 8.5) offers a powerful means to connect a growing collection of authors and titles. A similar approach can also be taken with the redundant 'subjects' column in Table 8.2. Both of the attributes

Table 8.3   Author table

author_id	author
1	Chatham
2	Brooks
3	Taylor
4	Overton

Table 8.4   Title table

title_id	title	pages	publisher
1	Beaches of Sand	204	XYZ
2	Sun of the Clouds	456	XYZ
3	High Dwellers	270	XYZ
4	Winds of Hope	352	QRS
5	Mountain Dreams	339	QRS

Table 8.5 The link_author_title linking table

author_id	title_id
1	1
1	5
2	2
3	3
4	4

Table 8.6 Revised title table

title_id	title	pages	pub_id
1	Beaches of Sand	204	1
2	Sun of the Clouds	356	1
3	High Dwellers	270	2
4	Winds of Hope	352	1
5	Mountain Dreams	339	2

Table 8.7 Publisher table

pub_id	pub_name
1	XYZ
2	QRS

in the new link_author_title 'linking table' are foreign keys, which were culled from the primary keys of the respective base tables.

As mentioned earlier, the title table (Table 8.4) is much improved but it still cannot claim to be at 2NF due to its troublesome duplication of publishers. This redundancy costs database storage space, may slow down performance as the table will have to be more fully scanned, and continues to risk spelling and other manual input errors. Luckily, this table can be brought into 2NF compliance by extracting the publisher data into a separate table.

Tables 8.6 and 8.7 are now operating under a one-to-many relationship, as in this scenario each book has only one publisher, and we already have evidence of QRS and XYZ publishing multiple titles.

Third normal form

At the third normal form, each column of a table should be directly related to the primary key (instead of being dependent upon another column). Another way of stating this is: 'a row [can] be uniquely identified by each column individually but ... no column [can depend] on any other column to identify the row'.[2] If a column does not meet this test, then it should be moved to a table of its own.

The revised title table (Table 8.6) could be further modified to attain 3NF status. The 'pages' field needs to be separated into another table as its uniqueness depends on the 'title' column. Technically, the 'pages' column may also violate 2NF as redundancies could eventually occur vertically. Yet for all but the largest databases, it would be practically nonsensical to create a keyed table full of page numbers. Simplicity would be the loser, and little would be gained by the effort.

A closely related construct of 3NF is called the Boyce-Codd Normal Form (BCNF). The stricter BCNF model (essentially 3NF+) can result in further 'decomposition' of tables to achieve even fewer dependencies. Generally speaking, 3NF (or BCNF) is considered the optimal normalisation form for regular production databases. Elmasri and Navathe note that:

> In practice, most relation schemas that are in 3NF are also in BCNF ... Ideally, relational database design should strive to achieve BCNF or 3NF for every relation schema. Achieving the normalisation status of just 1NF or 2NF is not considered adequate, as they were developed historically as stepping stones to 3NF and BCNF.[3]

In practice, however, some web developers do not always move beyond the 2NF.[4]

Much depends on the projected size of the database, its complexity, and how it will be managed and used. While the elimination of redundancy is an important consideration, at some point there can be diminishing returns. More tables usually mean more JOINS (SQL statements that process connections between primary and foreign keys in an effort to extract relevant data from related tables). More JOINS mean more SQL coding, and subsequently more taxing work for the DBMS which can result in decreased performance.

Sometimes too, from a very human perspective, it is convenient to have a somewhat larger table that may have an occasional non-keyed dependency. The ability to view important pieces of a record quickly on a single line (row) can be helpful. The creation of more tables usually means the increased splintering of individual records. Still, the design process should continually strive for increased normalisation so that data integrity is maintained. The entire process is a continual balancing act between theoretical perfection and 'real-world' performance, along with a dose of human–computer interaction sensibility.

One way to assess the quality of a database objectively is to run performance tests. When a query is run against a MySQL database, the DBMS always reports how long it took the system to process the query (e.g. 1.06 seconds). Experimentation with alternative table structures and SQL queries can sometimes lead to substantial performance gains. The MySQL DBMS also provides a table optimiser that can help identify trouble spots and offer clues that may lead to a better design. It can be rewarding to shave a few milliseconds (sometimes much more) off query times by gently tweaking a table or two. Database normalisation begins to become almost second nature with increased experience. Relationships between common pieces of data become obvious with practice. In the end, negotiating the ambiguities of effective database design is often as much an art as a science. A measure of concentration, tenacity and visual creativity can make all the difference.

Notes

1   Codd, E. F. (1972) 'Further normalization of the database relational model', in *Data Base Systems*, Courant Computer Science Symposia Series, Vol. 6, Englewood Cliffs, NJ: Prentice Hall. A number of helpful database design resources are available in print and online including: Riordan, R. M. (2005) *Designing Effective Database Systems*, Upper Saddle River, NJ: Addison-Wesley; Mullins, C. S. (2002) *Database Administration*, Boston: Addison-Wesley; Garcia-Molina, H., Ullman, J. D. and Widom, J. (2002) *Database Systems: The Complete Book*, Upper Saddle River, NJ: Prentice Hall; Elmasri, R. and Navathe, S. B. (2004) *Fundamentals of Database Systems* (4th edn), Boston: Addison-Wesley; Fells, D. (2004) 'Database normalization', available at: *http://www.devshed.com/c/a/Administration/Database-Normalization* (accessed 2 June 2006); Gilmore, W. J. (2000) 'An introduction to database normalization', available at: *http://www.devshed.com/c/a/MySQL/An-Introduction-to-Database-Normalization/* (accessed 2 June 2006); Wise, B. (2000)

'Database normalization and design techniques', available at: *http:/ /www.phpbuilder.com/columns/barry20000731.php3* (accessed 2 June 2006); Information Technology Services, University of Texas at Austin (2004) 'Introduction to data modeling', available at: *http:// www.utexas.edu/its/windows/database/datamodeling/rm/rm7* (accessed 2 June 2006); and Hillyer, M. (2004) 'An introduction to database normalization', available at: *http://dev.mysql.com/tech-resources/articles/intro-to-normalization.html* (accessed 2 June 2006).

2   Fells (2004), op. cit.

3   Elmasri (2004), op. cit. pp. 324–5. For a definition of BCNF, see Codd, E. F. (1974) 'Recent investigations in relational data base systems', in *Proceedings of the IFIP Congress* (Stockholm). The fourth and fifth normal forms have been defined, but they are mostly theoretical in nature. More recently, a sixth normal form has even been proposed: Date, C. J., Darwen, H. and Lorentzos, N. (2003) *Temporal Data & The Relational Model*, San Diego, CA: Morgan Kaufmann.

4   See Hillyer (2004), op. cit.

Building block V: MySQL

Build today, then, strong and sure,
With a firm and ample base;
And ascending and secure
Shall tomorrow find its place.
(Henry Wadsworth Longfellow, *The Builders*, 1850)

It is not accidental that MySQL has become the open source database of choice for many web developers. Its speed, flexibility, reliability and ease of use are renowned. Even novices can begin learning and experimenting with this powerful database management system after grasping some foundational concepts. For most 'entry-level' web developers, MySQL offers the perfect combination of power, growth potential and a rapid introduction to the world of database management.

Of course, no single DBMS is perfect in every way and for every use. While MySQL continues to gain market share in the enterprise-class arena, database vendors such as Oracle, IBM and Microsoft exude market dominance and have retained a special niche in the banking and financial industries because of their highly developed transaction features, stored procedures and strict data-type checking. These three titans alone control more than 85 per cent of the overall $10 billion DBMS commercial market.[1]

Unfortunately, not everyone can afford to pay titanic fees. The costs of pursuing the leading proprietary alternatives are prohibitive for many small businesses and not-for-profit organisations. Many groups are finding that open source database alternatives meet their needs quite well. According to computer research firm Evans Data Corp, the second half of 2005 saw overall open source database adoption rise 20 per cent. The deployment rate of MySQL alone increased by more than 25 per cent during this period.[2] MySQL has added more enterprise class features with the recent release of version 5 and is now poised to capture even greater market share.[3]

Due to its popularity among web developers, MySQL has become the open source database standard bearer, but there are other contenders, notably PostgreSQL. Initially developed at UC Berkeley in the 1980s, PostgreSQL has developed a following due to an advanced feature set and similarities with Oracle database functions. Generally speaking, MySQL's speed, ease of use and straightforward web interoperability probably account for its overwhelming popularity among web developers in both commercial and not-for-profit contexts.[4]

Getting started

This chapter assumes access to a Unix-like operating system with MySQL already installed.[5] The system administrator or web hosting service should supply specific information on how to access a MySQL server account. Specifically, the server address and port number where MySQL is installed (e.g. mysql.xyz.com:12345), and an administrative MySQL account username/password (e.g. root/aBcD123Z) should be supplied. This 'master' username/password combination grants *absolute* control over all databases and tables that may subsequently be created within the account. Due to its capability of adding, modifying and deleting all database structures and content, this login data must be guarded, and used carefully and sparingly.

A client program is used to administer and interact with an operational MySQL database server. In many environments, users will have access to the client's 'command line' prompt (e.g. mysql>), much like the traditional Unix prompt found within the operating system's shell. Somewhat confusingly (or redundantly), the name of the default 'command line' client used to access the MySQL DBMS is called 'mysql'. System administrators typically create a MySQL 'account' for each user (with a username and password), which lets them login to the MySQL database server via the mysql client (or some other administrative program).

Some web hosting services may only provide administrative access to the MySQL database server via a web-based interface such as the excellent phpMyAdmin open source program (*http://www.phpmyadmin.net*).[6] The following examples are based on the mysql command prompt because it is advantageous to understand the native MySQL environment before migrating to a mediated administrative tool such as phpMyAdmin. Both of these administrative interfaces have strengths and weaknesses and are particularly useful in performing specific functions. The command line is useful for granting permissions due to the automatic password encryption feature. It is also handy when testing queries, analysing tables and working to improve performance issues. Web-based administrative tools like phpMyAdmin can be especially handy for table creation, column and data type manipulation, and for rapid viewing and updating of content within individual rows.

The login process

To start the mysql program (so commands can be sent to the MySQL database server), enter the following login sequence at the operating system command prompt (e.g. prompt%):

prompt% mysql -u root -p **<Enter>**

A single 'space' should be provided between each parameter. The login sequence requests the opening of the MySQL client program (mysql) with an account username (-u) called 'root.' Appending the password option (-p) and pressing <Enter> (without supplying the expected password) is a good security precaution. This procedure forces a secondary password prompt ('Enter password:') to appear:

prompt% mysql -u root -p **<Enter>**
Enter password:

Entering the account password at this secondary prompt provides at least some extra protection. Visible text passwords entered on the initial command line (directly after the '-p') can potentially be captured. Passwords entered at this secondary prompt are not forwarded to the screen for display, making it more difficult for someone to acquire the password surreptitiously.

If the username and password are entered correctly, a 'welcome message' will appear followed by a mysql prompt (mysql>) ready to receive a command:

Welcome to the MySQL monitor. Commands end with ; or \g.
Your MySQL connection id is 3359 to server version: 5.0.20a
Type 'help;' or '\h' for help. Type '\c' to clear the buffer
mysql>

Creating a database

Creating a new database is very easy. At the mysql> prompt, simply enter the SQL command phrase 'CREATE DATABASE,' give the new database a name, and then close the command with a semicolon (;):

mysql> CREATE DATABASE books; **<Enter>**
Query OK, 1 row affected (0.00 sec)

The standard output ('Query OK...') from the SQL command (query) indicates that the statement was processed without error. All commands issued at the mysql> prompt must end with a semicolon (followed by pressing the keyboard's <Enter> button, which is assumed in the examples hereafter). MySQL is case insensitive regarding SQL commands and clauses, so either 'CREATE DATABASE' or 'create database' will function. The UPPERCASE rendering can be a helpful visual aid, especially when inspecting a lengthy statement. On Unix-type systems, the names given to databases, tables and columns are case sensitive (just as file and directory names).

Granting permissions

Immediately after creating a new database on the MySQL server, one of the most important operations is to establish a new user account. This account will govern all access and privileges associated with the database. Generally speaking, from that point forward the 'root' (master) password should no longer be used in conjunction with the new database. This is an important security precaution that helps cordon off the new database from all of the other databases that may already exist on the account. If some nefarious character discovers the new database login sequence they will only have the power to damage a single database, not every database established on the entire account. In addition, it is always a good habit to avoid using the 'root' password for general purposes as an innocent keyboarding error can have disastrous consequences for all databases under this master login.

Multiple accounts can be established, providing a means to limit access and constrain each user's ability to modify the database. Use can even be restricted to a specific database table or column. A variety of privileges can be granted including the right to SELECT, INSERT, UPDATE and DELETE database content. Specifying 'ALL' grants the user full rights to perform any of these commands when managing database content. To assign full rights to a user the following command could be issued:

```
mysql> GRANT ALL ON books.* TO 'booksadmin'@'%'
IDENTIFIED BY 'herpassword';
Query OK, 0 rows affected (0.02 sec)
```

This statement grants full privileges (ALL) to every table within the books database (books.*). Alternatively, full rights could have been declared for only a specific table within the books database (e.g. books.titles). A user named booksadmin may access the database from any location (%) by providing the stated password (herpassword). As a security precaution, it may be desirable to limit access to the database from remote systems. Instead of using the '%' host wildcard, a more conservative approach would allow database access from a narrower domain or IP address, for example:

```
'booksadmin'@'xyz.123.org'
'booksadmin'@'%.456.org'
'booksadmin'@'111.111.111.11'
'booksadmin'@'111.111.111.%'
```

If a database will be accessed by the public, it makes sense to create a limited 'read only' account that can be called from within PHP scripts. Users who access the database in this fashion may 'SELECT' (view/obtain) data, but are not empowered to add, delete nor modify database content in any way. This practice can help preclude an accidental coding error from causing damage to the database:

```
mysql> GRANT SELECT ON books.* TO 'readonly'@'%';
Query OK, 0 rows affected (0.02 sec)
```

Database and/or table privileges may also be rescinded from a user by invoking the REVOKE command:

mysql> REVOKE DELETE ON books.* FROM booksadmin;
Query OK, 0 rows affected (0.01 sec)

Such a command would remove the ability for the booksadmin user to DELETE records from all tables in the books database. The user would still be able to perform other commands previously granted unless these are also revoked (e.g. REVOKE ALL...).

For speedy access and retrieval, MySQL administrative tables (including the tables that record user privileges) are stored in memory. Immediately after establishing or adjusting any account permissions, always use the following 'refresh' command so MySQL will immediately recognise any changes to account privileges:

mysql> FLUSH PRIVILEGES;

After the FLUSH PRIVILEGES statement is issued, a quick way to review the current privileges of a user is to call the SHOW command:

mysql> SHOW GRANTS FOR readonly;

Output:

Grants for readonly`@'%
GRANT SELECT ON books.* TO 'readonly`@'%'

1 row in set (0.00 sec)

Creating tables

With the database created and appropriate permissions assigned, we can now begin creating tables and preparing them for incoming data. As a table could be created in any number of existing databases, there are two commands that are useful to know. The first command displays a list of available databases, while the second clarifies the database where we intend to place new tables:

```
mysql> SHOW DATABASES;
```

Output:

Database
archives
bibliography
books
plays

```
mysql> USE books;
```

Output:
Database changed

It is unnecessary to issue the SHOW statement if the database name is already known, but the USE command is always required before beginning work on a specific database. With the correct database selected ('changed'), our attention can turn to the matter at hand.

To create a table, several important pieces of information must be known about the fields about to be established. The data type for each column must be known along with any associated value settings. As the entries within a primary key column are typically numerals, the data type for this field should be set to hold an integer. Familiarity with the data to be inserted into the table is necessary as the fields must be large enough to hold any potential data, but not so large that valuable drive space is wasted due to setting aside far more field space than will ever be needed. For example, the maximum space limit for a basic alphabetical text field is 255 characters. As few authors have first (or last) names that would ever approach this length, it is probably safe to establish much smaller name fields.

Suppose that a table must be created to hold the names of a series of authors (Table 9.1). The table (descriptively named 'author') would need to provide columns for a primary key and each author's first and last name.

It could also be decided that including a TIMESTAMP column in the table would be useful for keeping track of when each author entry was last updated. The following command can be issued to create such a table:

Table 9.1	A proposed author table		
author_id	author_first	author_last	author_ts

```
mysql> CREATE TABLE author
(
author_id INT UNSIGNED AUTO_INCREMENT PRIMARY
KEY,
author_first VARCHAR(20),
author_last VARCHAR(20),
author_ts TIMESTAMP
);
```
Query OK, 0 rows affected (0.01 sec)

After declaring the name of the new table ('CREATE TABLE author') a parenthetical statement defines the nature of each tabular column. Each entry in the author_id field has been declared to be an unsigned integer (unsigned integers are non-negative numbers in the MySQL environment that range from 0 to 4294967295). Unsigned integers are ideal when specifying that a field should be automatically incremented (AUTO_INCREMENT) with each added row of data. Declaring the column as a PRIMARY KEY assures that every row will be given a unique number and that no row will have a NULL value in the field. These definitions ensure confidence that the table's primary key will always be a unique, positive numeral that can be absolutely relied upon to identify specific rows of data.

The author_first and author_last fields have been assigned a VARCHAR data type of up to 20 characters. This means that the field is configured to receive up to 20 characters of varying length.[7] VARCHAR is usually the best data type choice for general purposes, particularly if varying value lengths are expected. If it is certain that the column's value will always have the same number of characters (e.g. a 'year' column will always consist of four numerals), then CHAR is the better choice as MySQL is optimised to process fixed-row values. However, using the CHAR data type with entries of varying length can waste space as the entire field will be configured to receive the full specified value. If large blocks of text (e.g. the body of a web page) will be inserted into the table, the TEXT data type should be selected as it can hold up to 64K of information.[8] For the sake of performance, the goal is always to establish the smallest possible column size that will hold the largest piece of incoming data. The TIMESTAMP data type always consists of 14 characters in a 'year, month, day, hour, minute, second' format.[9] The TIMESTAMP is automatically updated to display the current date whenever the row is altered.

Please note that the CREATE TABLE syntax must be entered precisely. Even a minor syntax error will result in an error message. Fortunately, if an error message occurs, no damage is done. Simply re-enter the syntax being careful to make the necessary adjustments. Be sure to enclose the field data types and definitions within parentheses and to separate each clause with a comma. Extra 'whitespace' is permissible as is the extension of statements to multiple lines. The keyboard's 'up arrow' is a valuable timesaver as previously issued statements at the mysql command line can be reviewed (and then re-submitted with the <Enter> button).

Over time, multiple tables may need to be added to a database. The SHOW statement can help by providing a list of tables within the current database.

mysql> SHOW TABLES;

Output:

Tables_in_books
author

1 row in set (0.01 sec)

Issuing the following command provides a detailed look at the structure of a specific table:

mysql> DESCRIBE author;

Output:

Field	Type	Null	Key	Default	Extra
author_id	int(10) unsigned		PRI	NULL	auto_increment
author_first	varchar(20)	YES		NULL	
author_last	varchar(20)	YES		NULL	
author_ts	timestamp(14)	YES		NULL	

4 rows in set (0.00 sec)

Inserting data

With the author table now created and properly configured to receive content, little remains to be done except to begin loading data. For extremely small tables holding minimal data, content can be manually inserted directly from the mysql command line.

Usually it is far more efficient to upload data into MySQL from a comma-delimited text file or by importing content from another database via an ODBC connection.[10]

To insert a single row of data into a table manually, the INSERT query can be used:

```
mysql> INSERT INTO authors
(
author_id,
author_first,
author_last,
author_ts
)
VALUES
('0',
'Isaac',
'Brooks',
\N
);
Query OK, 1 row affected (0.02 sec)
```

Notice that the column names and the values to be inserted are arranged in the same order. The \N (NULL) value should be used to update the TIMESTAMP column. Note the absence of single quotes surrounding this value. An easy way to check the table and see what has occurred is to issue a SELECT command:

```
mysql> SELECT * FROM author;
```

Output:

author_id	author_first	author_last	author_ts
1	Isaac	Brooks	20060423164709

1 row in set (0.01 sec)

Everything looks in good order as the SELECT query confirms that the first row of content has been successfully inserted. Note that the primary key (author_id) has been incremented to '1' due to the AUTO_INCREMENT setting having been previously applied. Integers inserted into an AUTO_INCREMENT field should always have a value of '0' (zero), as MySQL will automatically install the 'next' number in proper sequence.

While this initial method of populating a table with data is straightforward and easy to understand, it is not an effective means of inserting large amounts of data. Tediously composing a host of such INSERT statements would soon become an objectionable chore, not unlike pouring a glass of water one drop at a time. A far superior method is to load all of the intended entries at once. Naturally, this does require some preparatory 'tweaking' of the incoming data so that the content will be properly organised and structured. If the content is amenable to being placed in a spreadsheet, systematising the data is not difficult. The columns of a database table and a spreadsheet share a similar vertical structure. Spreadsheets such as Microsoft Excel or the open source CALC product from openoffice.org can be used for this task (Figure 9.1).

No headers should be applied to the top of each spreadsheet column. The file should generally be saved in the 'Text (Tab delimited)' format,

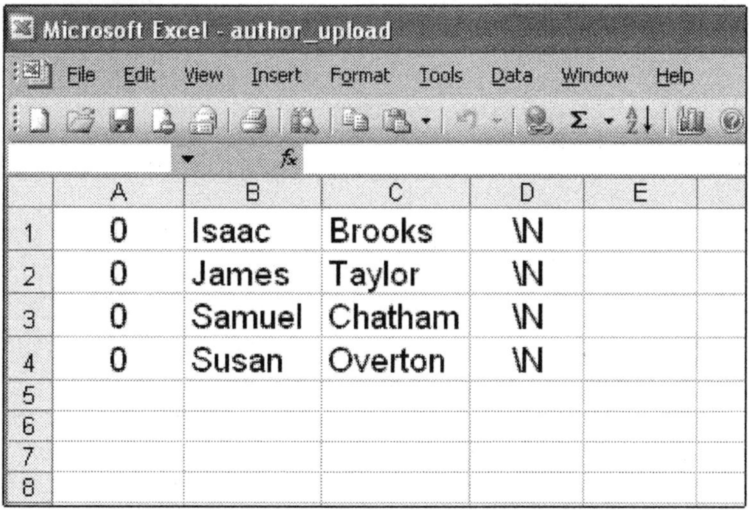

Figure 9.1   Use a spreadsheet to prepare data for loading

the default format for MySQL data loads.[11] The resulting file must be transferred (e.g. via FTP) to the local operating system where the MySQL server is installed. Due to security precautions it is not possible, for example, to upload files from a remote Internet location directly to a MySQL server. To be loaded into the database, the file must 'live' somewhere on the MySQL host's system. A 'temp' directory can be created on the host operating system to store the transferred file and provide a local path for loading the file into a MySQL table. The following command line statement accesses the 'author_upload.txt' file on the local system and loads it into the author table:

```
mysql> LOAD DATA LOCAL INFILE '/home/account/
temp/author_upload.txt'
INTO TABLE author;
Query OK, 4 rows affected (0.02 sec)
Records: 4 Deleted: 0 Skipped: 0 Warnings: 0
```

Note the path that specifies the location of the 'author_upload.txt' file on the Unix system. The data loading process appears to have been a success given the positive report indicating that four rows were added to the table. A quick SELECT statement reveals that all is well:

```
mysql> SELECT * FROM author;
```

Output:

author_id	author_first	author_last	author_ts
1	Isaac	Brooks	20061112164709
2	James	Taylor	20061112164709
3	Samuel	Chatham	20061112164709
4	Susan	Overton	20061112164709

4 rows in set (0.02 sec)

> **Data loading tip** By default, some spreadsheets automatically enclose delimited text fields with single or double quotation marks. Unfortunately, these marks are not always viewable from within the spreadsheet. Hidden quotation marks may be the culprit if data are only partially loaded into a table or if file loading errors occur. To resolve this issue, open the delimited file in a plain text editor (e.g. Notepad) and globally remove any quote marks that

may appear with the 'Find & Replace' editing function. Data to be loaded into a MySQL table should appear 'quoteless' and in tab-delimited format when viewed within a text editor:

0	Isaac	Brooks	\N
0	James	Taylor	\N
0	Samuel	Chatham	\N
0	Susan	Overton	\N

Updating data

The UPDATE statement is used to modify or edit content residing in a MySQL table.

Suppose that Susan Overton's first name has been unintentionally abbreviated and must be corrected. A correction can be easily made by issuing this command:

```
mysql> UPDATE author SET author_first = 'Susanna'
WHERE author_id = '4';
Query OK, 1 row affected (0.02 sec)
Rows matched: 1 Changed: 1 Warnings: 0
```

The resulting output indicates a successful revision. Susanna's entry in the author_first field can be checked like this:

```
mysql> SELECT author_first FROM author
WHERE author_id = '4';
```

Output:

author_first
Susanna

1 row in set (0.02 sec)

Deleting data

The statement used to DELETE a table entry is not unlike the queries previously demonstrated. The PRIMARY KEY (author_id) is again relied upon to ensure that the correct row is being targeted. Be sure to always include the WHERE clause as this protects all of the other rows in the table from being globally deleted.

mysql> DELETE FROM author WHERE author_id = '3';
Query OK, 1 row affected (0.01 sec)

A review of the table determines that the author entry for Samuel Chatham has been removed:

mysql> SELECT * FROM author;

Output:

author_id	author_first	author_last	author_ts
1	Isaac	Brooks	20061112174709
2	James	Taylor	20061112174709
4	Susanna	Overton	20061112174709

3 rows in set (0.01 sec)

Significantly, note that the primary key remains unchanged. The numerals established within the author_id field remain constant and are not somehow resorted due to the removal of the third entry. As expected, the authority of each row has been protected. Though perhaps well-meaning, inexperienced database users have been known to feel the inexplicable need to 'fix' the primary key column by starting over and renumbering the entries. This terribly misguided impulse will create disarray and undermine the authority control of the database. Though the number '3' will never again appear in the author_id column (which is the entire point), MySQL happily proceeds forward as it can automatically increment the primary key column over 4.2 billion times.[12] Once an entry has been assigned a primary key this unique number defines the row 'always and forever' and must never be altered.

To acquire a good understanding of how MySQL works there is probably nothing more profitable than sitting down before a mysql command prompt and beginning to practise and experiment. Try creating a database and then a table. INSERT data into the table, SELECT portions of it, UPDATE a few entries and then DELETE certain rows.

As the learning process unfolds, it is only natural that mistakes will occur. Sometimes there is nothing like a 'fresh start' after an unexpected data upload error, a keyboard mistake that imports data to an incorrect location, or a new table experiment that has gone slightly awry. On such occasions, sometimes the easiest way to begin anew is to delete all the rows of data in the table. The following command does not impact the structure of the table nor modify previously assigned column data types. It simply deletes all the rows of content. As alluded to earlier, use care when issuing this command:

```
mysql> DELETE FROM author;
Query OK, 0 rows affected (0.06 sec)
```

The resulting output is misleading because in reality all of the rows have been dramatically affected – they no longer exist! Another command line directive related to the concept of deletion is the DROP statement. It is perhaps most beneficially used during the process of creating a new table. Sometimes it can be easier to erase a newly minted (yet malformed) table than work to correct it. DROP, however, is a very powerful command that can easily ruin a nice afternoon if it is unadvisedly called. The command 'DROP TABLE author;' will immediately, irrevocably and permanently delete the author table and all of its content. Incidentally, the command 'DROP DATABASE books;' will have the same irreversible and eradicating effect upon all the tables and content within a database. If you love your database, do not drop it.[13]

Indexing columns

One way to improve overall database speed and performance (particularly when processing large tables), is to assign an index to columns that will be frequently searched or sorted. For example, whenever MySQL is instructed to SELECT a specific row, it must first 'look through' *every single row* in the table in search of the correct one. Strategically assigning an index to a limited number of certain types of columns can help speed up this process. In very simplistic terms, an index is often just another numeric column of the table, which has been advantageously sorted. Using sophisticated 'positioning algorithms' a database server can process indexes far more quickly than it can cycle through regular table columns.[14]

Luckily, it is not necessary to understand the inner workings of indexes to take advantage of them.

While indexes are an effective means of enhancing performance, there are also some good reasons to use this data-structuring technique judiciously. Indexes can consume sizable amounts of disk space and they must be continually updated as rows are added and removed. Indexing too many columns can result in diminishing returns as the database server will be forced to unnecessarily process data. One rule of thumb is to index the minimum number of columns necessary to improve performance. There is generally little benefit in indexing common text fields that are only intended for output (e.g. authors, titles, publishers, e-mail addresses, phone numbers, zip codes). Foreign key columns, fields that are frequently sorted, and fields that frequently appear in WHERE clauses are good candidates for indexing as they are heavily used. In general, consider indexing columns that have a 'linking' relationship with columns in other tables as they will probably be more frequently called upon to pull tables together.

Primary key columns are automatically indexed at the time of table creation, so it is not necessary to index these fields. In Tables 9.2 and 9.3, the author_id column in the author table and the title table's title_id column were indexed at table creation as the primary keys. It could be beneficial to index the author_id column in the title table as it acts as a foreign key and would be frequently used in queries to make connections between the two tables.

Table 9.2 An author table

author_id	author_first	author_last
1	Isaac	Brooks
2	James	Taylor
4	Susanna	Overton

Table 9.3 A title table

title_id	author_id	title_name	title_date
1	4	Winds of Hope	2003
2	1	Sun of the Clouds	1996
5	2	High Dwellers	1999

Fields may be indexed at the time of table creation or after the fact. The following statement would create the above title table and assign an index to its author_id column:

```
mysql> CREATE TABLE title
(
title_id    INT UNSIGNED AUTO_INCREMENT
PRIMARY KEY,
author_id   INT UNSIGNED,
title_name VARCHAR(20),
title_date CHAR(4),
INDEX (author_id)
);
Query OK, 0 rows affected (0.02 sec)
```

If the title table (Table 9.3) had already been created (without an index on the author_id field), the following statement could subsequently be used to add an index:

```
mysql> CREATE INDEX author_id ON title (author_id);
Query OK, 0 rows affected (0.11 sec)
Records: 0 Duplicates: 0 Warnings: 0
```

Summary

This chapter has highlighted some of the most important aspects of 'real-world' MySQL usage including account set-up, table creation and data management. Special attention was focused upon the MySQL command statements that are most frequently used in general web database development activities. Of course, this discussion only introduces a small portion of the possible activities and functions that a powerful database management system like MySQL can perform. The reader is encouraged to consult the official MySQL online documentation and related in-depth treatments of this exciting, powerful and functional database tool.

Notes

1   Mears, J. (2005) 'Open source databases grow', *Network World* (29 August), available at: *http://www.networkworld.com/news/2005/082905opendb.html* (accessed 2 June 2006).

2   Vaas, L. (2005) 'Open-source databases spreading like rabbits', *eWeek* (21 October), available at: *http://www.eweek.com/article2/0,1895,1875070,00.asp* (accessed 2 June 2006).

3   McCown, S. (2005) 'Long-awaited MySQL 5.0 makes its debut', *InfoWorld* (28 December), available at: *http://www.infoworld.com/article/05/12/28/01TCmysql_1.html* (accessed 2 June 2006); Cohen, N. and Fegreus, J. (2004) 'MySQL dials +99.999 for availability', *Open-Mag* (16 July), available at: *http://www.open-mag.com/features/Vol_101/MySQL/MySQL.htm* (accessed 2 June 2006); Vaughan-Nichols, S. J. (2005) 'MySQL 5 arrives', *eWeek* (24 October), available at: *http://www.eweek.com/article2/0,1895,1876702,00.asp* (accessed 2 June 2006); Niccolai, J. (2005) 'New MySQL version adds enterprise capabilities' *ComputerWorld* (17 October), available at: *http://www.computerworld.com/databasetopics/data/software/story/0,10801,105470,00.html* (accessed 2 June 2006); and Stafford, J. (2004) 'Why open source and MySQL are winning corporate hearts', *SearchOpenSource* (07 September), available at: *http://searchopensource.techtarget.com/qna/ 0,289202,sid39_gci1003753,00.html* (accessed 2 June 2006).

4   Vass, L. (2005) 'At last, a worthy open-source alternative to Oracle', *eWeek* (23 May), available at: *http://www.eweek.com/article2/0,1895,1819249,00.asp* (accessed 2 June 2006); Gilfillan, I. (2005) 'Open source databases: a brief look at Berkeley DB, Derby, Firebird, Ingres, MySQL and PostgreSQL', *Database Journal* (8 March), available at: *http://www.databasejournal.com/sqletc/article.php/3486596* (accessed 2 June 2006); 'Open source database comparison' (March 2005): *http://www.geocities.com/mailsoftware42/db/* (accessed 2 June 2006); Conrad, T. (2004) 'PostgreSQL vs. MySQL vs. commercial databases: it's all about what you need', *DevX* (12 April), available at: *http://www.devx.com/dbzone/Article/20743* (accessed 2 June 2006); and Drake, J. D. and Parmar, U. (2005) 'Open source database feature comparison matrix', *DevX* (14 October), available at: *http://www.devx.com/dbzone/Article/29480/* (accessed 2 June 2006).

5   Installation instructions for both MySQL and PHP are respectively available at: *http://dev.mysql.com/doc/refman/5.0/en/installing.html* and *http://www.php.net/install/* (accessed 2 June 2006).

6   Interestingly, phpMyAdmin is itself a PHP/HTML web application that is designed to administer and manipulate MySQL server databases, tables and data. The fact that this administrative tool is built with PHP demonstrates how well this language interacts with MySQL.

7   Prior to MySQL 5.0.3, VARCHAR columns varied in length from 0 to 255 maximum characters. More recent MySQL versions have extended VARCHAR to accept entries ranging from 0 to 65,535 characters.

8   The LONGTEXT data type can hold up to 4 GB of content. Incidentally, do not spend valuable time attempting to upload huge binary images to a MySQL database. It is far simpler to store image files on a large capacity free-standing file server. Textual links to the image filenames can then be inserted into a MySQL table and called via PHP as needed.

9   Prior to MySQL version 4.01 the TIMESTAMP format was represented by a string of 14 digits: YYYYMMDDHHMMSS. In subsequent versions the 14 digit format was revised to read: YYYY-MM-DD HH:MM:SS.

10   Though ODBC database connections are beyond the scope of this book, they can be a useful means of both loading data into MySQL and downloading data to a desktop database such as MS Access for convenient manipulation and backup. To get started, the 'free' MySQL Connector/ODBC (MyODBC) driver must be downloaded and installed on the operating system hosting your 'secondary' database. MyODBC driver and related information is available at: *http://dev.mysql.com/downloads/connector/odbc/* (accessed 2 June 2006).

11   Comma-delimited CSV (.csv) files may also be used by adding the following clause to the very end of the LOAD statement (just before the semicolon): FIELDS TERMINATED BY ','.

12   MySQL tables (with default MyISAM storage engine) can hold a maximum of 4,294,967,295 rows (far more than enough for most database driven web applications). For more information see 'MySQL numeric types' at: *http://dev.mysql.com/doc/refman/5.0/en/numeric-types.html* (accessed 2 June 2006).

13   As always, it is critical to back up valuable content in any computing

environment. MySQL provides some simple methods to help minimise the risk of data loss with the *mysqldump* and *mysqlhotcopy* utilities. Additional information is available at: *http://dev.mysql.com/ doc/refman/5.0/en/mysqldump.html*.

14   For an excellent overview of MySQL indexing, see Dubois, P. (2005) *MySQL* (3rd edn), Indianapolis: Sams, pp. 298–305.

Standards and accessibility

The power of the Web is in its universality. Access by everyone
regardless of disability is an essential aspect.

(Tim Berners-Lee, Web Accessibility Initiative, 2002)[1]

It should probably go without saying that one of the most consequential aspects of web design and development is compliance with international coding and accessibility standards. More than just a philosophical exercise, conforming to recognised standards promotes browser interoperability, 'universal usability', and prevents the raising of artificial barriers that may impede content access for people with disabilities. Beyond obvious ethical considerations, a growing number of legal requirements are increasingly mandating standards adherence. There is also a persuasive argument that it makes good business and public relations sense to provide equal information access.[2]

Accessibility standards

Most governments seeking to promote web accessibility generally recommend the adoption of international standards developed by the World Wide Web Consortium (W3C). Founded by Web inventor Tim Berners-Lee in 1994, W3C is an influential cyberspace organisation that is actively engaged in developing web specifications and resources on a number of fronts. W3C has established working groups to develop and extend specifications for HTML, CSS, XML and other important web protocols. The Web Accessibility Initiative (WAI) is a W3C working group specifically tasked with developing clear guidelines for making content more accessible to the disabled, but also for the broader online community.

WAI finalised a set of standards called the Web Content Accessibility Guidelines (WCAG) version 1.0 in 1999.[3] WCAG establishes a tri-level conformance framework. Sites that conform to 'Level A' have met the minimal accessibility recommendations described in a 'Priority 1' checklist. Sites in conformance with Level B meet both Priority 1 recommendations and the slightly more stringent Priority 2 guidelines. The ultimate level of web accessibility conformity is at Level 3 (satisfying Priority 1, 2, and 3 conditions).[4] These specifications are widely recognised and have been adopted internationally by the websites of governments, corporations, universities, associations, technology organisations and others.

Compliance: ethical and professional issues

A variety of professional organisations related to library and information science have for many years embraced the ideal of universal access. Deeply committed to intellectual freedom and avowing the human right of equal access to information, these groups have contributed much toward establishing open societies that embrace diversity and people with unique information accessibility needs. In many respects, library and information science professionals have been instrumental in influencing legislation, setting national information priorities and providing tangible leadership in adopting accessibility standards and encouraging others to follow suit.

Even a cursory historical study of major library and information science professional organisations reveals a strongly held belief in developing substantive ethical codes and standards in support of the establishment and protection of free and equal access to all forms of information. The preface of the American Library Association's (ALA) Code of Ethics includes the statement:

> We significantly influence or control the selection, organization, preservation, and dissemination of information. In a political system grounded in an informed citizenry, we are members of a profession explicitly committed to intellectual freedom and the freedom of access to information. We have a special obligation to ensure the free flow of information and ideas to present and future generations.[5]

In 2004, the ALA Council re-approved the following ALA Policy Manual statement on 'Access' as one of 11 'Core Values of Librarianship':

> All information resources that are provided directly or indirectly by the library, regardless of technology, format, or methods of delivery, should be readily, equally, and equitably accessible to all library users.[6]

The 1983 Code of Professional Conduct of the UK's Library Association stated that:

> In places to which the public has right of access ... members have an obligation to facilitate the flow of information and ideas and to protect and promote the rights of every individual to have free and equal access to sources of information without discrimination and within the limits of the law.[7]

The Chartered Institute of Library and Information Professionals (CILIP), the UK's recently unified body of library and information professionals, released the following statement on access in 2005:

> CILIP is committed to promoting a society where intellectual activity and creativity, freedom of expression and debate, and access to information are encouraged and nurtured as vital elements underpinning individual and community fulfilment in all aspects of human life. It is the role of a library and information service that is funded from the public purse to provide ... access to all publicly available information ... regardless of media or format, in which its users claim legitimate interest ...The principles of access are the same in the emerging networked society where the opportunities provided by information and communications technologies have revolutionised the way information is made available.[8]

Virtually every national member of the International Federation of Library Associations and Institutions (IFLA) explicitly embraces the principle of free and equal access to information.[9] The Code of Ethics of Czech Librarians is representative of the principles affirmed by many national library codes. Among its stated principles, the Czech Code affirms 'the basic right of the individual to information... [and] unlimited, equal, and free access to information and information sources in library collections'.[10]

Professional computing associations such as the Association for Computing Machinery (ACM) have promoted web accessibility efforts and expressed support for people with disabilities through research, publications and accessibility initiatives. ACM and its SIGACCESS special interest group host the biannual ASSETS international conference on computers and accessibility. These efforts help advance the development of computing and information technologies to assist disabled people.[11]

Library and information science organisations throughout the world have committed themselves to significant philosophical and ethical ideals related to the provision of equal access to information. Information media have changed dramatically over the last 15 years, and undoubtedly will take new forms in the future. Yet the foundational principles relating to information access, equality and basic human rights articulated by library and information scientists will likely serve as touchstones for new generations of information providers.

In some spheres, the idea of working a little harder or spending a little more to comply with accessibility guidelines that may directly assist a relatively small percentage of the population may seem a bit foolhardy or perhaps even a waste of resources. Those who devote their lives to helping others gain access to information often view such efforts in a different light. For them, every advance in improving accessibility is rightly prized as a tangible means of affecting the lives of real people, levelling the playing field, and directing the larger human society toward its best impulses, hopes and ideals.

Compliance: business issues

Major international web accessibility standards and guidelines are frequently discussed, written about, affirmed, celebrated and codified. Almost invariably (and for a variety of reasons), these same benchmarks are also routinely overlooked, neglected or ignored.[12] A recent study of American Fortune 100 company homepages revealed that 94 per cent are not fully accessible to people with disabilities. Only 18 per cent of these companies even meet minimum accessibility standards.[13]

Perhaps this is not terribly surprising as most commercial web developers are often working under strict deadlines and tasked to make things 'work'. Juggling database design, graphic design, coding issues, debugging activities and other project concerns may cause developers to concentrate their focus almost exclusively on results. Re-coding pages according to standards is difficult to perform after testing suggests problems at the end of a project. From the perspective of the busy developer, the relative success of a project may be both measured and influenced by the developer's individual style, computer configuration, browser preference, screen resolution, visual resources and other predispositions. Careful developers may even take the time to view a web page with different browsers and monitor resolutions to ensure that the presentation is uniform and pleasing to the eye. While such visual testing is widely appreciated and practised among professionals, the same kind of care and attention is not always paid to issues of accessibility for the visually disabled.

Based on many estimates, the disabled community represents a sizable portion of the population. According to the World Health Organization approximately 7–10 per cent of the global population (some 600 million people), has a disability.[14] Within the European Union (EU), one study found that approximately 24 million people of working age (roughly 10 per cent) have some form of disability. Other studies of the EU population have placed the percentage of all people with a disability in the 8–14 per cent range.[15] In the USA, Census Bureau research indicates that nearly one-fifth (19.3 per cent) of non-institutionalised citizens aged 5 and older (about 49.7 million), have a physical or mental disability. About 9.3 million US citizens (3.6 per cent) are believed to have a sensory disability involving sight or hearing.[16] Due to varying definitions, data collection techniques and research methodologies it is difficult to evaluate and compare the existing disability studies. Still, the available data suggests that sizable populations (~10 per cent) have disabilities of one form or another.

With the many varieties of disabilities, it comes as no surprise that web-accessibility issues can be exceedingly complex. People with visual disabilities may experience blindness, reduced vision or colour impairment. Those with hearing disabilities may have deafness or various levels of impaired hearing. Motor skill disabilities may lead to slower response times and may make it easier for some users to navigate a website primarily with a keyboard rather than a mouse. Cognitive and neurological disabilities such as dyslexia, attention deficit disorder (ADD), intellectual and memory impairments, and mental health issues can affect information access. While it is very difficult to address every possible disability that all users may experience, even some minimal accommodations can often make a significant difference for a majority of disabled users.[17]

With data indicating that disabled individuals are gravitating toward Internet use in great number, many commercial enterprises may be failing to take advantage of the buying power of this population group. One US study found that 50 per cent of working age adults with disabilities shop online.[18] Demographers have also noted that the average age of the population is on the rise in many countries. The decline of cognitive and physical functioning associated with aging can create numerous accessibility problems. Mobility disabilities (whether temporary or permanent) may create opportunities for people to increase their time interacting with web resources. From purely a business standpoint, it makes sense for business leaders to recognise that aging populations represent a significant segment of the potential market. In the UK, it is estimated that the disabled community has a collective spending power of £40–50 billion per year. The disabled market in the USA is valued at $175 billion.[19]

A National Organization on Disabilities/Harris Poll found that people with disabilities on average spend 30 hours per week online while those without disabilities are online for only 18 hours. Additionally, almost half of persons with disabilities claim the Internet has significantly improved their quality of life (versus 27 per cent of people without disabilities).[20] Furthermore, over 75 per cent of disabled people search for products and services with 50 per cent making online purchases.[21] A recent US government report found that 63.7 per cent of individuals in the workforce with severe vision impairment or blindness regularly use the Internet. The report also discovered that almost 59 per cent of individuals with multiple disabilities (e.g. vision, hearing, walking, typing, difficulty leaving home) regularly use the Internet.[22]

As businesses may not always appreciate the economic reach and online presence of the disabled community, they may also not recognise how a failure to adhere to standards may impede access to broader constituencies as well. One observer has noted that:

> Following good practice in web accessibility not only benefits disabled customers as the techniques used to create accessible websites open up online services to those using mobile devices, low bandwidth Internet connections and older technology platforms, maximising the potential audience … Accessible design frequently achieves a more usable and portable solution for the widest range of individuals and browsing environments.[23]

Content that is delivered via an accessible database delivery system is amazingly flexible and can be distributed via multiple media. As discussed previously, the practice of separating content from presentation has enormous advantages. When not tied to a single interface, content is 'skinnable' and can be easily presented in varying visual forms.[24] This same flexibility is important for non-visual presentations as content can be formatted and coded for improved accessibility.

With increased accessibility and a database platform, organisations can achieve device independence and are free to leverage content in fascinating new ways. PDAs, car information systems, RSS feeds, cell phones, kiosks, podcasts, desktops, and many other delivery systems and processes can be used to publish and distribute content. Well-designed sites that follow coding and accessibility standards intended to address the needs of the disabled are likely to make access and navigation easier and more dependable for all users. Creating an accessible website cannot help but be good for business, supportive of public relations efforts and helpful for practically anyone hoping to interact with the organisation online.

Compliance: legal issues

While good business practice and competitive advantage may encourage some entities to embrace web standards, there are other good reasons as well. A growing number of nations have begun to embrace and promote accessibility standards both as a 'best practice' and as a means of serving the common good. A frequent approach is for the national government itself to adopt international web standards for its own public sites. This is perhaps seen as a way to set a positive example and encourage other high-profile sites (both public and private) to follow their lead.

European Union: Voluntary compliance

The European Union, through the European Commission's Information Society initiative, helps fund the WAI and has proactively encouraged compliance with the WCAG standards in both public and private spheres. The European Commission (EC) has adopted the basic (Level A – Priority 1) WCAG guidelines for new and updated EU websites on the EUROPA server.[25] While there have been no EU legislative mandates on web accessibility, the EC has overtly promoted Internet accessibility initiatives.

The June 2000 'eEurope 2002 Action Plan' included an element entitled 'e-Accessibility' that sought to ensure that disabled people would fully benefit from the Internet and other technologies. The following year the EC adopted the Communication entitled 'eEurope 2002: Accessibility of Public Websites and their Content' that encouraged the adoption of WAI guidelines for all public websites among member states and European institutions. While the '2005 EC Communication on e-Accessibility' continued to encourage active support for the rights of people with disabilities, Yannis Vardakastanis, President of the European Disability Forum, expressed concern about waiting for voluntary compliance:

> The Communication explicitly recognises the right of 50 million people with disabilities to fully participate [in] the information society, and this already means great progress. But as long as the voluntary approach is not reinforced with effective legislation, there is no guarantee that disabled people will not be victims of the 'digital divide'.[26]

A November 2005 EU report noted that only 3 per cent of public European websites meet the minimum WCAG 'Level A – Priority 1' recommendation.[27] It remains to be seen whether the EU will pursue the enactment of legislation mandating compliance with accessibility standards for both public and private websites.

USA: Federal mandates and a state of uncertainty

The USA was the first nation to pass legislation specifying accessibility standards for the Web.[28] While an important step forward, this statement is not intended to even remotely suggest that web-related US disability and accessibility law is consistent, applicable in all contexts, or even fully settled in significant respects. The two most important legislative acts that impinge upon accessibility are the Rehabilitation Act (1973, amended in 1993 and 1998) and the Americans with Disabilities Act (ADA) 1990.[29]

Signed into law by President Bill Clinton, the 1998 amendment to the Rehabilitation Act marked a significant shift in how government formally viewed the interconnectedness between disabled individuals, content accessibility and technology. Both a declaration of a civil right and an historic assignation of specific standards to web-based communications, the revised Act signalled that people with disabilities would be afforded equal accessibility rights to governmental information, programmes and activities. Sections 504 and 508 are the most relevant components of the Rehabilitation Act concerning accessibility for the disabled. Section 504 states that:

> No otherwise qualified individual with a disability in the United States ... shall, solely by reason of her or his disability, be excluded from participation in, be denied the benefits of, or be subjected to discrimination under any program or activity receiving Federal financial assistance.[30]

Note that this 'civil right' for the disabled only applies in situations where federal monies are provided for specific programmes or activities. While on the surface this may seem to have a narrowing effect, the flow of federal money is so ubiquitous that s. 504 conceivably touches every citizen. All 50 states, plus thousands of local governments and agencies receive federal funds to support elementary and secondary education, health and human services, libraries and museums, agriculture, law enforcement, environmental protection, transportation services, workforce training, economic development and countless other significant concerns. Both public and private institutions of higher education routinely receive federal grants to conduct research, institute programming and provide other services. Even considered by itself, s. 504 could be seen as a remarkable piece of disability legislation.

However, s. 508 takes this general principle a step further by barring the federal government from purchasing 'electronic and information technology' goods and services that the disabled are unable to fully access. The government was not only setting an example – it was now changing all the rules for its suppliers. As any business seeking to sell technology at the federal level had to provide 'accessible' products, suppliers were forced to re-tool, re-adapt and re-engineer. Section 508 probably also caused many a quandary for well-intentioned bureaucrats attempting to evaluate and procure complex technologies needed to perform departmental responsibilities. Certain areas (e.g. military, intelligence) were exempted from the legislation and exceptions were made for cases where there was an 'undue burden'. Despite these caveats, the legislation generally encouraged technology suppliers to create more accessible products for federal procurement. The average consumer, whether disabled or not, likely benefited as product accessibility enhancements trickled down into the general marketplace.[31]

Section 508 established an historic precedent by laying out the first legal statement of accessibility standards for the Internet. All federal websites must comply with these specifications, which are based on WCAG 1.0. The respective state governments are also affected by this as they must each make assurances of website compliance to receive federal funds through the Assistive Technology Act 1998.[32]

The other piece of relevant legislation is the Americans with Disabilities Act 1990, which was signed into law by the elder George H.W. Bush. This law brought sweeping changes to physical space in facilities throughout the USA. Many aging structures, for example, had to be retro-fitted to allow for wheelchair entry and general passage. All newly constructed buildings must conform to the ADA's building design standards. The law also applies to both public and private entities offering 'public accommodations'. As a piece of foundational civil rights legislation, individuals with disabilities gained an equal right to participate in services, activities and programmes throughout the nation.

As ss. 504 and 508 only apply to programmes or activities receiving federal funding, groups representing disabled individuals have used the ADA as a vehicle for filing lawsuits against private corporations that fail to make their websites accessible. The suits have generally been grounded on the argument that websites are places of 'public accommodation'. Some of these cases have been settled out of court. In other instances, federal circuit courts have ruled both for and against the notion that the ADA applies to cyberspace. Cynthia Waddell, executive director of the International Center for Disability Resources on the Internet (ICDRI) has reflected on the current state of legal ambiguity by noting that:

> at this time in the US, our courts are split on the purely legal question as to whether or not the ADA applies to private websites. The First and Seventh Circuits have suggested that websites can be considered public accommodations and thus subject to the ADA. On the other hand, the Sixth, Third, and Ninth Circuits have held otherwise. Our case law is behind the times, hence the statement by the US Court of Appeals that this is a significant legal question.[33]

While governmental websites at all levels are increasingly drawn under s. 508, the status of private websites currently remains ambiguous. Given increasing lawsuits and the current state of legal uncertainty, pressure continues to mount on private US businesses and organisations to develop Web presences that are more accessible to disabled individuals.[34]

UK: The pursuit of public and private compliance

The UK has been at the forefront of legislatively mandating accessibility rights for disabled individuals. The relevant web accessibility component of this mandate was established by Part III of the Disability Discrimination Act 1995 (DDA), which came into effect in October 1999. Part III placed several obligations upon 'service providers' requiring that they must not refuse to provide services to disabled persons that they would normally provide to the general public, must not provide a lower standard of service to a disabled person, and must make 'reasonable adjustments' so that it is not impossible or unreasonably difficult for a disabled person to make use of a service.[35] The law has generally been interpreted to mean that all public and private websites in the UK must be made accessible for disabled users. Although websites were not explicitly mentioned in the legislation, specific reference is made to 'information services'.

The supplementary 'Code of Practice' for DDA Part III was published in May 2002 and makes specific reference to an airline reservation website as a service provider.[36] Martin Sloan, an expert on UK web accessibility law, has pointed out that DDA Part III does not mandate that actual products (books, newspapers, etc.) be made 'accessible' in alternative forms. Rather it holds that *access* must be provided to the product or service. It is generally believed and understood that for all practical purposes the law applies to both web services and to web content as it is difficult to sever the linkage. However, until tested in court, it technically remains somewhat ambiguous whether the law mandates that web content itself must be provided in accessible form, or that simply providing an online mechanism for making the content accessible is sufficient.

Neither the authorising legislation nor the Code of Practice makes overt reference to WAI/WCAG guidelines, but they are often cited in governmental accessibility recommendations. Over five years after the inception of DDA Part III, several studies have noted public sites failing to meet basic accessibility criteria.[37] An April 2004 formal investigation conducted by the Disability Rights Commission (DRC) found that 81 per cent of British websites were not accessible to disabled individuals.[38] This study led the DRC to commission the British Standards Institution to develop the 'Publicly Available Specification (PAS) 78'. Released in March 2006, PAS 78 provides formal guidance on web accessibility and is based on the WCAG.[39]

In addition to the USA, UK and European Union supporting web accessibility efforts, Australia, Canada, Japan and the Association of Southeast Asian Nations have also recommended the adoption of international standards or enacted accessibility legislation in varying forms.

Summary

Clearly, web accessibility is an important concern that is increasingly gaining the attention of international opinion makers and individuals from all segments of society. Political and business leaders are becoming increasingly knowledgeable (or at least aware) of web accessibility as legislative initiatives, lawsuits and legal challenges have recently come to the forefront. There are compelling ethical, business and legal reasons why it is important to understand accessibility standards and challenges when contemplating the development of a new website or web database application. While this discussion has explored the 'whys' of web accessibility, the following chapter will address the pragmatic concerns of *how* to go about complying with the major accessibility specifications impacting web development today.

Notes

1 Berners-Lee, T. (2002) Web Accessibility Initiative, available at: *http://www.w3.org/WAI* (accessed 2 June 2006). Berners-Lee is the W3C Director and inventor of the Web.

2 Schneiderman, B. (2000) 'Universal usability', *Communications of the ACM* 43 (August): 85–91.

3 For more information, see WAI (*http://www.w3.org/WAI*) and WCAG (*http://www.w3.org/WAI/GL*) (accessed 2 June 2006). WCAG 2.0 is currently under development, available at: *http://www.w3.org/WAI/intro/wcag20.php* (accessed 2 June 2006).

4   World Wide Web Consortium (1999) 'Web Content Accessibility Guidelines 1.0', available at: *http://www.w3.org/TR/WCAG10/* (accessed 2 June 2006). In practice, most organisations and governments are striving to meet the minimal 'Level A – Priority 1' recommendations. The WCAG 2.0 Guidelines are currently under development; see *http://www.w3.org/WAI/intro/wcag20.php* (accessed 2 June 2006).

5   American Library Association (1995) 'Code of ethics', available at: *http://www.ala.org/ala/oif/statementspols/codeofethics/* (accessed 2 June 2006). See also ALA (2006) *Intellectual Freedom Manual* (7th edn), Chicago: ALA Office for Intellectual Freedom.

6   American Library Association (1993) 'ALA policy manual', 53.1.14, available at: *http://www.ala.org/ ala/ourassociation/governingdocs/ policymanual/intellectual.htm* (accessed 2 June 2006).

7   The Library Association (1983) 'Code of professional conduct', Section 2e, available at: *http://www.ifla.org/faife/ethics/lacode.htm* (accessed 2 June 2006).

8   Chartered Institute of Library and Information Professionals (2005) 'Statement on intellectual freedom, access to information and censorship', available at: *http://www.cilip.org.uk/ professionalguidance/foi/ intellfreedom.htm* (accessed 2 June 2006).

9   See IFLA (2005) 'Professional codes of ethics/conduct', available at: *http://www.ifla.org/faife/ethics/codes.htm* (accessed 2 June 2006).

10 Association of Library and Information Professionals of the Czech Republic (2004) 'Code of ethics of Czech librarians', available at: *http://www.ifla.org/faife/ethics/czlacode.htm* (accessed 2 June 2006).

11 For more information on SIGACCESS, see: *http://www.acm.org/ sigaccess/* (accessed 2 June 2006).

12 Loiacono, E. T. (2004) 'Cyberaccess: web accessibility and corporate America', *Communications of the ACM* 47 (December): 83–7; Wallis, J. (2005) 'The Web, accessibility, and inclusion: networked democracy in the United Kingdom', *Library Review* 54(8): 479–85; Lewis, V. and Klauber, J. (2002) '[Image] [Image] [Image] [Link] [Link] [Link]: Inaccessible web design from the perspective of a blind librarian', *Library Hi Tech* 20(2): 137–40; Chavan, A. and Steins, C. (2003) 'Doing the right thing: how to build socially responsible web infrastructure', *Planning* 69 (July): 10–13; Williams, R., Rattray, R. and Stork, A. (2004) 'Web site accessibility of German and UK tourism information sites', *European Business Review* 16(6): 577–89; Sloan, M. (2001) 'Web accessibility and the DDA', *Journal of Information, Law and Technology* 2, available

at: *http://elj.warwick.ac.uk/jilt/01-2/sloan.html* (accessed 2 June 2006); and Loiacono, E. and McCoy, S. (2004) 'Web site accessibility: an online analysis', *Information Technology and People* 17(1): 87–101.

13 Loiacono (2004), op cit. p. 87. See also Romano, N. C. (2002) 'Customer relationship management for the web-access challenged: inaccessibility of Fortune 250 business web sites' *International Journal of Electronic Commerce* 7(2): 81–117; and Gutierrez, C. F. and Windsor, J. C. (2005) 'An evaluation of Fortune 500 company home pages for disability-access', *International Journal of Electronic Business* 3 (April): 137–53.

14 Brundtland, G. H. (1999) 'Interagency consultation on disability', Office of the Director-General, World Health Organization, available at: *http://www.who.int/director-general/speeches/1999/English/19990615_interagency_consulation.html* (accessed 2 June 2006); and World Health Organization (2006) 'Around the world an estimated 600 million people live with disabilities', available at: *http://www.who.int/disabilities/introduction/en/* (accessed 2 June 2006).

15 European Commission (2001) 'The employment situation of people with disabilities in the European Union', available at: *http://europa.eu.int/comm/employment_social/news/2001/dec/2666complete_en.pdf* (accessed 2 June 2006).

16 US Census Bureau (2003) 'Disability status: 2000', available at: *http://www.census.gov/prod/2003pubs/c2kbr-17.pdf* (accessed 2 June 2006).

17 Information Resources Council, North Texas University (2002) 'UNT web accessibility', available at: *http://www.unt.edu/webinfo/accessibility/accessibilitybackground.htm* (accessed 2 June 2006); Bohman, P. (2003) 'Introduction to web accessibility', *WebAim*, available at: *http://www.webaim.org/intro/* (accessed 2 June 2006).

18 Loiacono (2004), op cit. pp. 83–7.

19 Sloan (2001), op cit.; Wallis (2005), op cit.; Royal National Institute of the Blind (2005) 'Business benefits', available at: *http://www.rnib.org.uk/xpedio/groups/public/documents/PublicWebsite/public_businesscase.hcsp* (accessed 2 June 2006); Howell, J. (2006) 'DRC guidelines look to make accessibility easier to achieve', *New Media Age* (9 March): 15; and Henry, S.L. (ed.) (2005) 'Developing a web accessibility business case for your organization', *World Wide Web Consortium* (MIT, ERCIM, Keio), available at: *http://www.w3.org/WAI/bcase/* (accessed 2 June 2006).

20 National Organization on Disability/Harris Survey (2001) 'Impact of the Internet on community participation', available at: *http:// www.nod.org/index.cfm?fuseaction=page.viewPage&pageID= 1430&FeatureID=115* (accessed 2 June 2006).

21 Loiacono and McCoy (2004), op cit. p. 90.

22 National Telecommunications and Information Administration, and US Department of Commerce (2004) 'A nation online: entering the broadband age', available at: *http://www.ntia.doc.gov/reports/ anol/NationOnlineBroadband04.htm* (accessed 2 June 2006).

23 Wallis (2005), op cit. p. 481; and Sloan. D. (2002) 'Creating accessible e-learning content', in Phipps, L., Sutherland, A. and Seale, J. (eds) *Access All Areas: Disability, Technology and Learning*, York: TechDis.

24 Applying different visual 'skins', themes or appearances can add variety to a computer presentation.

25 European Commission 'EUROPA web accessibility policy', *http:// europa.eu.int/geninfo/ accessibility_policy_en.htm* (accessed 2 June 2006).

26 European Disability Forum (2005) 'The European Commission makes a first step towards disabled persons' access to the information society', available at: *http://www.edf-feph.org/en/news/ archive2005.htm* (accessed 9 June 2006). See also the '2005 EC Communication on eAccessibility' at: *http://europa.eu.int/ information_society/policy/accessibility/com_ea_2005/* (accessed 2 June 2006).

27 Muncaster, P. (2005) 'Government must champion accessibility', *VNU NET* (12 December), available from the *LexisNexis Academic* online database (accessed 2 June 2006).

28 WebAim. 'Section 508 of the Rehabilitation Act', available at: *http://www.webaim.org/coordination/law/us/508/* (accessed 2 June 2006); Williams (2004), op. cit. p. 579; Loiacono and McCoy (2004), op. cit. p. 89. See the European Commission's e-Accessibility initiative at: *http://europa.eu.int/information_society/policy/ accessibility/* (accessed 2 June 2006).

29 The Individuals with Disabilities Education Act (amended in 1997) and the Telecommunications Act 1996 (s. 255) respectively promote 'free appropriate public education' for students with disabilities and require that newly manufactured telecommunications equipment be accessible and usable by the disabled 'if readily achievable'.

30 Rehabilitation Act 1973 (29 U.S.C. 794d). Section 508 was significantly modified in the Workforce Investment Act 1998. See

http://www.access-board.gov/sec508/standards.htm (accessed 2 June 2006).

31 See *http://www.access-board.gov/sec508/guide/act.htm* (accessed 2 June 2006). There is evidence that federal websites continue to struggle with full compliance: Dizard III, W. P. (2002) 'Feds Keep Working on Section 508 Compliance', *Government Computer News* 21 (16 December), available at: http://*www.gcn.com/print/21_34/ 20608-1.html* (accessed 2 June 2006); and Daukantas, P. (2002) 'Survey says sites still lack accessibility', *Government Computer News* 21 (9 September), available at: *http://www.gcn.com/print/ 21_27/19906-1.html* (accessed 2 June 2006).

32 For more information see: *http://www.access-board.gov/sec508/ standards.htm* (accessed 2 June 2006).

33 See Waddell, Cynthia D. (2004) 'Letter to the editor regarding the Southwest Airlines accessible web case', *E-Access Bulletin* (8 November), available at: *http://www.icdri.org/CynthiaW/ eaccess_SWAir.htm* (accessed 2 June 2006).

34 *Miami Daily Business Review* (2006) 'Unusual strategy accuses target of denying blind access to online shopping', *Miami Daily Business Review* 52 (16 February): 10; *Disability Compliance Bulletin* (2005) 'Negotiations may trump lawsuits in dealing with tech accessibility' *Disability Compliance Bulletin* 29 (17 March), available from: *LexisNexis Academic* online database (accessed 2 June 2006); *Disability Compliance Bulletin* (2005) 'Attorneys convince banks to adopt web access guidelines' *Disability Compliance Bulletin* 29 (17 March), available from: *LexisNexis Academic* online database (accessed 2 June 2006). See *WebAim* 'Laws and Standards', available at: *http://www.webaim.org/ coordination/law/* (accessed 2 June 2006), for background data on specific court cases and the current state of international web accessibility law.

35 Sloan, M. (2002) 'Web accessibility and the Disability Discrimination Act', *DMAG*, available at: *http://www.dmag.org.uk/resources/legal/ dda.asp* (accessed 2 June 2006).

36 Disability Rights Commission (2002) 'Code of Practice for Part III of the Disability Discrimination Act (Rights of Access to Goods, Facilities, Services and Premises)' (Revised 27 May), available at: *http://www.drc-gb.org/thelaw/practice.asp* (accessed 2 June 2006).

37 *New Media Age* (2005) 'Government sites fail to meet own web accessibility targets', *New Media Age* (15 December), available from the *LexisNexis Academic* online database (accessed 2 June

2006); and Muncaster, P. (2006) 'Poor accessibility has a price', *VNU NET* (13 February), available from the *LexisNexis Academic* online database (accessed 2 June 2006).

38   Disability Rights Commission (2004) 'Formal investigation report: web accessibility', available at: *http://www.drc-gb.org/ publicationsandreports/report.asp* (accessed 2 June 2006).

39   Disability Rights Commission (2005) 'Making websites accessible', available at: *http://www.drc-gb.org/newsroom/newsdetails.asp?id= 805&section=4* (accessed 2 June 2006); and BSI (2006) 'PAS 78 guide to good practice in commissioning accessible websites', available at: *http://www.bsi-global.com/ICT/PAS78/* (accessed 2 June 2006).

In pursuit of accessibility

*Whenever you are asked if you can do a job, tell 'em, 'Certainly I can!' –
and get busy and find out how to do it.*

(Theodore Roosevelt, 1858–1919)

When the Western Illinois University Libraries were in the midst of a major website redesign project in 2003, we were fortunate to have a visually-impaired librarian participate in the development process. In the midst of a post-graduate MLIS internship at our main library, 'Michael' volunteered to join the library's web task force and to test several demo implementations of the library front page. The task force found that his feedback during the web page development process was invaluable. Michael used a familiar screen reader to navigate the demo pages and immediately found obstacles that the committee worked to address. With the benefit of vision, it is illuminating to spend even a little time observing how someone without sight navigates a web page.

When designing a web page, a great deal of time is typically spent addressing the aesthetics of header and banner sizing, colour selection, image positioning, icon usage, object dimensions, graphical design, buttons, borders and dividers. The futility of creating and struggling to perfect this 'eye candy' was quickly realised after seeing its irrelevance for Michael. During his first test of a leading demo page, he almost immediately struggled to activate an important 'drop down menu' that was actually devised to improve site navigation. The way this 'feature' was deployed brought Michael's ability to access the page's informational content to a screeching halt. Returning to the 'drawing board,' alternative methods were developed to address this accessibility flaw.

This is one example of the need for web developers to engage their user communities when creating a new website or web application. If a website is accessible to disabled users, chances are high that the site will be accessible to almost everyone. One method that can be used is for developers to utilise screen readers during the testing of new pages. This can help catch obvious design problems and is a step towards making pages more accessible. Still, there is nothing quite like running a page past an experienced disabled computer user. Such an individual is familiar with the keyboard shortcuts and navigational cues that accompany good page design. Sequentially breaking a page down into smaller pieces and analysing it alongside a disabled user can also help improve the overall navigational scheme and thematic design.

It is best to incorporate disabled users into the design process at the front-end of a web development project. Testing should be encouraged throughout each stage of development and implementation. It is probably not worth the effort to have testing commence solely at a project's conclusion. By that stage of the process, too much time, effort and cost will have been committed to make meaningful changes on behalf of accessibility. Rather, full accessibility is almost always achieved through planning and intentionality. Probably very few web pages have ever been created that were accessible by accident. While accessibility standards are not difficult to follow if they are built into the design process, they can become a real hardship for any developer who attempts to apply them retroactively. WCAG standards that are carefully applied at each stage of the coding process work to every user's advantage.

After a website or web application has been developed and put into production, it is important for the webmaster to remain vigilant. Over time, a perfectly accessible site can become difficult to navigate if care is not taken. Inevitably, new code and content will be added to meet the information needs of the website's organisation. Thus, accessibility testing should never end on the day a new website is unveiled. The site should be continually evaluated and monitored to ensure that standards are being met. The adoption of a 'continuous validation' policy helps bring the accessibility issue to the forefront. Web pages can be easily submitted to a series of no-cost online validators which assess conformance with WCAG, HTML, CSS, and other standards.[1] It only takes a little attention to detail to make a substantial contribution towards accessibility and interoperability. In addition, contributors are probably more apt to code in compliance with web accessibility standards if they know that their work will be validated.

It is unfortunate that many web developers do not seem to be attuned to the importance of universal accessibility and may even see standards compliance as a roadblock to success. Frankly, it generally does take more effort and planning to build an accessible website than an inaccessible site. Yet, in the final analysis, what is the point of providing content that is presumed worthy of being projected to the entire world if it is not made accessible to everyone? Luckily, resources are available to improve accessibility. In addition to numerous freely available validation services and accessibility resources, many university campuses have accessibility initiatives and communities of disabled users who are seeking to improve the information landscape. Disabled users are often generous with their time and willing to offer constructive and enormously helpful feedback.

Due to economics, legalities, or simply a sense of 'fair play,' many web developers are embracing accessibility standards and implementing them at the start of new projects. Sufficient consultation, planning, attention to detail and ongoing validation can pay great dividends over the life of a web development project. Whatever the motivation, making 'open source' web applications fully 'open to all' is a reasonable goal that developers everywhere should actively embrace.

Applying major web standards

In every day practice, most web developers should seek to have their code conform to at least a minimum of three basic groups of standards developed by the World Wide Web Consortium. Other standards may be promulgated by local authorities (with voluntary or mandatory compliance), but most bodies point to the recommendations developed by the W3C. While conformity with HTML/XHTML and CSS standards is not always mandated by accessibility protocols, it is good practice to adhere to these due to important browser and device interoperability issues that can significantly impact access.

The three main groups of standards related to web development are:

- *code*: HTML 4.01 and XHTML 1;

- *access*: WCAG 1.0;

- *style*: CSS 2.0.

'Code' refers to the group of standards related to the use of general web page markup languages. HTML (HyperText Markup Language) is considered by many to be the *lingua franca* for publishing content to the Web. HTML guidelines were formalised with the HTML 4.01 specification, which was released as a W3C recommendation in 1999.

HTML is very loosely based on the highly technical Standard Generalised Markup Language (SGML), and is the generally recognised standard upon which web pages are created. A related family of guidelines (XHTML 1.0) was created in 2000 to extend HTML and add XML (eXtensible Markup Language) capabilities.[2] In the words of the W3C, 'XHTML is the reformulation of HTML 4 as an application of XML'.

XML, a formal derivation of SGML designed for general usage, is particularly useful for describing data elements and giving documents a logical structure and form. XHTML is almost identical to HTML 4.01, but is considered a much 'stricter' version (e.g. every tag that is opened must be closed). HTML is a more flexible language that can be understood by browsers both old and new, while XHTML (though designed to be the successor to HTML) is not always 'backwards compatible' and has not yet been universally adopted. W3C formally recommends both HTML 4.01 and XHTML 1.0 for web development. Generally, it is perfectly acceptable to use HTML to develop most websites and web-based applications.

The 'style' group of standards relates to the cascading style sheet (CSS) guidelines created by W3C. CSS 1.0 (1996, 1999) includes properties for fonts, colours, margins and other significant aspects of presentation. The CSS 2.0 W3C recommendation (1998) includes all the properties of CSS1 and adds features such as auto-numbering, page breaks and the ability to 'absolutely position' elements on a page. Work continues on the proposed CSS 2.1 and CSS3 specifications.[3] CSS style sheets should always be used to format content for presentation on the Web. The final major group of the standards trio ('access') is concerned with the Web Content Accessibility Guidelines (WCAG 1.0) discussed throughout this chapter.

It is important to follow the guidelines for all three major groups as they interdependently operate to produce high-quality, accessible web pages. Unfortunately, the quality of web pages in general terms is quite uneven. In common practice, probably most web pages fail to conform to any of the three criteria. Webmasters who understand the importance of validating their pages for code and style are in a far better position to take the next step and address accessibility as well. As a general rule of thumb, most pages that conform to overall access standards already conform to code standards. Writing high-quality code and style provide a sturdy platform upon which to address accessibility. Developers who pay careful attention to code and style are more apt to avoid the kinds of accessibility issues that bedevil many pages found on the Web.

Automated HTML/XHTML validation

In many respects, too much time is spent talking about accessibility rather than actually tending to the task. Many helpful tools are available which can make the process of creating accessible pages manageable and even rewarding. Automated validation services remove much of the stress and frustration related to following complex accessibility instructions and rules. Web pages can be easily submitted to sophisticated programs that compare the code, style and access aspects of each page against major web-related standards. There is a sense of satisfaction that comes from testing a web page with an automated validator, making necessary changes, and having the code 'pass' the examination.

The origins of SGML date back to the 1960s when a 'strict' programming structure was needed to mark up complex governmental and aeronautical documents. Computer programs called parsers were developed to automatically analyse the syntax of documents that were structured with SGML. As descendants of the SGML family, HTML and XHTML code can also be strictly parsed by computer programs against the relevant specifications. The W3C's 'free' Markup Validation Service (*http://validator.w3.org/*) provides a convenient and easy means of evaluating HTML or XHTML code (Figure 11.1). Cut and paste a

Figure 11.1 Screenshot of W3C's Markup Validation Service

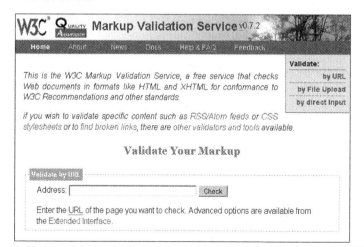

URL into the box, click 'check,' and the tool will deliver a detailed report indicating the line number(s) where a coding error has occurred. Helpful commentary explains the nature of the problem and suggests ways to improve the code. In terms of straightforward analysis and output, this dependable service performs well.

The WDG HTML Validator (*http://www.htmlhelp.com/tools/validator/*), produced by the Web Design Group, is another SGML-based parser that is widely used by professional web developers. Similar to the W3C service, the WDG validator issues text-based reports and excels in providing extensive documentation and resources for improving and correcting code. Both of these validators were designed for a very narrow purpose – to carefully compare web page code against formal HTML/XHTML specifications ('document type definitions') established by the W3C. These are the two recommended HTML/XHTML validators for achieving compliance with the established code specifications.

Many other markup 'validators' are available, but it is important to be aware that some of these commercial products may actually spend as much (or more) time searching for stylistic issues or proprietary browser tags as they do objectively comparing a web page with the official HTML/XHTML specifications. Many of these 'lint-like' parsers (programs named after the original Lint tool used to parse C language source code), are not primarily based on the SGML parser model. The reports they generate may attempt to find additional 'errors' based on the subjective opinion of a designer rather than on an objective evaluation of the code in comparison with a specification. That is not to say these products are not useful, but it does suggest that 'lints' may sometimes focus more attention on performing auxiliary tasks (e.g. testing retrospective browser support, link accuracy and spelling) than on formal validation.

CSS validation

Similar to W3C's Markup Validation Service, the consortium's CSS Validation Service (*http://jigsaw.w3.org/css-validator/*) is another recommended 'free' tool for checking CSS2 (Figure 11.2). Developers can submit a CSS style sheet for testing via a URL, file upload, or by directly inputting CSS syntax into a text box. The generated report lists errors, warnings, and the portions of code that validate successfully. WDG's complementary CSSCheck (*http://www.htmlhelp.com/tools/csscheck/*) provides expanded feedback and explanations along with

Figure 11.2 Screenshot of the W3C CSS Validation Service

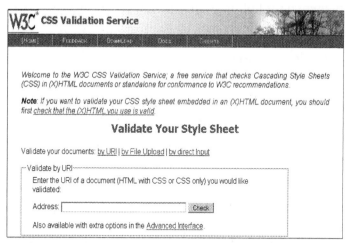

hypertext links back to the appropriate W3C CSS specifications. Unfortunately, CSSCheck primarily validates only the CSS 1.0 standard. CSS2 syntax may sometimes generate 'warning' messages.[4]

Accessibility validation

Most of the major accessibility validators are based on the WCAG 1.0 guidelines or the US s. 508 standards. Some validators provide an option for testing pages against either or both sets of specifications. The 14 web content accessibility guidelines formulated by WCAG 1.0 include a series of practical checkpoints that developers can use to evaluate their web pages. These guidelines can be summarised as follows:[5]

1. Provide equivalent alternatives to auditory and visual content.

2. Don't rely on colour alone.

3. Use markup and style sheets and do so properly.

4. Clarify natural language usage.

5. Create tables that transform gracefully.

149

6. Ensure that pages featuring new technologies transform gracefully.

7. Ensure user control of time-sensitive content changes.

8. Ensure direct accessibility of embedded user interfaces.

9. Design for device-independence.

10. Use interim solutions.

11. Use W3C technologies and guidelines.

12. Provide context and orientation information

13. Provide clear navigation mechanisms.

14. Ensure that documents are clear and simple.

Whereas the guidelines were intended to be broad and inclusive, the checkpoints provide detailed instructions and suggestions for creating more accessible pages. When WCAG 1.0 was created in 1999, the W3C's Web Accessibility Initiative also created an accompanying instrument, the Checklist of Checkpoints for Web Content Accessibility Guidelines 1.0 (Figure 11.3). This appended document extracted the series of checkpoints under each major guideline and prioritised them in a single listing. Most automated accessibility validators use this checklist as their standard for evaluating web pages.

Figure 11.3 Selected 'Priority 1 Checkpoints' from WCAG 1.0

In General (Priority 1)	Yes	No	N/A
1.1 Provide a text equivalent for every non-text element (e.g. via 'alt', 'longdesc', or in element content). *This includes*: images, graphical representations of text (including symbols), image map regions, animations (e.g. animated GIFs), applets and programmatic objects, ascii art, frames, scripts, images used as list bullets, spacers, graphical buttons, sounds (played with or without user interaction), stand-alone audio files, audio tracks of video, and video.			
2.1 Ensure that all information conveyed with colour is also available without colour, for example from context or markup.			
4.1 Clearly identify changes in the natural language of a document's text and any text equivalents (e.g. captions).			
6.1 Organise documents so they may be read without style sheets. For example, when an HTML document is rendered without associated style sheets, it must still be possible to read the document.			
6.2 Ensure that equivalents for dynamic content are updated when the dynamic content changes.			
7.1 Until user agents allow users to control flickering, avoid causing the screen to flicker.			
14.1 Use the clearest and simplest language appropriate for a site's content.			

Source: W3C (1999) 'Checklist of Checkpoints for Web Content Accessibility Guidelines 1.0' (*http://www.w3.org/TR/WCAG10/full-checklist.html*), Copyright © 1999 World Wide Web Consortium, (Massachusetts Institute of Technology, European Research Consortium for Informatics and Mathematics, Keio University). All Rights Reserved. *http://www.w3.org/Consortium/Legal/2002/copyright-documents-20021231.*

A list of free validation resources and services is presented in Table 11.1.

One of the most popular and well-known accessibility validators, Bobby, has recently undergone a major revision. Now called WebXACT (*http://webxact.watchfire.com/*), this no-cost accessibility validation service tests pages submitted via URL. WebXACT produces a detailed report displaying errors in coding and syntax and identifies related issues that may cause a page to be inaccessible. The report is divided into four major segments (general, quality, accessibility and privacy), each providing detailed information on the page's status. Offering both WCAG and s. 508 validation, WebXACT is one of the better ways to evaluate web pages for general accessibility.

One of the characteristics that set the major accessibility validators apart is how they report errors, warnings and potential issues. Cynthia Says (*http://www.cynthiasays.com/*) uses a predominantly text-based, tabular report structure that notes whether a site passes a series of checklist criteria (either WCAG or s. 508). Site Valet (*http:// valet.webthing.com/access/url.html*) displays the source code of each submitted page and divides it into blocks of related code. Errors or possible accessibility problems are noted along with the level of WCAG conformity at issue.

Hosted by the non-profit WebAim accessibility initiative, the WAVE 3.0 Web Accessibility Tool (*http://wave.webaim.org/*), produces a novel graphics report that displays the web page as it actually appears along with the insertion of numerous, specialised icons. Each coloured icon

Table 11.1 Free validation resources and services

HTML/XHTML validation	
W3C Markup Validation Service	http://validator.w3.org
WDG HTML Validator	http://www.htmlhelp.com/tools/validator
CSS validation	
W3C CSS Validation Service	http://jigsaw.w3.org/css-validator
WDG CSSCheck	http://www.htmlhelp.com/tools/csscheck
Accessibility validation	
WebXACT	http://webxact.watchfire.com
WAVE 3.0 Web Accessibility Tool	http://wave.webaim.org/
HERA	http://www.sidar.org/hera
Cynthia Says	http://www.cynthiasays.com
Site Valet	http://valet.webthing.com/access/url.html

symbolises an error (red); an alert to a possible issue (yellow); the identification of an accessibility feature (green); structural, semantic or navigational elements (light blue); or formatting (or other) elements (other colours). 'Hovering' the mouse cursor over each icon reveals descriptive information about the nature of the error, alert or element. In addition to WAVE, developers who appreciate a visual approach when tracking down accessibility issues may also wish to experiment with the multi-lingual HERA (*http://www.sidar.org/hera/*) validator. Validation reports generated by HERA display a series of icons, colours and other visual pointers noting possible issues that should be manually verified. Two views of each report are available including a 'normal page rendering' display and an 'HTML source code' display. A form also provides a way to record comments and then output a report for download or printing in XHTML and PDF formats.

Accessibility validation tools have improved considerably over the last few years and can yield impressive results. Still, despite the development of sophisticated algorithms and evaluation processors, accessibility issues remain complex and often have a somewhat amorphous quality. Virtually all accessibility validators require some post-test, 'manual' checking and evaluation to ensure that the page is in conformity. While validators can effectively check code and tags for possible error, they struggle with more 'subjective' tests such as determining whether colours are being relied upon to convey information or if 'the clearest and simplest language appropriate for a site's content' is being used.[6] Issues related to viewability often require the developer to manually 'eyeball' the page and determine if it has been created in keeping with both the spirit and letter of the established criteria. This reality demonstrates the importance of considering accessibility issues from the very conception of any new web project.

Addressing general accessibility becomes far more difficult if it is treated as an afterthought during the latter stages of a project. Countless web pages fail to meet minimum 'Priority 1' checkpoints for this very reason. The final row in the 'Priority 1 Checkpoint' table of the WCAG Checklist includes a special admonition under the heading 'And if all else fails':

> If, after best efforts, you cannot create an accessible page, provide a link to an alternative page that uses W3C technologies, is accessible, has equivalent information (or functionality), and is updated as often as the inaccessible (original) page.[7]

While this 'bail out' option at least provides a way to provide content in an acceptable form, in practice it does not always work very well.

Such 'supplemental' web pages are often forgotten by website maintainers and have been known to contain extremely outdated information. Of course, if a database driven approach is utilised it may be somewhat easier to overcome this particular shortcoming related to 'static' web design. Still, supplemental workarounds lead to redundancy of effort, unequal information access, and are often more trouble than they are worth.

Taking a proactive approach is the real key to developing web resources that are accessible for most users. Familiarising yourself with the problems that disabled users regularly confront on the Web is a crucial first step. Developers who take the time to understand the challenges that disabled users face can call upon the tools and resources discussed in this chapter to make a real difference. Even modest improvements can pay huge dividends as web pages that are easy for disabled users to access are generally more accessible to everyone. Finally, building accessibility into the fabric of a web project increasingly makes good business sense, benefits all users, and is the right thing to do.

'Win-Win' scenarios are sometimes difficult to come by. The active pursuit of universal usability is one worth seizing.

Notes

1   Free validators such as WebXACT (*http://webxact.watchfire.com/*), formerly called 'Bobby,' test web pages and note major accessibility issues (accessed 2 June 2006). Some accessibility testing (e.g. use of contrasting colours) must still be performed manually. W3C offers several free code validators including the 'W3C Markup Validation Service' (*http://validator.w3.org/*) for HTML/XHTML, and the 'W3C CSS Validation Service' (*http://jigsaw.w3.org/css-validator/*) to evaluate cascading style sheets (accessed 2 June 2006).

2   Or in the words of the W3C, 'XHTML is the reformulation of HTML 4 as an application of XML'. See W3C (2001) 'What is XHTML?', available at: *http://www.w3.org/TR/2001/REC-xhtml-modularization-20010410/introduction.html* (accessed 2 June 2006).

3   For more info, see W3C (2006) 'CSS Specifications', available at: *http://www.w3.org/Style/CSS/#specs* (accessed 2 June 2006). W3C identifies the forthcoming CSS 2.1 specification (based on CSS1 and CSS2, with corrections and updates) as a 'working draft'. At this

writing, CSS2.1 is not yet officially recommended by W3C, but many of its features have already been generally adopted.

4   Quinn, L. (2005) 'CSSCheck release notes', available at: *http://www.htmlhelp.com/tools/csscheck/release_notes.html* (accessed 2 June 2006).

5   W3C (1999) 'Web Content Accessibility Guidelines 1.0', available at: *http://www.w3.org/TR/1999/WAI-WEBCONTENT-19990505/* (accessed 2 June 2006).

6   W3C (1999) 'Checklist of Checkpoints for Web Content Accessibility Guidelines 1.0', 2.1 and 14.1, available at: *http://www.w3.org/TR/WCAG10/full-checklist.html* (accessed 2 June 2006).

7   Ibid. at 11.4.

Web development planning

It is a bad plan that admits of no modification.
(Publilius Syrus, 42 BCE)

Planning is an activity that many people either love or hate. Some are genuinely energised by the opportunity to peer into the future, marshal resources and develop sound strategy. Others feel drained by what they believe to be an excruciating process characterised by mindless meanderings, impenetrable flow charts and paralysing analysis. One person may call for an orderly approach that carefully and necessarily measures risk and opportunity ('plan your work, then work your plan'), while someone else may espouse the importance of grappling with the nuts and bolts of a project on an experiential level thereby understanding and overcoming the 'real' obstacles as they are confronted. Many fall to one side or the other depending on the nature of the project, the people around them, the proximity of a deadline, and the day of the week. Whatever our personality, birth order or general worldview, most of us probably have some sort of opinion on how work should get done.

Balance is important. There are moments when it may be important to step back and view the big picture. At other stages it is critical to be focused, detail oriented and quick to respond. The following sections describe some of the significant areas that may need to be addressed when overhauling a website or beginning the process of designing a new web application. Depending on the scope of a project, some of the sections may be more relevant than others. The discussion generally addresses elements involved in developing a sizable web project affecting multiple units of an organisation. The section headings can be used as a guide for thinking about the process of planning web development projects both large and small.

This chapter provides neither an overarching project management theory nor a grand conceptual framework for organising open source software development. There are numerous books on the market devoted to these important subjects.[1] Rather, the following discussion explores some of the common issues that arise in general web development within organisations and suggests ways that planning can be beneficial.

The chapter concludes with an overview of basic software engineering principles and suggests ways these can be incorporated into the planning of open source web database projects.

Identify resources

It may sound rather obvious, but it is always a good idea to know what resources are available when embarking on a new project. Particularly in larger academic settings, there is often an institutional commitment towards acquiring and teaching people how to better utilise new and emerging technologies. Those who tend to enjoy the comfort of their own cocoons, however, may easily miss some of the current trends and methods that are freely available across the hall or down the street. Seeking out others who use similar tools and software can be worth the effort as many developers are willing to share their insights and tips. Continuing education classes or local workshops can also help enhance skill sets. Technical resources and support are often extended by regional consortia, professional organisations and governmental agencies. In many organisations, there are special interest groups that provide a forum for sharing resources and support. Making contact with technology users in different departments or units of a large organisation can help everyone stay abreast of broader institutional resources and opportunities that may come available from time to time. Although the specifics may vary, people often face the same kinds of information management problems no matter what their job description. Networking with people beyond an immediate area can pay off as sharing ideas, approaches, and even code can help everyone avoid constantly 'reinventing the wheel'.

Of course, some of the more traditional resource challenges and questions always need to be addressed and considered. Some of these include: time and staffing (e.g. Do staff members have enough time to begin a major web re-design project? Is it possible to obtain short-term staffing to handle some chores?), budgeting (e.g. Are the financial components in place for obtaining needed hardware? Are there funds to hire a professional graphics designer to create a new series of logos and icons?), hardware and software (e.g. The open source software is free, but do we have the computing power necessary to run it? How long does it take to learn 'xyz'?), ISPs/hosts (e.g. Is our computing infrastructure reliable? Do we need to consider a change? Can we handle the maintenance and administration of our own server or is it easier and more cost-efficient to find a quality ISP?), ongoing maintenance (e.g. Who will be responsible for taking care of the database application once it is built? What happens if we lose our 'ace' database manager? Who will be responsible for uploading new content?).

Having a handle on the resources at your disposal can be a great aid when something 'goes wrong' or if an unforeseen roadblock happens to block the project's path. Perhaps more importantly, knowing and having confidence in local resources provides a sense of stability, support, and a sustainable foundation upon which to build. Database driven web development is not rocket science, but neither is it child's play. Having adequate resources and a dependable infrastructure is of critical importance to the development process. Though sometimes taken for granted, virtually all web development depends upon the existence of a reliable underlying framework.

Build a web team

Some web development projects can be effectively produced, managed and implemented by a single individual. In larger organisations, a team-based approach is often required to accomplish more complex web-based initiatives. Web developers can use teams, task forces and committees to their advantage by drawing from their input, creativity and insight. It is often most practical for the primary web developer to lead or chair group meetings, as this person will be most familiar with the overall scope of the project, fluent with the technology, and best positioned to answer questions and suggest alternatives. Though one person may facilitate the process, it is absolutely critical that other voices be included at *every* stage.

For a major redesign of a sizable website, form a team that is representative of the larger organisation. Try to gain representation from all quarters with the dual intention of keeping the team as small as possible. For a variety of reasons, not the least of which is finding mutually agreeable times to hold meetings, a smaller group (probably less than ten), can remain nimble enough and invested enough to make real contributions. 'Ownership' is a critical concept when developing a website or web application that will be used by many people in an organisation. People who are permitted (and encouraged) to 'buy in' and take part in the process can play an important role in ensuring its success.

The lead developer should remember to keep a very open mind, particularly during the early stages of a redesign process. In general, adopting the dual roles of 'facilitator' and 'educator' is a good way to get started. Some team members may know what they like when they see it but have difficulty communicating exactly what this is. Other team members may enter the process with definite opinions on the proposed site's 'look and feel' or its functionality. Instead of taking sides, be intentional about encouraging everyone to take a step back and explore all available options and possibilities. One way to begin is by having the team explore the websites of comparable organisations. Appoint a capable team secretary to take notes during all meetings, jotting down ideas, likes, dislikes, insights, comparisons and other verbal feedback.

As 'educator' the web team leader has the responsibility to inform the group about web accessibility issues, web page standards (both local and international), and how the development process will unfold. Some may need an overview of the database driven model so that they understand what the group is trying to achieve and the steps that must be taken to get there. Sharing background information and educating team members about important issues achieves at least two things. First, it reinforces 'ownership' and helps team members feel like they understand and are part of the process. Second, keeping the team 'in the loop' facilitates constructive information sharing and positive communication throughout the organisation. Team members can be the web developer's best allies in educating the entire institution about what is happening, what needs to be done and why the process can sometimes take longer than expected to complete.

During the early stages of the process, establish what it is the team will be doing, the general parameters of its activities, and a rough timetable for project completion. Hold regular meetings and be willing to divide responsibilities and appoint subcommittees as necessary. This can save the team valuable time and create a climate that is more conducive for sharing ideas and making contributions.

Know your content

Before the web team spends much time deliberating and peering into the future, it should take the opportunity to explore and understand the organisation's present information management status. The focus of the inquiry should be on how organisational content is gathered, accessed, organised, modified, preserved and distributed.

The overall analysis can be conducted in various ways, but it should seek to address at least the following questions:

- Who are our content sources, authors and providers?

- How do we obtain content?

- Does it come pre-digitised and properly formatted?

- How do we provide internal and external access?

- What information and 'products' (e.g. full-text articles) do we provide?

- How is the content inventoried and managed?

- How do we modify, enhance or constructively manipulate content?

- Is all content 'backed up' and securely stored?

- Is the content electronically 'browsable' and searchable?

- Is there important content that has not yet been digitised, and should be?

- What content distribution services do we currently offer?

At this stage of the process, the questions are intentionally framed to document factual information about how organisational content is managed. There will soon be opportunities for sharing new ideas, visions, opinions, hunches and perceptions. The focus of this section is simply establishing a shared understanding of the information environment. With everyone working from the same general frame of reference, we now turn to an exercise that is simultaneously interpretive, creative and certainly free-form.

Brainstorming and envisioning

Collective 'brainstorming' can be a powerful way of breaking old moulds, making new connections and exploring possibilities that have never been realised or even imagined. Brainstorming sessions can be a productive means of generating new ideas and exploring them in depth as groups of people can bring a diversity of experience and creativity to the process. Sessions can be led in a variety of ways, but no matter the approach, it is important that people have fun, be relaxed and feel comfortable sharing their ideas.

The leader of the session must reliably and consistently enforce the rule that no expressed idea may be ridiculed, judged, criticised or evaluated. An element of trust must be established as it can feel 'risky' to voice an idea that others could pounce upon as stupid, crazy or nonsense. The entire point of a brainstorming session is for each person to feel comfortable expressing whatever notion might occur to them. Participants should be encouraged to build upon any spoken idea, offering both pragmatic responses and 'wild' notions that may be funny, creative or 'off the wall'. An idea that may seem dumb or bizarre to one person at first hearing may inadvertently trigger a novel thought from someone else that may ultimately lead to a compelling new concept. In a spirit of cooperation and collaboration, encourage everyone to enthusiastically participate and refrain from criticism of any kind. A brainstorming session is specifically designed to generate innovative thinking which may lead to courses of action that could challenge the status quo. There can always be post-session opportunities for thoughtful analysis, reflection and selection of sound courses of action. A brainstorming session, however, is not one of these times.

The session leader may want to have a list of words or phrases that can be used to 'prime the pump' and keep the process lively. Allow the discussion to move wherever it will. Before idea streams begin to run dry, renew the process by offering a new word or phrase to keep energy up and interest high. A large whiteboard or sheet of paper and markers can be useful for noting ideas and connections that may emerge.

A related 'idea generation' method that can be employed is holding an 'envisioning session' where participants can respond to a series of questions. The questions can be distributed beforehand or asked spontaneously. This kind of session can be used to encourage people to express their views, hopes, ideas and 'wish lists' for the future. Less 'free-form' than a brainstorming session, a colloquium can provide an opportunity for individuals who may feel more comfortable sharing in a forum allowing for thoughtful exchanges of reasoned views. Some of the questions that could be posed include:

- How can we better realise our organisation's mission through our web presence and online activities?

- What goals do we have for our online presence and for our physical facilities?

- How do these intersect?

- How is our website used?

- What web-based content is used most (and least)? Why?

- Who uses this content? Why?

- Who doesn't use this content enough? Why?

- How can we reach out to them?

- What are our two most important web resources or services that are underutilised?

- What are the two most important resources or services not currently on our website that could be?

- What two changes would really make a difference for us internally?

- What two things do we like best and (dislike most) about our current site?

- Are there ways to expand (or provide focus to) our existing content?

- What opportunities do we see on the horizon?

Finding answers to questions such as these can be helpful in developing a vision for an organisation's web presence and for prioritising other web development activities. An 'envisioning session' could be convened specifically for a web team or expanded to embrace the ideas of the larger community.

Discover 'what's out there'

Fortunately, the weight of the world need not solely rest on a web team's shoulders as it strives to innovate a new vision for its strand of the World Wide Web. Thousands of international organisations both large and small have already made their very best attempt to harness the power of the Internet and to create an online presence that will dazzle, educate, inform and influence people around the globe. The absolute best they could muster is on display 24 hours a day 'at a URL near you'. With all of this content, graphic design and functionality freely available for the viewing, it makes sense to explore the landscape and see if there are lessons to be learned and general approaches that could be adopted.

But where to begin? It is easy to get bogged down in Google searches and Yahoo! subject directories without finding anything particularly relevant to explore. One useful approach is to target the websites of 'peer institutions' – organisations with a similar size and mission as your own. This method establishes a kind of baseline and can help provide a sense of what is possible based on comparable resources and objectives.

There is more than one way to proceed. A web team can work from a pre-selected list of peer websites, or a list of URLs can be generated by each member for consideration. For example, participants could be asked to contribute five or more URLs of peer institutions with which they are familiar based on their knowledge and interests. A combination of selection schemes can be used to render a balanced, reasonably sized pool of sites for further exploration. Remember to include your organisation's current site on the list.

There are also numerous ways to go about evaluating the sites. One method is to have each person independently visit the sites on the list, making note of features, design, navigation and general 'look and feel' characteristics. The group can later reconvene, view the site together, and begin sharing notes and comments. Another rather enjoyable technique for external site exploration is to organise an informal 'focus group' session for the team. With the team secretary taking notes on a whiteboard, randomly begin screening the selected websites with a projector. Initially, give the participants only a couple of moments to see each site. Immediately have them vote on whether they 'like' or 'dislike' the site based only on their first general impression. When voting concludes, go back and review each site more carefully, giving participants a chance to make comments, explain their initial reaction, and to reconsider their vote after further discussion and analysis. If possible, it is preferable to conduct this exercise in a computer lab where team members can individually connect to each site, click the links, and explore the layout. Frequently, general themes and even a vague sense of consensus can emerge from such sessions as team members become more familiar with the process and begin to identify features they find convenient and useful or confusing and cluttered.

It can be helpful to guide the team through asking a series of questions as they evaluate the various sites, including:

■ What styles and colours are popular?

- What features stand out and are being frequently used?

- Where are search boxes and 'help icons' located?

- What kinds of navigational tools or menus are employed?

- How are the sites structured in terms of categories, subject headings and providing access to content?

- Is information easy to find?

- Is contact information and general information readily available (e.g. hours, location, addresses, personnel directories)?

- What kinds of technologies are used? (e.g. JavaScript, AJAX, etc.)

- Do you immediately 'like it' (or not)? Why?

- What is your overall impression?

After working through the list of sites, have the group explore some of the 'major' sites that team members consider to be generally popular or well-known. These could be news, business, government, art, music, search engine or general interest websites. At the conclusion of the session, have the participants pick their favourite sites and discuss the characteristics that make them compelling, easy to use, or somehow enjoyable to visit.

Find out 'what people think'

Once the web team has been through this process, consider having the team lead similar focus group sessions for broader constituencies. These constituencies could be internal or external. In a university library setting, any single group, combination or mixture of professional librarians, library staff, library student workers, teaching faculty, administrators, other university personnel, and general undergraduate or graduate students are among the stakeholders who could be consulted. These sessions can work from either the original list of sites or from a smaller selection based on the knowledge gained from the web team's original session. Try to ensure that there is diversity in style, navigation and colour among the pages shown so that feedback is not skewed. Again, be sure to include your organisation's current site in the mix. Having large sheets of paper available to record participant feedback can be useful.

Evaluate

After the session(s), a subcommittee can consolidate the information recorded on the sheets and share the results with the entire team. This review process can help the web team glean valuable information as it spots trends, preferences and themes. It is best to review the focus group data while it is still 'fresh' in everyone's mind. Discuss how each group reacted to the 'first impression' of a website as it was quickly flashed on the screen. Tally the votes from each group to see which sites were ranked the highest (from both the beginning and end of each session). Based on participant comments, try to determine why certain sites rose to the top. In particular, gauge how content, layout, 'look and feel' and ease of navigation played a role. After careful consideration of all of the focus group data, the web team can begin drawing overall conclusions about what was learned, what can be used, and what else needs to be explored.

Study your current site

Just because it may be time to redesign an organisation's website (or a web database application's interface), does not necessarily mean that nothing can be learned from it. In many cases a great deal of thought and planning may have preceded its original creation. It is possible that some aspects of the site's structure, categories or navigational elements still serve users well. Web teams should not be afraid to retain elements that work well simply because a site overhaul is long overdue. Of course, the difficult question that immediately rises is 'how do you know if something is working well?' Fortunately, two valuable techniques are readily available that can be described in succinct phrases: 'listen to what they say' and 'see what they actually do'.

Website usage statistics are an invaluable aid in documenting and understanding how users discover and access content. Most quality web log analysis programs can pinpoint search phrases, website entry and exit points, and the paths users follow to access specific content. This kind of information can be extraordinarily useful in making frequently used items that are 'buried' (two or more clicks down) easier to access. Usage data may also assist in enhancing navigation, renaming or redefining subject categories, and reclaiming valuable front page real estate by repositioning or eliminating rarely used links.

While usage stats probably paint the clearest picture of what is actually happening, it can also be useful to ask users for their comments, suggestions and perceptions. Developing an online survey instrument can assist the team in collecting user feedback of a more qualitative variety. Using checkboxes, radio buttons, drop-down menus, and text boxes, a web survey can elicit answers to a variety of questions including:

- How often do you use the website? (choice of: this is my first visit, daily, weekly, several times a year, rarely)

- Do you primarily use the site while on campus or off campus?

- Based on this screenshot of the front page [displayed within the survey], please respond to these questions:

  - What do you LIKE about this page?

  - What do you DISLIKE about this page?

  - Feel free to comment on this or any other page of the website...

- When visiting the library website, do you use? (select all that apply):

  - Online catalogue, journal/magazine databases, electronic reserves, interlibrary loan forms, etc.

  For each selection, a secondary question can ask 'how easy is it to find?' (choice of: easy, somewhat easy, somewhat difficult, difficult, no opinion).

- What information or services have you had difficulty finding on the library website?

- What would you like to see added to the library website?

- Please provide additional comments or suggestions...

By focusing the survey on the present site, the team may be able to identify both problems and opportunities based on commonly voiced concerns. Ideally, the data gathered via the survey will be buttressed by qualitative information already gleaned from the prior (or concurrent) focus group sessions. Used in conjunction, an analysis of the web statistics and opinion data can help the team better understand user satisfaction, preferences, content access trends, and navigational strengths and weaknesses. Interestingly, the results may also be useful in challenging the web team's initial perceptions concerning the major elements that need to be addressed.

Make decisions and continuously circle back

After all the work of facilitating focus group sessions, developing surveys and reviewing and compiling feedback, it is time for the web team's 'heavy lifting' to finally begin. With data, analysis and brainstorms in hand, the group must now tend to the business of synthesising, prioritising and giving form to a website. Not surprisingly, this is a key stage for the lead web developer, who will soon attempt to construct a series of demonstration pages based on the recommendations of the team. The developer needs to be attentive to the process and help the team work through the advantages and disadvantages of possible paths. Some website designs could take more time to develop and implement than others, potentially straining the limited resources identified at the beginning of the process. A particular approach that could improve general navigation for some users may negatively impact accessibility for others. An innovative 'cutting edge' technique one person proposes could be detrimental to the 'continuity' valued by another. It is a time to be simultaneously ambitious, sagacious, forward-leaning and commonsensical. Collaboration, flexibility and some 'give and take' are required of all participants.

As this segment of the process unfolds, the group will benefit from continuously 'circling back' through the previous stages of insight and discovery. The mission and the priorities highlighted early on need to be continually expressed and reinforced as do the lessons learned from the focus groups, the web usage statistics and the online survey. Moving through this cyclical process (Figure 12.1) can help the team grapple with what is critical and what may be superfluous.

'What *must* we have?' could be the mantra of the team as it comes to terms with concept, content, objective, aesthetics, category, navigation and design. Almost undoubtedly, the technical side of database driven web development is far simpler than the artful political process of achieving design consensus through dialogue, diplomacy, tact, persuasion and perseverance. These are precisely the skills needed to help organisations create effective websites reflecting the diversity of resources and services provided by complex organisations made up of human beings with varied ideas, values and specialised skills. As a matter of course, decisions must be made to move forward.

Fortunately, the decision-making process is made far simpler by having invested the time to build the web team. Once the concrete decision-

Figure 12.1 Continuously 'circling back'

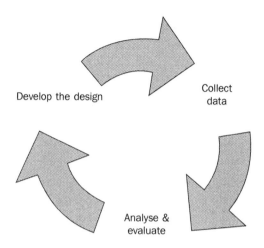

Develop the design

Collect data

Analyse & evaluate

making stage is finally reached, the web team members will have already come together to conduct focus group sessions, participate in discussion forums, design online surveys, review statistics and absorb many lessons. By this time, team members will have had every opportunity to 'buy in' to the project fully. If the lead web developer can surrender a measure of control over the process, the end-product has a better chance of benefiting from the collective contributions of the team. By facilitating and listening instead of imposing and proscribing, the developer can support the creative process and help it naturally unfold.

Draft demos

Upon general agreement on the basic characteristics of the layout (which can be sketched out with the team), the web developer can begin creating a 'mock up' of the website's front page. The layout of the front page is critical because secondary and tertiary-level web pages are often dependent upon the navigational structure and general design initially established. As designing graphics and crafting the code for a new page can be time-intensive, it can be advantageous to use a desktop publishing program to create the initial demos. Additions, deletions and modifications can be easily made and redistributed as feedback is received. Once the layout has taken shape and gained critical acceptance, actual HTML, CSS and PHP coding can begin. Once the 'live' demos are in place, team members can benefit from experiencing the actual functionality of the site. The demo pages should be continually tested and retested against online validators as the underlying code will provide the foundation for all that will follow.

Circle back, again

The continual encouragement of feedback and constructive criticism can help team members feel free to express concerns. It is far better to forthrightly address any possible issues in the early stages of the development process than to retrospectively attempt to 'fix' them at the end. Once a reasonably stable demo is approved, it is again time to 'circle back' and ask broader constituencies again for comments, suggestions and feedback on access, usability and appeal. This can be achieved by hosting open forums, focus group sessions or by inviting participants to comment on 'live' demos individually. Whatever methods are selected, the web team can use the responses to make further recommendations, modifications and improvements.

Once the 'final' versions of primary, secondary and tertiary-level pages are complete, the web developer can finally begin the work of transferring the 'old' site into the new format. In a certain sense, a website is an 'open' publication that is never truly complete. Indeed, if using a 'database driven' model, it is theoretically possible to have multiple web interfaces facilitating the access of the exact same content. In practical terms, most organisations are probably seeking a design that can be essentially 'fixed' for an extended phase. A simple, accessible layout that users can depend upon can even serve as a 'value added' feature that entices considerable return traffic.[2] Perhaps, more importantly, the web team, larger organisation, and certainly the lead web developer will at some point need to seize a sense of finality and closure. A well-advertised 'unveiling' can generate excitement for the new site, validate the contributions of all who participated in the effort, and celebrate the conclusion of a collaborative process that produced tangible results for the world to see.

Software and web engineering

This chapter has been primarily devoted to general website planning and web interface development. Traditional software engineering methodologies have not been frequently adopted by many open source web developers, partly due to the more informal arrangements that have helped make these communities thrive and flourish.[3] For many functional web-based applications (such as those reviewed in the later case studies), the development planning process need not be terribly sophisticated, but it does need to be intentionally thought out. Some familiarity with the basic elements of formal software engineering can be useful when attempting to put together a substantial database driven web application.

Paul Vixie, an influential software programmer and open source developer, has enumerated the basic elements of the formal software engineering process:

1. *Marketing requirements*: creation of a document describing target users and why they need the software (i.e. 'What should we build, and who will use it?').

2. *System-level design*: a 'high-level' description of the software outlining the requisite modules or programs and how they will interact.

3. *Detailed design*: each module named in element 2 is thoroughly described, interfaces are determined, charts are created to show the work sequences and dependencies, a time estimate for construction of each module is set, and the kinds of tests that will be needed to verify that the modules function correctly must be specified.

4. *Implementation*: each module must be coded or programmed, tested (see element 3), and successfully used by another module(s).

5. *Integration*: system-level integration can occur when all modules are essentially complete. The modules must be compiled, linked and packaged as a whole. System-level testing must be performed to ensure that all parts work in tandem.

6. *Field-testing*: begun internally, the developers and employees of the organisation run the software on their own computers. Developers must be available for support and 'triage', particularly when external testing begins. Determination must be made if defects can be 'fixed' in the documentation, if they need to be addressed before the version is officially released, if improvements can wait until a subsequent release (or if it is impractical to ever fix it).

7. *Support*: defects discovered during field-testing should be entered into a tracking system and assigned to a software engineer who will propose changes to system documentation or how a module is defined or implemented. Changes must be subjected to new testing requirements, which must be integrated with the original system-level tests. Customer service and engineering must work together to properly define and characterise bugs and to create solutions.

Vixie notes that no element should be started before the prior ones are substantially complete, and that a change in one element demands that all of the other elements undergo a review process and be reworked (if necessary) due to the modification. All elements should be submitted for general review by multiple parties (e.g. peers, management) and each should be assigned a version number so that the history of the process may be audited.[4]

It may come as no surprise that most open source software projects, developed by a collection of unpaid volunteers contributing for the fun and love of their work, lack the formal strictures and structures of a quintessential software engineering paradigm. Many web developers, partly due to the advantages of working in a web-based context that is more markedly defined, have not found it necessary to adopt the kinds of development processes used by commercial software firms. Still, all web developers can learn from the elements described in the preceding model. The general web developer's planning process need not be terribly sophisticated, but it does need to be intentional.

As a starting point, the developer must unambiguously know what the web application is for and what it will be expected to do. This usually necessitates meeting with the people who will be using the finished product. The developer will need to ask many questions, helping the users grapple with what they need, what they think they need and the advantages and disadvantages of pursuing various options. Sometimes clients may think they need the functionality of a complex database system when what they really need is to be shown how to use a spreadsheet. The web developer should not begin writing the first line of code before having a mutually agreed understanding of what is to be built, what it will do, and what it will not do. Such an agreement helps minimise confusion and the possibility of a misunderstanding when the product is delivered. It usually takes more than one meeting to ensure that everyone is 'speaking the same language' and truly understands both the limitations and benefits of any proposed application.

Vixie states that the software engineering elements dealing with design (elements 2 and 3) are frequently ignored by open source developers. He writes that:

> There usually just is no system-level design for an unfunded open source effort. Either the system is implicit, springing forth whole and complete straight from Zeus's forehead, or it evolves over time (like the software itself). Usually by Version 2 or 3 of an open-source system, there actually *is* a system design even if it doesn't get written down anywhere.[5]

Paying due attention to the design phase can save an abundance of time and effort for web developers. The process of writing down or mapping the scope of the project, even in an abbreviated way, makes it possible to conceive the various modules that will be needed and how the entire project 'hangs together'. Simply put, if the developer knows where the project is headed, it is a lot easier to get there. PHP easily lends itself to being programmed in modular form. For instance, one module of code may provide a database editing function while another block may allow the user to add more entries. Each module can be called only when needed, thus saving computer processing overheads and improving general performance.

Planning the necessary steps and documenting code is not always the most exciting part of a project, but it is a valuable guide as the coding begins to take shape. Good documentation is also an indispensable resource when an application must be updated or revised many weeks, months or years later. As time passes and memory fades, even the developer who originally wrote an application may have difficulty interpreting what the various blocks of code were intended to perform. Designing and documenting a web project pays big dividends in the long term.

The implementation and integration phases of web development (elements 4 and 5) are among the most enjoyable aspects of a project. The process of coding and debugging a script is interesting, challenging and rewarding work. There are often many ways to go about writing a stanza of code that performs correctly. One method may not be necessarily superior to another, but as the developer's coding skills increase, more efficient techniques often emerge. Finding these advanced 'shortcuts' is part of a larger (and longer) learning process that keeps the process fresh, engaging and worth the effort.

Integrating the various modules to create a functioning web-based system is, of course, immensely satisfying as all the pieces come together to serve a higher purpose.

Any newly developed database driven web application must be thoroughly tested to ensure that all functions and features are performing properly. Of course, most developers who have taken the time to build an application will take the time to make sure it works. Yet, almost without fail, one bug or another will manage to sneak through the developer's own tests. Field-testing is essential to effective development and a necessary precursor to releasing a web application into actual production. When real users put recently developed software 'through the paces', they tend to stumble upon issues and bugs that the developer has missed. Sometimes this is because the developer (who after all knows how the application *should* be used) cannot have foreseen nor can presently fathom why someone would even attempt to use the application in such a novel or painfully misguided fashion. Discovering these 'blind spots' provides new opportunities to improve and enhance the code, leading to more effective and successful programs that are dependable and ready to be used by the novice or the professional.

Finally, any web developer worth their own salt must stand behind the application and provide ongoing support. Knowing that this continuing responsibility lies at the end of process can give the developer incentive to exercise care and thoroughness with each passing stage. Acquiring a certain patience and humility with the process can also be helpful, particularly when the time comes to assist the almost inevitable disgruntled or unhappy user. Almost no web application is ever totally completed. There is always room for improvement and the startling pace of technological innovation practically ensures that any application built today will probably be surpassed by a superior undertaking in the future. However, the current and pressing information needs of people and organisations are real and must be addressed in the moment. Open source web development tools such as PHP and MySQL can have an impact in the near term and provide opportunities for future migration and enhancement possibilities. Making the time to plan the development process gives each web application a better chance to be successful and make a real difference.

Summary

Many of the planning elements described in this chapter require time and patience to employ. The planning phase is sometimes difficult to undertake, especially when time seems limited, the needs are pressing, and the database development tools are within easy reach. Still, carefully planning each phase of the project and knowing what each piece of code will be designed to achieve makes for good design and creates software that will effectively respond to the organisation's information needs.

Being the dynamic information management systems that they are, it is difficult to plan advanced web interfaces without adopting a flexible approach that can respond quickly to change. The preceding discussion also expresses a sense of trust in the process and in the professionalism of the people who participate within it. A website can be viewed as an outgrowth of the mission, values and expertise of the larger organisation. As every organisation and situation is unique, it may not always be realistic to address each of the elements presented here due to time constraints, lack of resources, staffing models and other factors. Still, many of these ideas can be adapted to address and overcome the challenges, circumstances and particulars of diverse environments. It is hoped that this discussion will be used as a starting point for thinking through how to effectively engage and manage the process of planning successful web-related endeavours.

Notes

1   The IEEE Standard for Software Project Management Plans (IEEE Std 1058-1998) provides a model that has been adopted in many contexts (e.g. see State of Texas: Department of Information Resources (2003) 'Project development plan', available at: *http://www.dir.state.tx.us/eod/qa/planning/projplan.htm* (accessed 2 June 2006)). A recent 'classic' in the software development field is Brooks, F. P. (1995) *The Mythical Man-Month: Essays on Software Engineering*, Reading, MA: Addison-Wesley. More recent studies include Thayer, R. H. (ed.) (2000) *Software Engineering Project Management* (2nd edn), Los Alamitos, CA: IEEE; Glass, R. L. (2002) *Facts and Fallacies of Software Engineering*, Boston: Addison-Wesley; and Ghezzi, C., Jazayeri, M., and Mandrioli, D. (2003) *Fundamentals of Software Engineering* (2nd edn), Upper Saddle River, NJ: Prentice Hall. One of the more popular web planning models is the feature driven development (FDD) methodology, see: Bauer, M. (2005) 'Successful web development methodologies', available at: *http://www.sitepoint.com/article/successful-development* (accessed 2 June 2006).

2   The Google website (*http://www.google.com*), one of the world's most popular, is known for its simple and understated interface.

3   Vixie, P. (1999) 'Software engineering', in DiBona, C., Ockman S. and Stone, M. (eds) *Open Sources: Voices of the Open Source Revolution*, Sebastopol, CA: O'Reilly, p. 96. There are new efforts underway to apply scientific engineering principles to web development activities, much like in traditional software development. See Mendes, E. and Mosley, N. (eds) (2006) *Web Engineering*, Berlin: Springer-Verlag.

4   Vixie (1999), op. cit. p. 91.

5   Vixie (1999), op. cit. p. 97.

The dynamic duo

Invisible harmony is better than visible.
(Heraclitus, 535–475 BCE, *Fragmente der Vorsokratike*)

PHP and MySQL complement one another so beautifully that there is little wonder the two resources have become such a popular combination for database driven web developers. As PHP was specifically created to be a web scripting language, it integrates seamlessly with HTML and dexterously interacts with MySQL and other web-based relational database systems. For its part, MySQL is a relational web database solution providing a rare combination of power, speed, simplicity and agility. The two relate to one another exceptionally well, offering webmasters (without skills in either the language or the database) an opportunity to move quickly towards incorporating a database driven approach with a variety of web projects. The earlier 'building block' chapters on PHP and MySQL provided an introduction showing how each tool can be used independently. This chapter shows how they work together to create dynamic, database driven web possibilities.

Making the connection

As demonstrated previously, PHP can be embedded within HTML-coded web pages to perform a variety of tasks. Some of these functions are routinely implemented in relatively 'static' webpage environments. However, the act of initiating a PHP connection with a MySQL database changes everything. This harbinger of the 'database driven' web model is as simple as it is powerful. Only a few lines of code create immense opportunities to dynamically, and interactively, publish practically any form of content to the Web. The possibilities for information gathering, management, manipulation, distribution and storage increase exponentially as PHP and MySQL are purposefully aligned in common cause.

The essential elements required to make a PHP connection to a MySQL database from a web page are:

- a MySQL server address and port number (e.g. mysql.xyz.com:12345);

- a username/password combination that has been created for an existing MySQL database (e.g. Gaylord/CUcamel88 'books').

The 'webpage.php' file (Figure 13.1) contains a snippet of PHP code embedded within the parameters of a web page coded with HTML. PHP's mysql_connect() function (line 4) performs most of the work as it locates a MySQL server and logs in with a username/password combination. The mysql_select_db() function signals the MySQL server that the database to be selected is 'books.' If the connection to 'books' fails, the die() function outputs an error message and terminates the script. Assuming PHP and MySQL are functioning properly, a failure to connect is almost always due to at least one of three very common factors: (1) spelling errors, (2) PHP syntax mistakes (such as missing quote marks or semicolons), or (3) failure to have granted the user sufficient privileges to access the database (see Chapter 9).

Note that while it is possible to embed the username/password and other login data directly into the PHP script (as in Figure 13.1), it is better practice to make use of variables and call the actual values from a secure file located elsewhere on the server.[1] This promotes security as other operating system users will be unable to view the password data; in addition, this method also makes it easier to keep track of the various user accounts that may need to be called sequentially within the PHP script or application. The very small PHP file in Figure 13.2 assigns the login information to specific variables. The file ('books1.php') can then

Figure 13.1 A MySQL database connection from a PHP file called 'webpage.php'

```
1  <html><head><title>A Webpage</title></head><body>
2  <?php
3
4  mysql_connect ("mysql.xyz.com:12345", "Gaylord", "CUcamel88");
5  mysql_select_db (books) or die ("Unable to select!");
6
7  ?>
8  </body></html>
```

Figure 13.2 A 'connection file' for MySQL database access (books1.php)

```
1 <?
2 //USER: Gaylord GRANTED: SELECT
3 $mysql_path = 'mysql.xyz.com:12345';
4 $mysql_user = 'Gaylord';
5 $mysql_pswd = 'CUcamel88';
6 $mysql_db = 'books';
7 ?>
```

be placed in a directory specifically created to hold various 'connection files' of this type. This 'private' directory should normally be created outside the regular 'http' directory path accessible to the general public.

With books1.php in place, the following block of code can be substituted for lines 4 and 5 in Figure 13.1. Note the PHP include function, which essentially pulls the entire books1.php connection file directly into the script when it is run.

```
include '/home/account/MySQLconnections/books1.php' ;
mysql_connect ("$mysql_path", "$mysql_user",
"$mysql_pswd");
mysql_select_db ($mysql_db) or die ("Unable to
select!");
```

The include function pulls the contents of books1.php directly into the script, supplying the required MySQL login information. Oddly, parentheses are not used with PHP's include function.

The include function is a marvellous invention that saves space and promotes clarity when writing code. As will be shown later, it is a particularly helpful device for calling modules to perform specific tasks in complex PHP applications. Even in the above example, more could be accomplished with the include statement by placing the entire MySQL connection sequence within a revised books1.php file (Figure 13.3).

Figure 13.3 The revised books1.php file contains all of the necessary data for a MySQL connection

```
1 <?
2 //USER: readonly GRANTED: SELECT
3 $mysql_path = 'mysql.xyz.com:12345';
4 $mysql_user = 'Gaylord';
5 $mysql_pswd = 'CUcamel88';
6 $mysql_db = 'books';
7
8 mysql_connect ("$mysql_path", "$mysql_user", "$mysql_pswd");
9 mysql_select_db ($mysql_db) or die ("Unable to select!");
10 ?>
```

A single command can now be called in the initial PHP webpage script to efficiently make the database connection. Thus, lines 4 and 5 in Figure 13.1 are replaced with:

```
include '/home/account/MySQLconnections/books1.php';
```

Querying the database

The most straightforward way to ensure that the database connection is functioning properly is to begin querying it immediately to retrieve information. Most SQL statements that can be run from the mysql command prompt (mysql>) can also be run via PHP from a web page. This wonderful capability enables web pages to interact dynamically with databases, respectively pulling and pushing content from and to one another.

For example, suppose that it would be helpful to display the last names of all the authors currently found in the books database (a similar search was run from the mysql prompt after inserting author data in Chapter 9).

Note that the SELECT statement in Figure 13.4 has been assigned to the $query variable (lines 8–9) for use in PHP's mysql_query() function

Figure 13.4 'Webpage2.php' queries the books database and displays data from the author table

```
1  <html><head><title>A Webpage</title></head><body>
2  <?php
3
4  //make database connection:
5  include '/home/account/MySQLconnections/books1.php';
6
7  //create an SQL statement:
8  $query = "SELECT author_last FROM author
9    ORDER BY author_last";
10
11 //query the database and retrieve the results:
12 $result = mysql_query($query) or die("Error in: $query");
13
14   print "Here are the authors: <BR>"
15
16 //display the results
17 while ($row = mysql_fetch_array($result))
18   {
19   print "$row[author_last]";
20   print "<br>";
21   }
22
23 ?>
24 </body></html>
```

(line 12). This function sends the query to the MySQL server and returns a result that is, quite reasonably, assigned to a variable called $result.[2] Lines 17–21 represent a 'while' loop statement, which is used to print multiple rows to the page. Essentially, the 'while' loop commands that all rows must be processed for as long as (while) any 'untouched' rows remain. Meanwhile, the mysql_fetch_array() function is called upon for a special task. Each row of data represented by the $result variable is divided into a more manageable series of containers called an array. Automatically, each container in the $row array is conveniently named after its respective 'column name' within the table. The contents of each container (e.g. $row[author_last]) can then be printed in turn (line 19). Line 20 inserts an HTML line break tag (<br>) after the printing of each author's name, for a more pleasing vertical listing. Figure 13.5 presents a screenshot of the output generated by this.

At this point, some readers may feel the sudden urge to drop everything and begin creating their own database driven website. While there is always more to be learned, the general principles for creating such a site have now been presented. Most experienced webmasters possess the skills to take their site to the 'next level' once they know how to pull text from a database and send it directly to a web browser. By sprinkling

Figure 13.5 Screenshot of the output generated by 'webpage2.php'

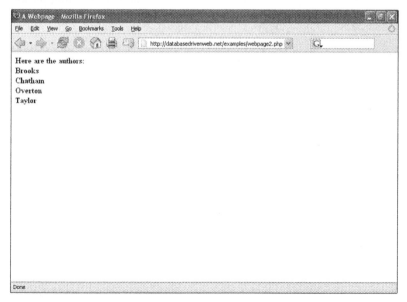

a little HTML and CSS into the mix, the possibilities are practically limitless.

Summary

This chapter explored how PHP and MySQL work hand in hand. Only a few lines of code are required to establish a MySQL database connection and rapidly return content to a web page. Further details about database driven website development are discussed in the later case studies. The focus now turns to the use of functions, which can be leveraged to create interactive web applications.

Notes

1   As always, consult your system administrator for details on local practices and procedures for enhancing PHP security. For example, some systems place special restrictions on certain filename extensions (e.g. '.sphp'), making these files inaccessible to all but their creator/owner.

2   This variable (or any variable) could be named anything as long as it is prefaced with the '$' sign and begins with a letter (A–Z or a–z) or an underscore (e.g. $_QRS_variable5). Variables must also consist of only alphanumeric characters (including the underscore).

The indispensable function

Still glides the Stream, and shall for ever glide;
The Form remains, the Function never dies...
(William Wordsworth, 'After-Thought', 1820)

One of the more important and useful devices related to PHP coding and web application development is the function. While it is possible to program web applications without using functions, it is difficult to imagine why anyone would. Once the simple technique of using functions is grasped, it can be applied in almost limitless ways. The use of functions makes it possible to modularise blocks of code so they can be re-used at various points within an application (or series of applications). Instead of laboriously and redundantly re-inserting a valuable block of code throughout a script, functions make it possible to write a segment of code only once, and then call it into action whenever desired.

By using functions, scripts can be significantly shortened, thus improving performance and processing speed. A complex application that needs to repeatedly execute a variety of code segments can easily run to several hundred lines (or more) long. Debugging such a lengthy script can be onerous as it can be difficult to keep track of line positions. Furthermore, if a correction needs to be made to a frequently used segment, every instance of the stanza will have to be touched. By using functions, corrections can be performed at one place and time.

Jeffersonian functions

Though perhaps best known as the author of the Declaration of American Independence and third President of the USA, Thomas Jefferson was also an accomplished agronomist, architect, educator, diplomat, political philosopher, scientist and inventor. He either invented or substantially perfected numerous devices including the 'Moldboard Plow of Least Resistance', the portable copying press, and the wheel cipher for coding messages.[1]

If the resourceful and imaginatively inventive Thomas Jefferson lived in the present age, it seems well within the realm of possibility that he would find time to develop his own website (perhaps even a PHP/MySQL database driven site). If such fantastic reveries may be entertained, consider Mr Jefferson's dilemma as he seeks to enhance his 'textish' web pages. After some study, he determines that the deployment of PHP functions will provide an effective mechanism for enhancing his development efforts.

Functions may be created directly within a script, or more elegantly (and often preferably), by placing them in a separate file and calling them into the script with the include() function. A function is not difficult to form. Simply declare its existence (with the word 'function'), give it a name (following the same naming rules as apply to variables), and enter one or more statements for it to process (e.g. print).

Mr Jefferson decides to visually 'break up' his lengthy web pages of prose by devising a simple PHP function. Naming the function 'divider()', he uses it to assist in inserting occasional image file dividers (Figure 14.1).

It is clear that Mr Jefferson appreciates the practicality of inserting the function at the very beginning of the web page script so that it can be accessed whenever desired (Figure 14.2, lines 3–9). He begins calling the function where the image should display (lines 15–17). Towards the end of the script, Mr Jefferson makes an aesthetic modification, remembering that the PHP 'function call' may alternatively be rendered on a single line (line 23).

The Jefferson web page example (Figure 14.2) is somewhat oversimplified, as it could be easily argued that the <img> tag might have been inserted with straight HTML. However, far more sophisticated

Figure 14.1 Jefferson's divider() function

```
1 function divider() {
2 {
3 print "<img src=\"divider.gif\" border=0>";
4 }
5 } //close the function
```

Figure 14.2   Jefferson's web page declares the divider() function and uses it

```
1  <html><head><title>jefferson.php</title></head>
2  <body>
3  <?
4  function divider() {
5    {
6    print "<img src=\"divider.gif\" border=0>";
7    }
8  } //close the function
9  ?>
10
11 <P>
12 [This line represents several paragraphs of text.]
13 <P>
14
15 <?
16 divider();
17 ?>
18
19 <P>
20 [This line represents several more paragraphs of text.]
21 <P>
22
23 <? divider(); ?>
24
25 </body></html>
```

functions may be called into the body of a page by using the same basic technique.

With his web pages becoming more readable and drawing attention, Mr Jefferson decides to display general contact information at the bottom of each web page on his site. By creating a simple function, Mr Jefferson devises a means to avoid manually retyping the contact information on every page (Figure 14.3).

Figure 14.3   The contact_info() function is saved to a file named 'mycontact_info.php'

```
1 function contact_info () {
2   {
3     print "For more info, contact me:<br>";
4     print "Thomas Jefferson<br>";
5     print "Monticello, VA<br>";
6     print "TJ@mymonticello.org";
7   }
8 } //function closes
```

Mr Jefferson saves his newly minted contact_info() function to a single file (e.g. mycontact_info.php) and uploads it to a directory on his website. As his contact information now exists at a single location, Mr Jefferson can easily alter the file and see the change immediately reflected on every page of his website. Whenever Mr Jefferson wishes to have his contact information display at the bottom of a web page, he embeds the following statement at that location:

```
include '/home/account/myfunctions/
mycontact_info.php';
```

Similar to include(), the require() function is an excellent choice for calling headers, footers and vital PHP code that must always be inserted into a page or script. While require() forces code insertion *in all cases*, the include() function is dependent upon surrounding conditional statements (e.g. if an if-else condition is met). If not embedded within a conditional statement that could possibly negate it, include() can generally be relied upon for inserting PHP code into web pages.

Another important concept related to functions involves the use of inputs called arguments. It is often desirable to pass an argument into a function for processing. For instance, perhaps one page on Mr Jefferson's website is devoted to the natural habitat around his home. Wanting to make his site more interactive, Mr Jefferson decides to develop a light-hearted web script that will enable his visitors to construct simple, first-person narratives about his meanderings in the hills around Monticello.[2] As the visitors will be able to choose from several wildlife options, Mr Jefferson needs a way to display a variety of potential sentences on the web page. Mr Jefferson determines the best approach is to pass a series of variables to a printing function he names wildlife().

Note that on line 1 (Figure 14.4), the wildlife() function is prepared to receive three arguments in the form of variables. The order of the arguments is critical. The arguments listed in the wildlife() function must be listed in the exact same order as those listed in the call of the wildlife() function. The function will return disordered results if these arguments are listed out of sequence. Using a series of if-else statements, Mr Jefferson devises a way to test the variables that are sent to the function. For example, if a web visitor forgets to select an animal to help complete the story (i.e. the $animal variable is not passed to the function), a reminder message is displayed to the screen (lines 15–20). Finally, Mr Jefferson creates a Boolean conditional statement to determine if all three variables have been received (line 22). If one or more variables

Figure 14.4 The wildlife() function processes a series of arguments and conditions

```
1  function wildlife($tree,$flower,$animal)
2  {
3  if ($tree) {
4    print "I sat under a tall, sturdy $tree tree. ";
5    }
6    else {
7    print "<B>(Please select a tree!)</B><BR>";
8    }
9  if ($flower) {
10   print "Unexpectedly, I saw movement near the lovely $flower.
     ";
11   }
12   else {
13   print "<B>(Please select a flower!)</B><BR>";
14   }
15 if ($animal) {
16   print "There stood a growling, and very unhappy, $animal! ";
17   }
18   else {
19   print "<B>(Please select an animal!)</B>";
20   }
21
22 if (($tree) AND ($flower) AND ($animal)) {
23       print " --<i>Thomas Jefferson</i>";
24       }
25   else {
26   print "<p><b>Part of my tale remains untold. ";
27   print "Please, won't you finish the story?!</b><p>";
28   }
29 }
```

is missing, the user is encouraged to complete the tale (lines 26–27). However, if $tree, $flower and $animal all pass through the function successfully (meaning the narrative has been completed), the print statement on line 23 'signs' the story, as though it were written by Thomas Jefferson himself.

With wildlife() completed, saved to a file (wildlife_func.php), and uploaded to his web server, Mr Jefferson begins work on coding a web user interface (Figure 14.5). He decides to create three 'drop-down' menu sequences from which participants may make their selections for the narrative. The variables $tree, $flower, $animal (and $submit), will be automatically generated by the forms once the 'View the Story' button is clicked. These variables are registered for use on lines 2–5.[3] Note that the $ prefix does not need to be embedded within the HTML code on lines 12, 19 and 26. As the script engages, the variable information is invisibly sent back to the server (and processed by the same script), via the form's 'POST' method (line 11).

Figure 14.5 monticello.php enables visitors to create a story about Jefferson's adventures

```
1  <? //declare variables:
2  $tree = $_REQUEST[tree];
3  $flower = $_REQUEST[flower];
4  $animal = $_REQUEST[animal];
5  $submit = $_REQUEST[submit];
6  ?>
7  <html><head><title>Nature Story</title></head><body>
8   Thomas Jefferson is going on a nature walk.
9   Please select what you think he will discover on his outing... <p>
10
11 <form action="monticello.php" method="POST">
12 <select name="tree">
13 <option value="">Select a Tree:
14 <option value="oak">Oak
15 <option value="maple">Maple
16 <option value="pineapple">Pineapple
17 </select><p>
18
19 <select name="flower">
20 <option value="">Select a Flower:
21 <option value="roses">Roses
22 <option value="chrysanthemums">Chrysanthemums
23 <option value="petunias">Petunias
24 </select><p>
25
26 <select name="animal">
27 <option value="">Select an Animal:
28 <option value="grizzly bear">Grizzly Bear
29 <option value="polar bear">Polar Bear
30 <option value="teddy bear">Teddy Bear
31 </select><p>
32 <input type=submit name=submit value="View the Story">
33 </form>
34
35 <?
36 if ($submit) {
37   print "<hr><center>";
38   print "<b>Thomas Jefferson\'s Nature Walk Story:</b>";
39   print "</center><hr><p>";
40   include '/home/account/myfunctions/wildlife_func.php';
41   wildlife($tree,$flower,$animal);
42 }
43 else {}
44 ?>
45 <form action="monticello.php" method="POST">
46 <input type=submit name=restart value="Start Over">
47 </form></body></html>
```

POST is generally the preferred, and more secure, method of sending variable data. Data sent via POST is streamed to the server along with the process request. The alternative 'GET' method embeds the variable data within a URL string for processing. This is both advantageous and potentially dangerous. As the URL generated by GET is publicly viewable, malicious individuals (either online or looking over your shoulder in a public venue), could conceivably capture or view the variables within the string and use them for ill purposes. While this may not particularly matter in the case of Mr Jefferson's wildlife web project, there could be serious implications if GET were used in an online shopping application that passed credit card information to a retailer.[4] Furthermore, the use of GET comes with limitations on the amount of data that can be passed over the URL. Few web developers want this kind of structural limitation imposed upon them when building a robust web application.

On the other hand, GET's ability to embed variables directly into the URL of a web page can be desirable. There are occasions when it is useful to grant users the ability to bookmark web pages and return to them later. A URL created with GET makes this possible. As POST does not make use of the URL to pass data, a page generated with this method cannot be saved for future access. GET is also a particularly useful device for script debugging. As GET sends all of the variable data directly to the browser's URL window, web developers can immediately confirm which variables are being passed along and which are being dropped due to a coding error. Frequently, it can be beneficial to employ GET when initially writing and testing a script, and then change to POST when making the script available for production use.

Lines 35–44 of the monticello.php script are designed to include() and process the wildlife() function (along with three variables), but only if the $submit variable has been passed to the script. Mr Jefferson uses this technique to avoid engaging the wildlife() function until the user has had the opportunity to make initial selections and click the 'View the Story' button. Significantly, this enables the page to display appropriately (without any wildlife()-generated error messages), when it is viewed for the first time.

Summary

This chapter explored how the use of functions can save time and effort, while providing an effective means to process incoming variable data. By placing conditional statements within functions, the coder can gain control of the incoming 'variable stream' and creatively manipulate user inputs to process commands, call queries, and generally manage the operations of the application. The following chapter demonstrates how variables, functions and purposefully designed command sequences can be intertwined to create interactive database driven applications.

Notes

1 Though dated, see an illuminating and memorable review of Jefferson's scientific activities in Oliver, J. W. (1943) 'Thomas Jefferson – Scientist', *The Scientific Monthly* 56 (May): 460–7. See also Bedini, S. A. (1984) *Thomas Jefferson and His Copying Machines*, Charlottesville, VA: University Press of Virginia; and Thomas Jefferson Foundation (2003) 'Reports and research tools', available at: *http://www.monticello.org/reports* (accessed 2 June 2006).

2 Jefferson's interactive web script can be accessed online, at this book's companion website: *http://databasedrivenweb.net*.

3 As a security measure, the PHP development community decided to change the default value for the 'register_globals' directive from ON to OFF (as of version 4.2.0). This means that PHP users must manually register (i.e. 'declare', 'grant permission for') each variable to be passed through an HTML form to a PHP script. Only incoming form variables (external to the script) need to be registered in this way. Variables may be declared at the very beginning of the PHP script. Consult your system administrator and the PHP manual for important security issues related to global variables (e.g. see 'Using register globals', available at: *http://www.php.net/register_globals* (accessed 2 June 2006)).

4 Regardless of the method chosen, sensitive data should always be processed in the web environment with secure socket layer (SSL) encryption (via the https protocol).

Database driven web applications

Lowly faithful, banish fear,
Right onward drive unharmed;
The port, well worth the cruise, is near,
And every wave is charmed.
(Ralph Waldo Emerson, 'Terminus', 1867)

Many components come together in the development of a database driven web application. HTML and CSS provide a means for displaying web pages that are inviting and accessible. PHP variables, conditional statements and functions channel user input, process commands, create connections and generate output. MySQL provides a reliable and speedy backend for data storage, access and retrieval.

Developing a database driven web application is really nothing more than sensibly organising segments of working code to perform tasks. At one moment the task may be to pull data from a table. At another, it could be displaying a search result or editing an entry. Tasks tend to be performed in sequence and are usually initiated in response to a variable or series of variables that have been passed through a conditional loop (e.g. if-elseif-else). Conditional statements and functions that perform important tasks can be placed in their own PHP files and called upon when needed (as described in Chapters 13–14). Dividing major application tasks into smaller, more manageable modules improves performance and makes debugging easier as an identifiable segment of code is responsible for each task's success or failure.

While the idea of developing a database driven web application may seem daunting, the process should be thought of and approached in terms of logically stringing together a small collection of modules and conditional statements into a unified whole. Rather than spend the next few pages conducting an exhaustive walk-through of a single application (which is unlikely to have general relevance), the space is better used demonstrating how to manage and integrate a practical collection of components that can be broadly implemented. This book's companion website (*www.databasedrivenweb.net*) includes fully functioning open source examples that may be downloaded, re-used and explored.

Pulling it all together

Many web applications consist of a single script (e.g. datamanager.php) that calls upon external modules to perform certain tasks. An easy and dependable way to call upon modules to perform tasks is to use an if-elseif-else conditional statement at the very top of the script (immediately after registering any variables). Figure 15.1 displays a block of code from *datamanager.php* that can be useful for initiating specific tasks based on variables sent to the script by an HTML form. Line 2 automatically inserts a PHP file (functions.php) containing a set of functions that can be called upon whenever needed (including calls from the external modules). The subsequent if-elseif-else conditional statement

Figure 15.1 Conditional statements and variables can be used to initiate tasks

```
1  <?
2  require 'myfunctions/functions.php';
3
4  //modules called based on incoming variables:
5  if   ($add) {
6     include 'mymodules/add.php';
7     }
8  elseif ($edit) {
9     include 'mymodules/edit.php';
10    }
11 elseif ($askfirst) {
12    include 'mymodules/askfirst.php';
13    }
14 elseif ($delete){
15    include 'mymodules/delete.php';
16    }
17 else {
18 ?>
19
20 <html><head><title>DataManager</title></head><body>
```

ensures that a specific module will be executed (e.g. edit.php) if one of four variables (e.g. $edit) passes through it.

Sending commands with forms and variables

An important aspect of any web application is the inclusion of an appropriate user interface for making selections and submitting them for processing. A convenient way to display a primary 'control panel' or default web page is to make use of the 'else' condition shown on line 17 (Figure 15.1). If none of the four modules is activated by incoming variables (e.g. at initial login), the 'else' condition instructs the script to display a default, primary web page where the application's controls can be displayed.

The 'controls' generally consist of one or more HTML forms used to initiate tasks. The submission of a form can activate a specific module (e.g. add.php) by passing a variable (e.g. $add) back to the script (e.g. datamanager.php or an external PHP script). Variables may be set within a form by any of the standard HTML form elements (e.g. text fields, textarea fields, drop-down menus, checkboxes and radio buttons). Of course, many users will probably never be aware that they are setting and passing PHP variables, only that they are making desirable choices and button clicks.

'Hidden' (non-displayed) HTML form input tags are useful containers for holding variables that must be passed to a module or script for processing. These 'variable containers' are particularly handy for passing variables via submission buttons that are designated for initiating tasks. The following simple HTML form will pass a variable called $add to the datamanager.php script (Figure 15.1), thus activating the add.php module:

```
<form action=datamanager.php method=POST>
<input type=hidden name=add value=add>
<input type=submit name=submit1 value="Add a New
Entry">
</form>
```

As a module completes its assigned task, it can sometimes be advantageous to pass specific variables back to the default web page (or to another page). These variables (e.g. a database row's ID number) can be actively embedded within dynamically generated HTML forms to initiate additional tasks.

For instance, someone might complete an HTML form that adds an entry to a database table. After completing this task, the person could be presented with a page that confirms the addition, and then offers the user buttons for performing additional tasks such as viewing or editing the same entry. To perform a task on the correct database entry, these buttons would need to activate HTML forms already embedded with specific variable information (i.e. the entry's database row ID number). An easy way to achieve this effect is by embedding HTML forms with PHP statements:

```
<form action=datamanager.php method=POST>
<input type=hidden name=edit value=edit>
<input type=hidden name=id value="<? echo $id;
?>">
<input type=submit name=submit1 value="Edit Title">
</form>
```

This form will pass the $edit variable to the datamanager.php script. The $id variable is dynamically inserted so the correct entry will be selected for editing.

Adding entries

The add.php module (Figure 15.2) is activated by the first of the two forms previously given. The if-else statement beginning on line 4 tests whether a valuable called $submit passes through the module (! = NOT). Indeed, the module has not yet encountered a $submit variable as the statement used to activate add.php used a variable named $submit1. This technique enables lines 7–13 to be displayed, offering the user an opportunity to enter information into the books database. When this form is submitted, the variables $add and $submit will pass through the module (along with the information contained in the $title and $year variables). As the conditions of the if-else statement are met, the necessary commands are initiated to insert the data into the title table.

Figure 15.2 The add.php module inserts data into the title table of a MySQL database

```
1  <?
2  if ($add) {
3
4  if (!$submit) //no submission yet, so offer form:
5  {
6  ?>
7  <html><body>Enter Title Info:<br>
8  <form action=datamanager.php method=POST>
9  Title: <input type=text name=title value=""><br>
10 Year: <input type=text name=year value="">
11 <input type=hidden name=add value=add>
12 <input type=submit name=submit value="Add Entry">
13 </form></body></html>
14 <?
15 }
16 else
17 {
18 //open database connection to book
19 include '/home/account/MySQLconnections/books2.php' ;
20
21 //escape any quotemarks
22 $title = addslashes($title);
23 //trim any whitespace
24 $title = trim($title);
25 $year = trim($year);
26
27 //insert data into the 'title' table:
28 $query = "INSERT INTO title (title_id, title_name,
29     title_year, title_ts)
30   VALUES('0', '$title', '$year', NOW())";
31 $result = mysql_query($query) or die("Error in: $query");
32
33 print "<html><body>
34 <b>Update successful</b>.<BR>
35 <form action=\"datamanager.php\" method=POST>
36 <input type=submit name=submit value=\"Return to Main\">
37 </form></body></html>";
38 }
39 ?>
```

Editing entries

Modules created to edit database entries can be designed in much the same way as 'add entry' modules. The first half of the if-else statement in the edit.php module is assigned the task of dynamically creating a web page and pre-populating an HTML form (Figure 15.3). The SELECT query on line 3 obtains a specific row of data (specified by the value of $id) from the title table.

Each row pulled from the query result is defined as an 'object' by using the mysql_fetch_object() function. The main advantage of this function over mysql_fetch_array() is the simplicity with which the 'data

Figure 15.3 Selected lines from edit.php demonstrate the process of creating an HTML form that is pre-populated with object data (see Figure 15.4)

```
1  <? if (!$submit) {
2  include '/home/account/MySQLconnections/books2.php' ;
3  $query = "SELECT * FROM title WHERE title_id = '$id' ";
4  $result = mysql_query($query) or die("Error in: $query");
5  $row = mysql_fetch_object($result);
6  ?>
7
8  <html><body><form action=datamanager.php method=POST>
9  Title:
10 <input type=text name=title value="<? echo $row->title_name; ?>">
11 <br>Year:
12 <input type=text name=year value="<? echo $row->title_year; ?>">
13 <input type=hidden name=id value="<? echo $id; ?>">
14 <input type=hidden name=edit value=edit>
15 <input type=submit name=submit value="Update">
16 </form></body></html>
```

Figure 15.4 The resulting web page (produced by the code in Figure 15.3), enables the user to modify the entry and re-submit it to the database

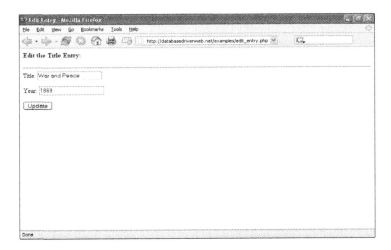

pieces' in each row can be inserted into HTML via a beautifully concise statement (echo $row->fieldname;). The database row number of the present entry (the value of $id) is retained and embedded into the form (line 13) along with the other variables. It is important to consistently pass the $id variable identifier through the module with each form submission. This ensures that the correct entry will be accessed, modified and updated.

The resulting, dynamically produced, web page (Figure 15.4) has helpfully inserted the original content into text fields for easy modification.

Upon clicking the 'Update' button, the directives in the second half of edit.php's if-else conditional statement overwrite the data in the appropriate row of the title table (Figure 15.5).

Viewing entries

Some web applications may not require a 'view' module, either because the editing module suffices for data viewing, or the output is streamed to an external web page that can be seen independently. Viewing modules can be worthwhile additions to certain types of programs, particularly web-based content management systems (CMS). Web pages under development can be pulled directly into a viewing mode already pre-formatted with the site's CSS. Such an approach can yield savings such as decreasing the amount of time spent toggling between the CMS and a separate browser application.

A viewing module can be formed directly from the code used to construct edit.php (Figure 15.3). Instead of (or in addition to) populating HTML forms, the database content can be pulled into the regular body of the page. One useful technique is to immediately assign the incoming elements of an object row to a series of variables. The variables can then be easily dispersed (within print() or echo() statements) throughout the page code or placed within conditional if-else statements for managed output:

```
<?
$row = mysql_fetch_object ($result);
$title = $row->title_name;
$status = $row->title_status;
if (1 == $status) {
print ("You are in luck! <b>$title</b> is
available.");
}
elseif (0 == $status) {
print ("Sorry, <b>$title</b> has been checked
out.");
}
?>
```

One of the other more common tasks associated with calling data into a viewing module or web page is the creation of hypertext links. As it

Figure 15.5 Selected lines from edit.php update the data in the title table

```
16 } else {
17 $query = "UPDATE title SET title_name = '$title',
18    title_year = '$year', title_ts = NOW()
19    WHERE title_id = '$id' ";
20 $result = mysql_query($query) or die("Error in: $query");
21 }
```

is inefficient (and usually quite unnecessary) to store anchor tags in database table URL fields, the following code can be used to create a clickable hypertext link:

```
<?
$hyperlink = "<a href=\"$row->myURL\">$row->myURL</a>";
?>
Related URL: <? echo $hyperlink; ?>
```

Deleting entries

Designing a module to delete a row of data is exceedingly simple. Before calling it, however, it is usually a good idea to give users one last chance to change their mind before deleting a row forever. The askfirst.php module (Figure 15.6) provides just such an opportunity.

Figure 15.6 The precautionary askfirst.php module

```
1 <? if ($askfirst) {
2 ?>
3 <html><body>
4   <b>Are you sure you want to delete this entry?</b><P>
5 <form action=datamanager.php method=POST>
6 <input type=hidden name=delete value=delete>
7 <input type=hidden name=id value="<? echo $id; ?>">
8 <input type=Submit name=submit value="Yes-Delete">
9 </form>
10
11 <form action=datamanager.php method=POST>
12 <input type=submit name=submit value="No-Save">
13 </form></body></html>
14 <? }
15 ?>
```

Figure 15.7 The operative lines of the delete.php module are short (and unforgiving)

```
1 <? if ($delete) {
2 include '/home/account/MySQLconnections/books2.php';
3 $query = "DELETE FROM title WHERE title_id = '$id'";
4 $result = mysql_query($query) or die("Error in: $query");
5 } ?>
```

Upon clicking the askfirst.php web page's 'Yes–Delete' button, the passing of the $delete variable (line 6) immediately executes delete.php. As a result, the specified entry is permanently and irrevocably purged by the DELETE statement in Figure 15.7.

Keyword searching

Probably one of the most sought after features that developers wish to incorporate into their database driven web applications is keyword searching. There are many ways to go about optimising searches and crafting the perfect 'regular expression' syntax for handling search strings. The search.php module (Figure 15.8) demonstrates one effective way to provide keyword searching capabilities for an application. The script uses a regular expression to match submitted keywords with database entries. The Boolean 'AND' operator is automatically inserted between terms to improve relevancy and precision. The procedure matches 'whole' words and is case insensitive, so a search for 'read' finds both 'read' and 'Read,' but neither 'reader' nor 'Reading.'

The HTML form in Figure 15.9 can be used to pass keywords to the search.php module for processing.

The search.php script is flexible and can be easily modified to perform various types of keyword matching. Different iterations of the script may be called within the same application by passing distinct variables (e.g. $booleanAND, $booleanOR) through if-else loops. Alternate search modules can be created by inserting varying 'WHERE' clauses at line 16 (Figure 15.8). For instance, substituting the following line will institute 'whole word' matching with the Boolean 'OR' operator:

```
$WhereClause .=" REGEXP
'[[ :<:]] $theKEYwords[ $i][[ :>:]]' OR ";
```

Figure 15.8 The search.php module searches the title_name field of the title table for matches

```
1  <?
2  $keywords = $_REQUEST[ keywords] ;
3  if ($keywords)
4  {
5  //escape quotemarks
6  $keywords = addslashes($keywords);
7
8  //create an array of keyword strings
9  $theKEYwords = explode(" ",$keywords);
10 $WhereClause = "";
11 $howmanywords = count($theKEYwords);
12
13 //generate a WHERE clause
14 for($i=0; $i<$howmanywords; $i++)
15 {
16 $WhereClause .=" title_name REGEXP '[[:<:]]$theKEYwords[$i][[:>:]]' AND ";
17 }
18
19 //remove the trailing 'AND' [ '-4' = (1 space + 3 characters)]
20 $WhereClause = substr($WhereClause, 0,strlen($WhereClause)-4 );
21
22 include '/home/account/MySQLconnections/books2.php';
23 $query = ("SELECT * FROM title WHERE ".$WhereClause."");
24 $result = mysql_query($query);
25
26 //the number of results:
27 $totalrows = mysql_num_rows($result);
28 if ($totalrows === 0) {
29 print "Sorry. Your search for <b>$keywords</b> returned no results.";
30 } else {
31 print "Your search returned <b>$totalrows</b> results.<p>";
32 }
33 while ($row = mysql_fetch_object($result))
34 {
35 echo $row->author_last;
36 echo "<br>";
37 }
38 }
39 ?>
```

Figure 15.9 This simple HTML form queries search.php

```
1 <html><body>
2 <form action=search.php method=POST>
3 Search by Author (enter a last name):<br>
4 <input type=text name=keywords value="">
5 <input type=hidden name=search value=search>
6 <input type=submit name=submit value="Search">
7 </form></body></html>
```

The following clause makes use of the LIKE 'operator' (and the % wildcard) to automatically truncate word endings and simultaneously perform a Boolean 'AND' search. Using this clause, a search for 'pol' will find 'pole,' 'political' and 'polyester':

```
$WhereClause .=" LIKE '$theKEYwords[ $i] %' AND ";
```

Another technique is to totally dispense with lines 8–20 (Figure 15.8)

and insert LIKE constructs directly into the SELECT statement (line 23). Similar to the previous example, this method begins by matching the first few characters of a string (moving from left to right), but then performs automatic truncation on word endings (due to the wildcard). A search for 'read' will find 'read,' 'reader,' and 'Reading' (but not 'proofread'). As this statement does not make use of the AND operator, it is perhaps best used for abbreviated 'exact title' searching:

```
$query = ("SELECT * FROM title WHERE title_name
LIKE '$keywords%' ");
```

Summary

While the modules and examples reviewed in this chapter provide the necessary tools to begin developing database driven web applications of all kinds and in widely divergent contexts, the following chapter presents case studies of web applications that have been constructed to address diverse information challenges in a university library setting. It is difficult to build 'one size fits all' web applications because the information needs of every organisation vary. While the genesis and formulation of these applications sprung from the many concepts presented throughout this book, they were also created for, and influenced by, the people and organisational environment from which they emerged.

It is hoped that this book generates creative ideas and practical inspirations for developing consequential database driven web endeavours in your context. The opportunities, possibilities and synergies are waiting to be realised and discovered. Through ascertaining needs, gathering resources, facilitating feedback and assembling building blocks, you can make a real difference in your organisation and in the lives of the people around you. Brave journey!

> *It is brave to be involved,*
> *To be not fearful to be unresolved.*
> (Gwendolyn Brooks, 'Do not be afraid of no', *Annie Allen*, 1949)

16

Case studies

In case of doubt, decide in favor of what is correct.[1]

(Karl Kraus, 1874–1936)

The following case studies represent 'real-world' projects, assembled to take advantage of the possibilities provided by open source database driven web development tools such as PHP and MySQL. Unfortunately, due primarily to long-standing university intellectual property rights (not unlike the matters discussed in Chapter 2), the source code for these projects is not associated with the term *libre*. Still, it is hoped that these overviews may generate ideas and perhaps lead to the development of innovative tools that will solve other information management problems

Modules of PHP code that are proven effective can be re-used in subsequent projects. Numerous similarities can be seen in the application interfaces discussed in these case studies. Code that functioned well and met pressing needs was immediately re-deployed. This saved valuable development time and eliminated the necessity of building every application from scratch.

The components and techniques illustrated in this book can be used to develop database driven web tools much like the ones detailed in the following case studies. Each application was specifically created to address actual problems. Similar information challenges are likely experienced by individuals working in a variety of organisations, large and small. Experience suggests that a great many challenges can be overcome by developing basic skill sets and applying these proficiencies with a measure of curiosity, tenacity and good humour.

Visit this book's companion website (*www.databasedrivenweb.net*) for resources, tips, links and access to additional free and open source software information.

Case study 1: A database driven website

The website of the Western Illinois University (WIU) Libraries was completely overhauled during 2003 and 2004 as scores of 'static' HTML web pages migrated into a database driven PHP/MySQL framework featuring templates developed with cascading style sheets (CSS). Built from the ground up, the completely redesigned site adopted a database driven model to improve efficiency and data currency. Along with a new 'look and feel', the site featured a newly designed navigation structure and came into compliance with the W3C's Web Content Accessibility Guidelines (WCAG), federal s. 508 standards, and the Illinois Web Accessibility Standards published by the State of Illinois (Figure 16.1).

Figure 16.1 Website of the Western Illinois University Libraries

The library's web task force surveyed library website users, led focus group sessions, developed wish lists and studied historical usage statistics and trends. The websites of peer institutions and major information services providers were reviewed with an eye toward embracing the latest technologies, techniques and navigational frameworks for providing access to diverse information resources. Multiple demos were tested and usability studies were conducted before a design was finally selected in spring 2004.

The summer of 2004 was spent pulling content out of the 'static' HTML pages that had become weighted with proprietary browser code and outmoded style tags. All content was processed by a PHP script that was specifically designed to strip out all 'non-valid' HTML tags.[2] The tags considered valuable and worth keeping (e.g. paragraph tags (<p>) and hypertext linking tags (<a href>)) were declared 'valid' within the script and left unharmed. 'Cleanest possible content' became the unofficial rallying cry. After undergoing the stripping process (which saved much time), the content of each 'page' was automatically uploaded into a MySQL database, associated with a specific library department or function, and assigned a unique number to serve as a primary key.

A web-based content management system (called WebAdmin) was developed with PHP/MySQL to help manage the newly stripped content. An editing module provided direct access to the remaining text and HTML so that necessary changes could be made. A minimal amount of manual editing proved necessary for putting the content in good order.

As August, and the start of a new academic year approached, a series of templates was created using a combination of PHP, HTML and CSS. As a CSS style sheet had already been created for the approved design, few stylistic changes needed to be made. Separate templates were designed for the front page, secondary and tertiary level pages, and for 'general pages' that did not conveniently fall into these hierarchical categories. Templates were generally crafted so that banner or header text could be pulled directly from the database along with any necessary sidebar content (e.g. navigation menus). The templates also provided an open space for the 'body' of the pages to be pulled in.

Each template included a PHP mechanism to insert appropriate 'footer' information (e-mail addresses, phone numbers, etc.), based on the nature of the page's content.

Each major secondary-level page (e.g. the Reference Unit's front page) was placed in a unique directory and named 'index.php' so that a call to the directory would deliver this file first by default. This technique allowed each unit to retain a more direct (and more attractive) primary URL (e.g. *http://www.wiu.edu/library/units/reference/*). Without adopting such an approach, major areas of the site would have had lengthy and unmemorable URLs laden with cryptic identifiers such as '*http://www.wiu.edu/library/units/reference/refhome.php?id=285*'. To achieve this effect, the ID number (primary key) of each major page was called within the template instead of appended to the URL, for example:

```
//parameters:
$unitid = '3'; //Reference (this unit's pages
only)
$id = '189';  //the Reference Unit's front page
id#
$query = "SELECT * FROM libweb WHERE libweb_id
= '$id'
AND libweb_unitid = '$unitid'
AND libweb_status = '1' ";
```

A $unitid variable was included within the query parameters to help ensure that each unit's pages are appropriately routed to the correct template. Finally, each row in the database included a column field called $libweb_status. This field can be switched from '1' to '0' based on whether the page is considered 'active' or 'inactive'. Pages with a value of '0' are automatically suppressed, as the query demands that entries must possess a value of '1' to display. Additional parameters (outside of the query) were added to reveal a unit's customisable sidebar, a library-wide default sidebar, or no sidebar if the page's body needed to fill the entire screen.

It would be impractical to create a unique 'URL template' for every page. This would also substantially undermine the beauty of the database driven approach. Instead, a generic template was constructed for each unit. The template could then call from the database only the 'pages' associated with that unit. For example, a template entitled reference_web.php was created for the Reference Unit. Within this page was embedded the $unitid parameter (so only content associated with the Reference Unit could be pulled into the body of the template). As a 'pristine' URL was considered less important for sub-level pages, the $id variable could be appended to these addresses (e.g. /.../ reference_web.php?id=37).

As the process drew to a close, templates were established, links were created and the entire system was carefully monitored and tested. The conversion process ultimately transferred a moderate-sized site of about 300 static pages and forms into the new paradigm. Fortunately, the entire project was completed in late July, a few weeks before the beginning of the new academic year. The multi-stage process of establishing a functional website design that was embraced by all parties required approximately a year to complete. The technical work related to the migration process, not counting the related WebAdmin CMS development project, lasted only ten weeks.

The 'static' HTML approach to web development has effectively ended for the WIU Libraries. No longer is a series of 'dead' files cobbled together to resemble a web presence. The database driven model now provides library users with a reliable system of interconnected dynamic links. These links pull fresh database content into web pages 'on the fly', improving performance, accessibility and data currency. The WIU Libraries serve a university community of approximately 13,000 students and some 600 faculty. As measured by increasing levels of usage and reach (over 2.2 million annual page views and approximately 1,900 unique visitors daily),[3] the library's transition to a database driven website model has been a successful undertaking. Websites can always be improved, however, and are continual 'works in progress'. In response to ever-changing user needs and information seeking behaviour, it is anticipated that the WIU Libraries' website will continue to expand, adapt and evolve in the years ahead.

Case study 2: A web content management system

The WebAdmin content management system (CMS) was specifically developed for managing the database driven website of the WIU Libraries. WebAdmin's components are highly customised, reflecting the organisational structure of the Libraries and have been tailored to meet the needs of the information systems staff.

Developed solely with PHP and HTML, the CMS interface is connected to the library website's MySQL database, providing direct access to virtually all website textual content. Entries may be added, viewed, edited or deleted using the system. Recently updated entries automatically appear in the left column of the main menu due to a query that searches the TIMESTAMP of each entry (Figure 16.2). All entries may be searched

Figure 16.2 WebAdmin's main menu

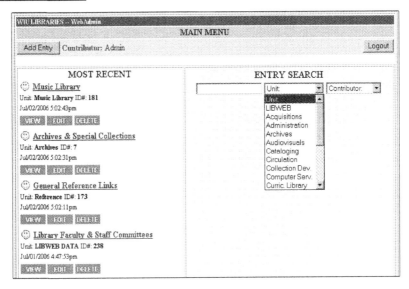

by keyword and limited to a specific library unit (or activity), and/or content contributor.

The WebAdmin editing module enables users to modify content in either a 'word processing' mode or native HTML mode (Figure 16.3). Any changes made to an entry are automatically saved to the MySQL database, which is backed up on a regular basis.

If a new entry is added to the database, a unique ID number is automatically assigned to the row (via the MySQL AUTO_INCREMENT statement that establishes the primary key). This ID number is then embedded in a PHP template file or appended to a template file's URL so that the related content can be inserted into the body of an appropriate page.

Case study 3: A searchable online database

The WIU Libraries' periodicals holdings list (PHL) has manifested itself in a variety of forms and undergone multiple transformations over the last couple of decades. Originally little more than a printout of the library's journal and magazine subscriptions, the PHL is now a searchable

Figure 16.3 WebAdmin's editing console

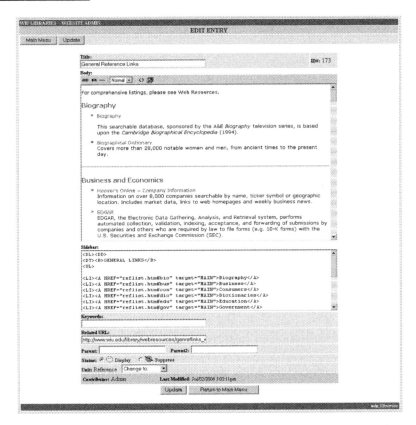

online database providing location information for traditional periodicals and direct access to more than 24,000 'full-text' e-titles.[4]

Like the other case study applications, this resource was developed with PHP/HTML scripting and a MySQL database backend. The 'basic' PHL interface features keyword title searching and the ability to limit searches to only 'full-text' titles. The 'advanced search' interface (Figure 16.4) offers additional search options including keyword title (AND), keyword title (OR), exact title and ISSN. Limits that can be applied to these searches include: 'full-text titles', 'full-text newspaper titles' and the default 'all titles' setting. An alphabetical 'browse' function is available as well as an alphabetical listing of all 'full-text' e-titles organised by subscription databases, aggregators and publishers. Full-text title coverage dates are provided along with hypertext links to specific titles or appropriate database search screens.

Figure 16.4 A PHL search result

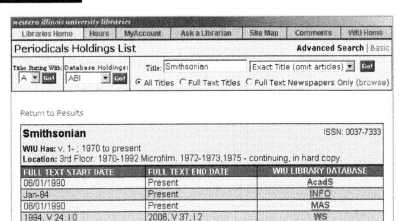

Case study 4: A digital object management system

A substantial collection of historic images related to the west central Illinois region is housed in the Archives and Special Collections unit of the WIU Libraries. Until 2003, the unit had stored its digital images in a proprietary, single-workstation database. The unit faced an information management challenge when the database would no longer accept new image entries. As a number of PHP/MySQL database applications had already been developed within the Libraries, it was relatively easy to modify and extend existing code to create a functional web-based digital object management system (DOMS). A searchable public interface was also developed and came to be known as the Digital Image Database.[5]

The public interface enables users to search virtually all textual fields including image description, location, photographer, date, keyword, and subject heading (Figure 16.5). Subject headings may be browsed alphabetically. An 'AnyWord/AnyWhere' keyword matching function feature offers simultaneous searching of all public fields. To easily achieve this multi-field searching functionality, whenever a record is added or modified by the DOMS cataloguing module, all field-specific data are simultaneously saved to a single TEXT field (in addition to each piece of data being saved to its respective column). Instead of crafting a complex series of SQL statements or trying to manipulate data with a

Figure 16.5 The Digital Image Database front page

post-search PHP routine, a simple query of this 'free-text' field allows rapid global matching of keyword terms within specific entries.

The descriptive entry fields within the cataloguing module were designed to comply with Dublin Core metadata standards (Figure 16.6). These standards were followed to ensure interoperability and preserve data export options with future DOMS products. Non-public fields were created to hold donor information and other data for staff use (e.g. the physical location of original photographs, slides and negatives). By toggling a 'radio button', staff may display or suppress individual records depending upon the extent of descriptive cataloguing achieved.

The library's decision to provide online access to this collection of images has made it possible for researchers, teachers, students and the general public to learn more about the historic west central Illinois region that lies alongside the Mississippi River, just upstream of metropolitan St. Louis. By 2006, the Digital Image Database contained more than 3,000 fully catalogued images, already making it one of the largest image depositories of its kind in Illinois.[6]

Figure 16.6 The Digital Image Database's cataloging console

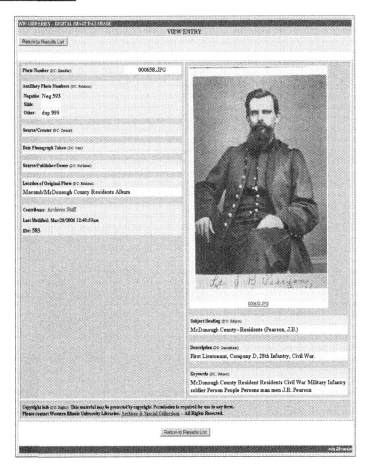

Case study 5: A searchable URL database

The Reference Desk of Western Illinois University's main Leslie F. Malpass Library is a busy public service location. Adjacent to an 'always full' computer lab/classroom on the library's main floor, the desk is staffed by a contingent of 11 professional librarians who collectively answer approximately 13,000 reference questions per year. In addition to a substantial collection of reference books and access to numerous bibliographic databases, librarians increasingly rely upon Web sources to assist library researchers.

One of the earliest database driven web applications developed within the WIU Libraries was the Reference Unit's URLs database. The need for an information management tool became apparent as librarians were having difficulty keeping track of valuable websites uncovered during the course of the working day. At least 11 people were 'bookmarking' websites at the desk's two computer workstations, sometimes on more than one browser. Although several strategies for bringing order to the chaos were attempted, it became increasingly difficult for staff to locate previously identified sites efficiently.

A solution was found by developing a database driven application that librarians could quickly access to store and retrieve website URLs. By analysing the overburdened bookmark lists, a group of diverse categories were selected to serve as a subject authority file for database entries (see Figure 16.7). An important design decision was to create the URLs database to be an 'open' system so that all reference librarians could contribute websites and all could benefit from the accumulated results.

Librarians may login to the system under their own names or anonymously. Logging in as an individual and adding a new site has the advantage of automatically connecting the entry with the contributor.

Figure 16.7 The main menu of the URLs database (showing the subject authority limit)

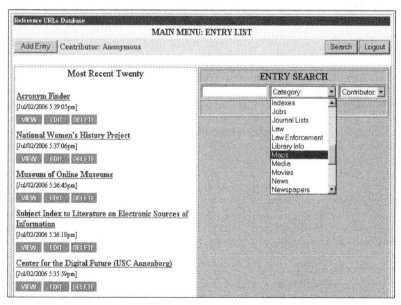

This relationship allows users to quickly limit database searches to entries they personally contribute. The search mechanism offers the ability to conduct contributor searches (an alphabetical listing of websites entered by specific librarians), category searches (an alphabetical list of websites assigned to a major subject categories), and global keyword searches that can be limited by contributor and/or category.

Contributors may add URLs to the database by clicking the 'add entry' button. Website titles and URLs can be quickly pasted into their respective text boxes (Figure 16.8). A drop-down menu enables the librarian to select a single authority subject that most closely describes the nature of the website. A 'keyword' text box provides a means for supplying additional descriptive terms that could potentially be used to search for the website.

The default web page at the Reference Desk workstations includes a search box enabling librarians to conveniently enter terms and begin searches limited by category or contributor. Used continuously since 2002, the database now contains several hundred entries, and provides WIU librarians with a reliable mechanism for managing disparate online reference resources.

Case study 6: A link management system

Reaching more than 6,000 students in library classrooms annually, WIU librarians lead approximately 250 bibliographic instruction sessions per

Figure 16.8 The 'add entry' module of the URLs database

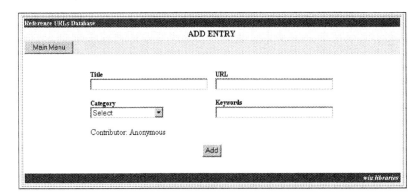

year. These sessions introduce students and faculty to library resources and services, provide instruction in conducting effective research, and demonstrate how to get the most out of sophisticated reference databases.

The library website includes a specialised gateway for locating instructional class guides, handouts and tutorials developed by librarians. Users may search for guides by the library instructor's name, by official course number (e.g. GEOG 505), or by the title of a specialised tutorial or workshop resource. As librarians began developing more sophisticated resources, and in greater number, it became more difficult to manage all of the continually changing links and entries on the 'class guides' gateway page. In addition to growing information management challenges, instructors needed a convenient means (and ideally an 'around the clock' capability) for adding, modifying or deleting links posted on the gateway under their names.

Once again, the PHP/MySQL combination made it possible to develop a workable solution based on already existing code modules. As the class guide gateway typically consists of less than 200 rows of data, it was not necessary to normalise the data relationships fully. A single class_guides table was created to hold the significant elements (Table 16.1).

With the table in place, a familiar-looking interface (drawn from previous library database projects) was reconfigured to interact with

Table 16.1 Selected columns from the class_guides table

cg_id	cg_status	cg_contribid	cg_course	cg_title
13	0	7	AG 320	
3	1	1	PHYS 150	Energy and the Environment
2	0	1	EIS 500	Searching ERIC
253	1	7	LEJA 101	Survey of Criminal Justice
253	1	7	MGT 490	Resources for Strategic Analysis
251	1	8	His 491A (Hall)	Locating Primary Sources
250	1	8	His 510	Research Seminar in US History
249	1	9	SOC 472	

the class_guides table. Standard 'add entry' and 'edit entry' modules were included in the resulting class guide link manager, so that librarians can easily modify the links and titles appearing on the gateway page (see Figure 16.9). As instructors are given separate user accounts, they are prevented from accidentally modifying or deleting the links of others. An 'entry suppression' feature enables instructors to remove a link from the gateway temporarily without having to delete it. This can be useful when updating a class guide or when wanting to suppress a guide that will not be needed until a future semester.

With the class guide link manager in production, library instructors are free to make last minute (or late night) changes to their class guide entries. This database driven web resource has empowered busy librarians and streamlined the process of keeping an important library information access point current and relevant.

Case study 7: A database management system

The rise of web-based citation databases and full-text periodical services has transformed the environment of many academic libraries. An expansive, state-of-the art CD-ROM network that less than ten years ago was the bibliographic workhorse of the WIU Libraries is now a slumbering dinosaur. It only occasionally spins an arcane disc when awakened for bleak duty – usually involving a solitary grad student

Figure 16.9 Class guide link manager's editing console

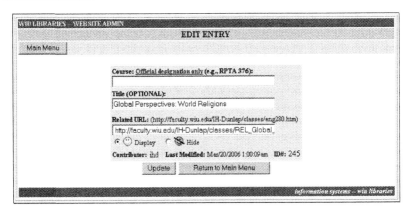

seeking access to corporate financial statements from the late 1980s. Numerous professional conferences and reams of library literature are exclusively devoted to issues related to the acquisition, assessment, management, preservation and delivery of electronic (and usually web-based) library resources.[7] Not surprisingly, this 'brave new world' of online digital librarianship has impacted workflows, altered professional responsibilities, changed user research patterns and influenced educational pedagogy.

The WIU Libraries began acquiring significant numbers of web-based, bibliographic citation subscription databases in the late 1990s. In addition to new contracts, vendor pricing conundrums, complex legal licensing terms and related acquisition issues, an entire range of new technical challenges began to emerge. These included 'password only' database access models, technical support issues, IP address communiqués, A–Z e-serial list generations, proxy server implementations, and the more recent introduction of 'meta-tools', such as link resolvers and federated search systems, that require substantial maintenance and configuration.

In this environment, keeping up with the altogether separate task of providing reliable information to library users about current database options can be somewhat daunting. Online subscription databases seem to remain in a constant state of flux. Ever-changing database URLs, interface updates and system upgrades contribute to the disorder, as do frequent vendor mergers and acquisitions. Wonderful new products are released on a regular basis, further encouraging libraries to 're-mix' their collection of database subscriptions while attempting to wisely expend precious resources and maintain some degree of platform consistency. Most academic library webmasters are intimately familiar with ongoing database additions, modifications, deletions and fiscal year 'remixes'.

In a 'static' web environment, it can be cumbersome to respond to these kinds of changes on a continual basis. Quite sensibly, however, most modern researchers come to an academic library website with the understandable expectation that links to subscription databases will function appropriately and that information provided about each database will be accurate and complete. There had to be a better way to manage database titles, URLs, descriptions, vendor names, coverage dates and related pieces of information.

Employing the tried and tested PHP modules that had successfully met other information management challenges, development work began on a database manager web application. A 'database of databases' was about to be born.

To make the project work well, two separate PHP scripting mechanisms needed to be created. First, a robust administrative interface was needed to manage all of the pertinent information related to each subscription database. Much like the applications displayed in the previous case studies, the database manager was designed to have adding, editing, viewing, deleting and searching capabilities. A supplemental subject linker' module also needed to be developed, so the administrator would be able to easily attach pre-defined subject categories to each record. Second, a 'smart' user interface would be required to pull content out of the MySQL database and present it on a web page. A pure 'template' approach might suffice, but so much more could be achieved by leveraging the dynamic nature of the PHP/MySQL combination. Instead, a 'database gateway' was designed so users could interactively discover and access databases in different ways.

The database manager administrative module makes it simple to add and modify subscription database entries. Numerous text boxes are provided for entering important data about each entry. Drop-down menus are dynamically generated from a MySQL table so that the administrator may consistently define settings such as each database's current vendor. As bibliographic databases tend to vary in both content type and format, drop-down menus are available for noting whether the database includes scholarly, peer-reviewed content and/or access to full-text articles.

To solve the issue of constantly changing database URLs, the underlying database manager PHP script automatically generates a unique URL for each new entry. Within the unique URL is embedded a database identifier ($bibdb_id) based on the entry's primary key ID (317), thus:

http://www.wiu.edu/library/databases/access.php?name=GeoAbs&**bibdb_id=317**

This unique URL effectively becomes the library's eternal 'persistent link' to the external bibliographic resource. The persistent link passes the $bibdb_id variable to a MySQL SELECT statement within a supplemental script (Figure 16.10).[8] Whenever a library researcher clicks the persistent link, the script 'grabs' the bibliographic database's 'actual' URL from the MySQL database and seamlessly forwards the user to the external bibliographic resource via a header redirect (line 8).

Whenever a bibliographic database's 'actual' URL changes, the 'main URL' text field for that entry can be easily updated (Figure 16.11). This approach has numerous advantages including the fact that database

Figure 16.10 Segment of a supplemental script that processes persistent links and redirects users to 'actual' bibliographic resources

```
1  $query = "SELECT actual_bibdburl FROM bibdburls
2   WHERE primary_bibdbid='$bibdb_id'";
3  $result = mysql_query($query) or die ("Error in: $query");
4
5  if ($row = mysql_fetch_array($result))
6  {
7  $link = $row["actual_bibdburl"];
8  header ("Location: $link");
```

Figure 16.11 The database manager's editing console

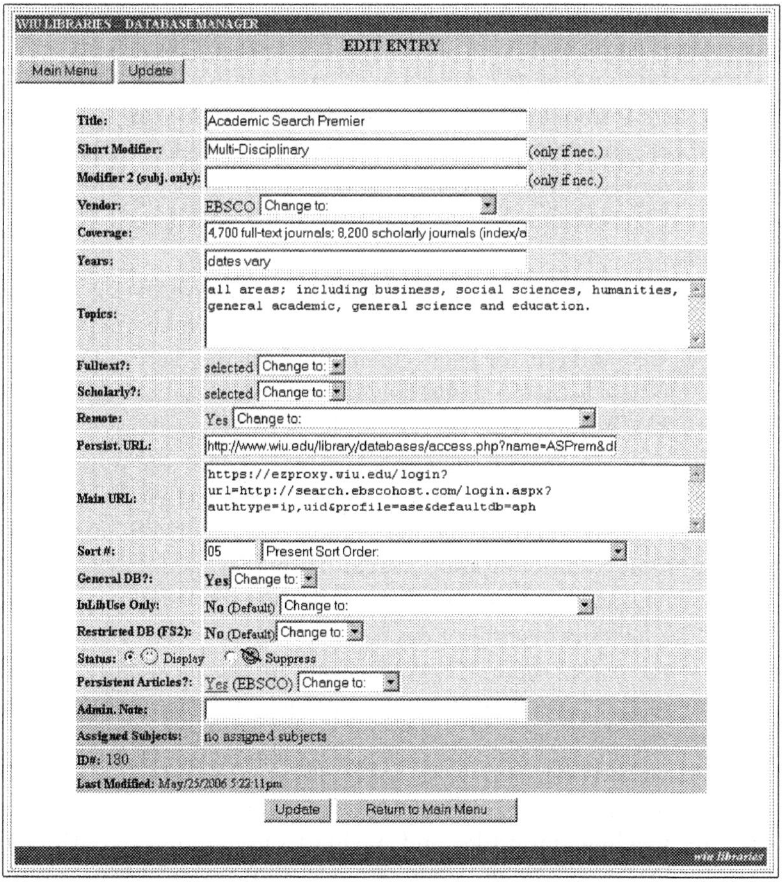

links embedded in online course modules, tutorials, faculty web pages (and library website pages), never need to be updated again. A simple edit to a single field in a MySQL database immediately 'refreshes' every distributed link in existence.

As bibliographic databases are often given names sporting unusual abbreviations and acronyms, it can be difficult to effectively sort on a database's regular title. Yet due to local sorting conventions, it may be desirable to output a list of bibliographic databases in a certain ordering scheme. The database manager provides a way to establish a manual sorting order (Figure 16.11), by giving the administrator the opportunity to insert a preferred sorting position in a text box. An adjacent, dynamically created drop-down menu, lists the current sorting order for all entries in the database. This list can be conveniently consulted before specifying a sorting position for the entry.

A PHP script dynamically queries a MySQL database to produce the WIU Libraries' 'Select A Database' web page (Figure 16.12). An alphabetical list of all library databases is presented by default. Users may click the 'info' button adjacent to each database entry to reveal complete details about the resource. A 'preferences' button (located at the top of the rightmost column of the alphabetical table), enables users to select a variety of page display options. For instance, a different set of informational columns can be displayed in the table for viewing and/ or printing.

In addition to a 'general' multidisciplinary resources display, a 'subject' drop-down menu provides users with a list of databases organised by major disciplines. Like all the pages emanating from the 'Select a Database' gateway, database listings organised by subject are dynamically generated (Figure 16.13). A 'linking table' within the MySQL database is used to match the primary key of each database entry with the appropriate primary key of entries in a 'subject' table. As additional indexes and abstracts are located in the reference area, it was decided to intersperse these important traditional resources in the smaller (and more focused) subject displays, rather than add them to the already lengthy (and ever-growing) alphabetical listing of databases.

The 'Select A Database' gateway is one of the most heavily used resources on the library website. Given the growing importance of electronic resources within the WIU Libraries, it made sense to devote some time toward developing an administrative interface that could help address some of the challenges their existence creates. Instead of constantly juggling static files and having to update links continually

Figure 16.12 The 'Select A Database' gateway

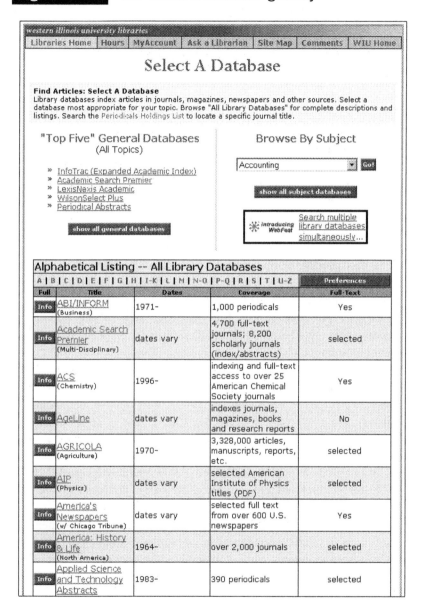

throughout the library website, the database manager web application has made managing electronic database resources practically a pleasure.

Figure 16.13 A dynamically generated listing of 'Art' databases and resources

Art Databases			
Title	**Dates**	**Coverage**	**Full**
Architectural Index	Print Source (Reference Area, Main Library)		Info
Art Abstracts	1984–	285 periodicals	Info
Arts and Humanities Search	1980–	about 8800 periodicals	Info
Bibliography of the History of Art	Print Source (Reference Area, Main Library)		Info
Saskia Digital Archive	Antiquity – Present	30,000 digital images of paintings, sculpture, architecture	Info

Notes

1 See Zohn, H. (1990) *Half-Truths and One-and-a-Half Truths*, Chicago: University of Chicago Press, p. 59.

2 The first portion of the script declares the tags deemed 'valid' and places them in an array. The script 'protects' these tags from deletion by using the str_replace() function to substitute all instances of < > with [ ]. The strip_tags() function then deletes the remaining undesirable tags. Finally, str_replace() returns the valid tags to their former state (< >).

3 'The 2005 data indicate a record number of library webpages viewed (over 2.28 million), a 23% increase in the number of library website visitors (129,465 more than in 2004), and an average of 6,271 library webpages viewed every day of the year (a 26% increase)'. Source: Information System Unit (2005) 'Annual Report', WIU Libraries, IL.

4 During 2005, the PHL contained 9,076 print titles and 24,179 (17,589 distinct) electronic periodical titles. Source: Information System Unit (2005) 'Annual Report', WIU Libraries, IL.

5 The complete story concerning the planning and development of this web database application is available: Dunlap, I. H. (2005) 'Open source digital image management', *Computers in Libraries* 25 (April), available at: *http://www.infotoday.com/cilmag/apr05/dunlap.shtml* (accessed 02 June 2006).

6 The Digital Image Database is available at: *http://www.wiu.edu/library/units/archives/* (accessed 02 June 2006).

7 The inaugural Electronic Resources in Libraries (ER&L) national conference was held at Atlanta's Georgia Institute of Technology in early 2006 (*http://electroniclibrarian.org*), drawing participants from

academic institutions throughout the USA. Conceived and organised by an e-community of librarians, ER&L is an example of professionals coming together to share findings and concerns, discover resources and devise strategies for addressing significant information challenges.

8   When passing a variable to a script (particularly via a 'public' URL), it is considered good security practice to immediately 'test' the variable (e.g. make sure the variable only contains desirable alphanumeric characters). Consult a security guidebook or your system administrator for details.

Further reading

Accessibility and standards

Bohman, P. (2003) 'Introduction to Web Accessibility' WebAIM (October); available at: *http://www.webaim.org/intro/* (accessed 2 June 2006).

Disability Rights Commission (2005) 'Code of Practice'; available at: *http://www.drc-gb.org/thelaw/practice.asp* (accessed 2 June 2006).

European Commission (2005) '2005 EC Communication on eAccessibility'; available at: *http://europa.eu.int/information_society/policy/accessibility/regulation/com-ea-2005/* (accessed 2 June 2006).

IT Accessibility & Workforce Division, US General Services Administration (2006) 'Section 508'; available at: *http://www.section508.gov/* (accessed 2 June 2006).

Phipps, L., Sutherland, A. and Seale, J. (eds) (2002) *Access All Areas: Disability, Technology and Learning*, York: TechDis.

Sloan, M. (2002) 'Web Accessibility and the Disability Discrimination Act', Digital Media Access Group; available at: *http://www.dmag.org.uk/resources/legal/dda.asp* (accessed 2 June 2006).

WebAim. 'Laws and Standards', available at: *http://www.webaim.org/coordination/law/us/508/* (accessed 2 June 2006).

World Wide Web Consortium (1999) 'Web Content Accessibility Guidelines 1.0', available at: *http://www.w3.org/TR/1999/WAI-WEBCONTENT-19990505/* (accessed 2 June 2006).

CSS

Briggs, O., Champeon, S., Costello, E. and Patterson, M. (2004) *Cascading Style Sheets: Separating Content from Presentation* (2nd edn) Berkeley: Friends of ED.

Meyer, E. (2001) *Cascading Style Sheets 2.0 Programmer's Reference*, Emeryville, CA: McGraw-Hill Osborne Media.

World Wide Web Consortium (2006) 'Cascading Style Sheets Home Page'; available at: *http://www.w3.org/Style/CSS/* (accessed 2 June 2006).

Database design and normalisation

Codd, E. F. (1972) 'Further normalization of the database relational model', in *Data Base Systems*, Courant Computer Science Symposia Series, Vol. 6, Englewood Cliffs, NJ: Prentice Hall.

Codd, E. F. (1974) 'Recent investigations in relational data base systems', in *Proceedings of the IFIP Congress, Stockholm.*

Elmasri, R. and Navathe, S. B. (2004) *Fundamentals of Database Systems* (4th edn), Boston: Addison-Wesley.

Garcia-Molina, H., Ullman, J., D. and Widom, J. (2002) *Database Systems: The Complete Book*, Upper Saddle River, NJ: Prentice Hall.

Mullins, C. S. (2002) *Database Administration*, Boston: Addison-Wesley.

Riordan, R. M. (2005) *Designing Effective Database Systems*, Upper Saddle River, NJ: Addison-Wesley.

Free and open source software

DiBona, C., Ockman, S. and Stone, M. (eds) (1999) *Open Sources: Voices from the Open Source Revolution*, Cambridge, MA: O'Reilly.

Dixon, R. (2004) *Open Source Software Law*, Boston: Artech House.

Kavanaugh, P. (2004) *Open Source Software: Implementation and Management*, Amsterdam: Elsevier.

Koch, S. (2005) *Free/Open Source Software Development*, London: Idea Group.

Overly, M. (2003) *The Open Source Handbook*, Silver Spring, MD: Pike & Fischer.

Ritchie, D. and Thompson, K. (1974) 'The UNIX time-sharing system', *Communications of the ACM* 17: 365–75.

Rosenberg, D. K. (2000) *Open Source: The Unauthorized White Papers*, Foster City, CA: IDG Books.

Raymond, E. S. (2001) *The Cathedral and the Bazaar*, Cambridge, MA: OReilly.

Stallman, R. M. (2002) *Free Software, Free Society: Selected Essays of Richard M. Stallman,* Boston: GNU Press.

Wayner, P. (2000) *Free For All: How Linux and the Free Software Movement Undercut the High-Tech Titans*, New York: HarperBusiness.

Wendel De Joode, R. van, Bruijn, J. A. de, and van Eeten, M. (2003) *Protecting the Virtual Commons*, The Hague: TMC ASSER Press.

General web development

Mendes, E. and Mosley, N. (eds) (2006) *Web Engineering*, Berlin: Springer-Verlag.

Yanks, K. (2004) *Build Your Own Database Driven Website Using PHP and MySQL*, Collingwood, Victoria: Sitepoint.

Wandschneider, M. (2006) *Core Web Application Development with PHP and MySQL*, Upper Saddle River, NJ: Prentice Hall.

Welling, L. and Thomson, L. (2003) *PHP and MySQL Web Development* (2nd edn), Indianapolis: Sams.

Williams, H. and Lane, D. (2002) *Web Database Applications with PHP and MySQL*, Cambridge, MA: O'Reilly.

MySQL

DuBois, P. (2005) *MySQL* (3rd edn), Indianapolis: Sams.

Dyer, R. J. T. (2005) *MySQL in a Nutshell*, Cambridge, MA: O'Reilly.

Koffler, M. (2005) *The Definitive Guide to MySQL 5*, Berkeley: Apress.

MySQL AB (2006) 'MySQL reference manual', available at: *http://dev.mysql.com/doc/* (accessed 2 June 2006).

PHP

PHP Documentation Group (2006) 'PHP Manual', available at: *http://www.php.net/manual/en/* (accessed 2 June 2006).

Sklar, D. and Trachtenberg, A. (2003) *PHP Cookbook*, Cambridge, MA: O'Reilly.

Ullman, L. (2004) *PHP for the World Wide Web* (2nd edn), Berkeley: Peachpit Press.

Ullman, L. (2001) *PHP Advanced for the World Wide Web*, Berkeley: Peachpit Press.

Index